HOW 401(K) FEES DESTROY WEALTH AND WHAT INVESTORS CAN DO TO PROTECT THEMSELVES

This book could save you hundreds of thousands of dollars over your investing lifetime. A must-read for anyone planning for retirement

CHUCK EPSTEIN

Printed in the United States of America

ISBN 978-0-9000000-0-0

1. Personal Investing —Investments—Investment disclosure. 2. 401(k). 3. Department of Labor—Disclosure regulations 4. Fiduciary standards. 5. Investment conflicts-of-interest 6. Financial media

First Edition

14 13 12 11 10 / 10 9 8 7 6 5 4 3 2 1

ISBN: 1477657991

ISBN 13: 9781477657997

About the Author

Chuck Epstein is an award-winning writer and marketing professional, who also has held senior-level marketing and communications positions in the mutual fund, hedge fund, and listed futures industries. He has held senior positions at the New York Futures Exchange, Chicago Mercantile Exchange, Lind-Waldock, Zacks Investment Research, Russell Investments and Principal Financial, and won national awards from the Mutual Fund Education Alliance. His website, http://mutualfundreform. com, was named best small blog in 2009 by the Society of American Business Editors and Writers.

He has written articles for more than 50 financial publications, and worked on teams that introduced futures and options based on the S&P 500 Index, Russell stock indexes, the CRB Index, Eurodollars and certificates of deposits. He is the editor of *Managed Futures in the Institutional Portfolio* (Wiley, 1992) and *The Handbook of Corporate Earnings Analysis* (Wiley, 1994), as well as numerous other corporate and personal investing financial articles. He can be reached at cepstein@prodigy.net.

Acknowledgments

This book recognizes the persistent efforts of the U.S. Department of Labor's Employee Benefits Security Administration and its Assistant Secretary Phyllis C. Borzi, who protected and advanced the rights of millions of current and future retirees through the new 401(k) fee and expense disclosure regulations.

The positive efforts of financial professional groups, such as the Committee for the Fiduciary Standard and the Fiduciary Society for Ethical Financial Practices, which are promoting the adoption of a pro-investor universal fiduciary standard, must also be noted.

In addition, I would like to acknowledge my wife, Laurie, who never knew why I was spending so much time at the computer. Beau LaGrange and Charles Rusus also provided valuable industry and editorial insights when reviewing this manuscript. This book is for Sydney Soto Epstein and all future retirees.

Table of Contents

"The financial system puts up zero percent of the capital and takes zero percent of the risk and gets almost 80 percent of the return, and you, the investor in this long time period, an investment lifetime, put up 100 percent of the capital, take 100 percent of the risk, and get only a little bit over 20 percent of the return.

"That is a financial system that is failing investors because of those costs of financial advice and brokerage, some hidden, some out in plain sight that investors face today. So the system has to be fixed."

– **John Bogle**, founder of the Vanguard Investment Group[1]

Introduction

HOW EXCESSIVE 401(K) FEES DESTROY WEALTH AND WHAT INVESTORS CAN DO TO PROTECT THEMSELVES

Since the formation of the American republic, one of the main ideas driving the development of "American exceptionalism" has been the unrestrained ability of its citizens to more or less consistently make money. But by the end of 2008, investors realized they had suffered through one of the worst periods of wealth destruction in U.S. history. The wealth creation plans for millions had been derailed.

The "Lost Decade" of equity returns, combined with the unprecedented loss in home equity, wasted the two main engines of wealth creation available to millions of Americans: their home equities and investment portfolios. This helps explain why the average American family's household net worth declined 23% between 2007 and 2009, from $125,000 to $96,000.[2] But the story of American wealth destruction is actually decades in the making.

Wealth destruction is not a topic the financial services industry and elected officials want to discuss. After all, wealth managers are well paid to pursue near-uninterrupted wealth creation through profitable investing, estate planning and tax management. Any critical assessment of a declining American standard of living is the third rail for politicians, wealth managers and investment advisors, who will avoid explaining the disruptive forces of market volatility, bank failures, and errant investment strategies that produced financial losses of 30% or more.

While more investors are openly questioning the forces that drive their investment returns, the financial services industry continues to evade the subject of wealth destruction for a fundamental reason: The very concept erodes the authority of wealth managers since it casts doubt on their ability to predict future investment results. This perceived authority to divine the future is why fiat currencies derive their power from the full faith and credit of national governments backing paper money. Without that unquestioned confidence, the money becomes worthless.

Similarly, investment professionals derive their perceived authority from their ability to produce significant returns over time. If they cannot do this, investors have little reason to pay for their services. When portfolios suffer losses on a large scale—accompanied by declines in home equity, savings, job security, and unnerving global economic and financial problems—the average investor has every reason to question whether investment professionals have the ability to create sustained positive market returns. When these positive returns falter, investors can reasonably ask whether the financial advisor's recommendations are working in their best interests.

Millions of Americans are concerned about the role and ability of investment professionals to profitably navigate today's increasingly complex and volatile global markets. While this presents a serious credibility issue, the financial services industry would rather not discuss it. There are many reasons for this, and we will soon see that the interests of the financial services industry are often *not* the same as the interests of their own customers. In some cases, stripped of embellishments and formalities, many client-advisor relationships are essentially adversarial.

While the Great Depression, that ran from 1929 to about 1941, devastated the stock market, it only affected the 3% of Americans who owned stock during that period. At that time, there were no 401(k)s and the only old-age financial support available to some Americans (before the passage of the Social Security Act in 1935) was pensions. More than 80 years later, the system and numbers are very different: At the end of 2010, there were about 50 million 401(k) retirement accounts, which held an estimated $4.5 trillion in assets under employer-sponsored defined contribution (DC) plans.[3] This was about one-quarter of the total $17.4 trillion in U.S retirement assets in 2010, according to the *2011 Investment*

Company Fact Book; Of that amount, private DC plans accounted for $4.5 trillion and individual retirement accounts (IRAs) held $4.7 trillion.[4]

The estimated $1 trillion in investment losses, combined with the $1 trillion in lost home equity resulting from the Great Recession of 2008, has shattered, seriously destroyed or delayed the ability of millions of Americans to enjoy a financially secure future or leave a family legacy. These losses have fallen disproportionately on middle- and lower-income families and have also come at a time when real wage growth for most Americans has been stagnant. From 1979 to 2009, productivity grew 80%, but the hourly wage of the median worker grew by only 10%, and even then, all of the wage growth occurred from 1996 to 2002, reflecting the strong economic recovery of the late-1990s.[5]

Stagnant wages translate into a reduced savings rate, another reason for curtailed wealth creation. But rising prices and an uncertain job market have made the savings rate for Americans very volatile. This has produced an uncertain situation where "Americans are in a cycle of save-and-splurge–building up their nest eggs to fund their spending sprees before retreating to start the cycle over again," according to the *Washington Post.*[6]

Adding to the uncertainty about adhering to any consistent wealth-building plan is the unsteady job market, where layoffs, age discrimination, and a steady stream of new applicants willing to work for low salaries pose constant threats. It's no wonder that in 1997, then-Federal Reserve Board Chairman Alan Greenspan noted that when workers had poor job security, they were more reluctant to ask for raises. This would eliminate a major cause of inflation, he said.[7]

This is the reality check American investors face today. The main engines for building wealth–portfolio returns, gains in home equity, personal savings, and to a lesser extent, Social Security and inheritance–have all been seriously eroded. Worse, as we will see, portfolios and real estate do regain value, but slowly. In the case of real estate, any significant price appreciation could take place decades in the future. Real estate price gains are also regionalized, so the pace of any national recovery will be erratic.

All this makes it critically important for investors to re-evaluate their investments, strategies, investment relationships, and most important, the fees and expenses that are constantly eroding the value of their investment portfolios.

This is important for three reasons:

- Fees and expenses are two critical investment variables that investors can directly and easily control;

- Low-cost bond and equity funds historically have produced better net returns than more expensive funds;

- The investment and insurance industries have not provided full, truthful disclosures about the actual costs their customers (retail and institutional) are paying.

Full disclosure is a critical issue because investment fees are charged on a regular basis (monthly, quarterly or annually) over the entire length of most investment relationships. Over decades, these cumulative fees and expenses can reduce very large investors' portfolios, both in and out of their 401(k)s, by as much as 28% over 30 years. Not only are investors overpaying for services they may never receive, but this is money that investors can never recover.

In essence, overcharges on fees and expenses amounts to a major source of wealth destruction. And it comes from the very people—company 401(k) administrators, 401(k) plan specialists, investment experts, mutual fund and insurance companies—who are *supposed* to be overseeing these complex plans in the best interests of their less-sophisticated customer-investors. But as we will see, this has not always been the case.

One glaring example has been the complete absence of full fee and expense disclosures in 401(k) plans. In a consumer society, it is unthinkable that these critical costs would not be explained and disclosed to investors, many of them unsophisticated. But after decades of debate, reviews, studies, and comment periods, the U.S. Department of Labor (DOL) finally enacted new regulations that took effect in mid-2012 to address these disclosures inside 401(k) plans.

This is a historic action affecting millions of 401(k) participants and plan sponsors.

These new far-reaching disclosures–innocuously disguised by their section citations as DOL rules 408(b)(2) and 404(a)(5)–will start a process that allows 401(k) plan sponsors and everyone participating in a 401(k) plan to begin comparing fees and expenses charged to administer their plans. For decades, 401(k) service providers and some employers allowed their employees and customers to be overcharged for services they did not receive. These errant practices would be forbidden in any other corporate department, yet they were tolerated, sometimes knowingly, in some 401(k) plans.

While enacting these fee and expense disclosure regulations is a simple and seemingly straightforward action, it has never been done before. Why has it taken decades for this to happen? Who profited from this inaction? This is a question that should puzzle and irritate owners of the nation's 50 million 401(k) accounts.

But, as we will see, the simple disclosure of fees and expenses has the potential to re-shape the entire mutual fund and annuity industries. This is the 401(k) industry's version of the scene in the *Wizard of Oz*, when the Great Oz cautions Dorothy to "pay no attention to that man behind the curtain." But investors must disregard this directive because the man behind the curtain has extraordinary control over your entire retirement future, including how much you will have in retirement and ultimately, your quality of life for decades to come.

The DOL's disclosure rules have focused the attention of millions of 401(k) investors, many of them unsophisticated, on "the man behind the curtain." In many cases, these discoveries will not build confidence in some segments of the financial services industry.

This story cannot be told, however, outside the context of what contributed to other sources of wealth destruction and the major events inside the financial services industry that have shaped it into what it is today.

What This Book Covers

This book explains the 2012 DOL 401(k) fee and expense regulations, what they require, and their expected impact on the nation's 700,000 401(k) plans. But this is much larger story than one about federal regulations. It also discusses the historic origins of retirement; changing employer-employee relations; the 401(k); its big brother, the pension industry; and how these plans were shaped by larger forces in politics and financial services that have come to control the 401(k) industry.

Sadly, an essential part of this story is the inherent conflicts-of-interest that exist between many financial advisors, mutual fund companies and even some employers and their employees. These inherent conflicts make it difficult, or impossible, for average investors to gain the objective, low-cost advice they need to attain future financial security.

This book also works in the larger context of the 2008 Great Recession (which officially lasted from December 2007 through June 2009, the longest recession since the Great Depression), and the significant wealth destruction it caused in portfolios and home equity. While attention must be paid to this event, this story also covers the destruction of pension plans and related workplace changes that have been developing over the past 50 years.

This book is based on seven key premises, which, as readers will see, are based on attributed facts and personal observations about the state of the financial services industry:

1. The financial services industry today is essentially anti-customer. It suffers from conflicts-of-interest, which should put all investors on notice that many financial salespeople have different priorities and interests than their own customers. Unless investment product salespcople make an extra effort to align their interests with those of their customers, investors should assume they are entering into relationships where their interests may not align with their advisor's. Often, this means investors should watch for investments that perform better for the salesperson than for themselves.

2. Active investment management has a role in any portfolio, but it should be limited. Investors should seriously

investigate the benefits of passive investment strategies for the long term. If an investor strongly believes in active management, they should consider alternative strategy funds, which have the ability to go long and short.

3. Buy-and-hold is a precarious investment strategy. Over time, this strategy benefits financial professionals and the industry more than investors. When this strategy is used with expensive load funds, it often generates significant fees for managers and fund companies, regardless of fund performance.

4. Based on the discovery of significant overpayments of fees and expenses from 401(k) plans, as well as the wholesale abandonment of pension plans by corporate America, employees should realize there is a new employer-employee relationship. Many corporations today view employees as expenses, not assets. This has been demonstrated through mass layoffs, pension abuses, increases in executive compensation, outsourcing, the use of perma-temp employees, and severe reductions in employee benefits. All of this has been accompanied by stagnant real wage growth over the past decade, despite large productivity gains.

5. Employers and investment professionals have shifted an extraordinary level of financial risk to large numbers of ill-equipped individuals, who must now manage their own investments. This risk transfer occurred as corporations largely abandoned their professionally-managed pension plans and used many of those pension assets to fund new acquisitions and pay lucrative executive compensation and retirement packages to their top executives.

6. The full impact of the wealth destruction wrought by the 2008 Great Recession will continue to ripple through the economy for at least a decade. While not widely discussed, the lost wealth, depressed job market, delayed entry of

many young workers into the job market, and lower wages will seriously hurt younger workers entering the workforce. Cumulatively, younger workers will lose the extraordinary benefits of accruing the compound interest from any modest 401(k) savings during their crucial early working years.

7. Attempts to privatize Social Security should be recognized as the transfer of significant financial risks to ill-equipped individuals. Under a privatized system, participants will pay higher fees and expenses for the prospect of facing a more insecure financial future.

To more fully explain the specifics behind these premises, this book is divided into six chapters.

Chapter 1, "A Brief History of Retirement and the Fiduciary Standard," provides an overview of the fiduciary rules that formed the basis for the Employee Retirement Income Security Act (ERISA), the historic legislation that established how individuals must act when entrusted with managing and investing pension assets. Since the Middle Ages, when knights went to fight in the Crusades, protecting the assets of people who were unable to represent their financial interests in person has been the subject of intense legal debate, which ultimately found its way into common law.

The adherence to fiduciary obligations continues today in the management of pension funds, which are governed by ERISA. Some investment professionals and consumer advocates are trying to extend those same high standards into the investment advisory industry, including the way 401(k) plans are managed.

But this proposal has not been universally embraced. And while it has developed a small, dedicated, professional following among Registered Investment Advisors, the adoption of the broader fiduciary standard and its resulting changes in sales and investment practices, remains a contentious issue in the financial services industry.

Chapter 2, "Why Fund Expenses Matter," explains the importance of fees and expenses inside mutual fund and 401(k) accounts, the responsibilities of 401(k) plans under DOL Rule 404(a)(5), and how fees benefit financial firms and salespeople. The disproportionate benefits paid to fund industry professionals explains how mutual fund firms and insurance companies maintain leverage over their own customers, and why they have resisted decades of repeated attempts to disclose fees in an understandable, comprehensive way to their own customers.

Chapter 3, "The Power of Disclosure: Introduction to the DOL's 2012 Fee Disclosure Regulations," presents how the disclosure regulations evolved, what they require, and their impact on 401(k) participants, plan sponsors and some investment products.

Chapter 4, "The Great Wealth Transfer and Wealth Destruction," discusses the extraordinary amount of financial risk individual investors now assume. This occurred as professionally-managed pensions were phased out and replaced by 401(k)s.

Chapter 5, "Show Me the Money: Why Average People Do Not Become Great Investors," specifies steps investors can take to protect and assume control over their retirement funds.

This chapter includes a short discussion about the benefits of the increasingly popular exchange traded funds (ETFs), including their lower expenses; and how the rise of the financial media helped develop market bubbles, day trading, and market manias.

Chapter 6, "What Investors Gained—and Lost—From Poor Disclosure," summarizes the huge costs of poor disclosure over the past decades. The amount of investor money lost to this deficiency is an incalculable, unnecessary, and irrecoverable loss to millions of working individuals. Many of these people were unsophisticated investors, who trusted investment professionals to act in their best interests. This betrayal helps explain the reason why the financial services industry is held in low public esteem.

While the chapters containing information on the new DOL regulations cannot avoid the use of legalistic language, readers should not be intimidated. This is language used by 401(k) industry professionals to refer to specific sections of the regulations.

If investors take the time to become familiar with the key concepts and regulations, they will be able to speak the language that drives investment and 401(k) discussions and gain power in discussions about fees, fund expenses, conflicts-of-interest, and the fiduciary standard.

This book does not provide any short-term, actionable investment advice or fantastic trading strategies. That type of investment advice is readily available elsewhere, although it is often obsolete by the time it reaches a mass audience.

Instead, this book encourages investors to take control over their own investment choices, discover the sources of their wealth destruction, and how they can take steps to prevent their hard-earned wealth from being destroyed again in the future. One of the book's main goals is to inform 401(k) investors about the negative impact of fees, and how some in the financial services industry work against their own clients' interests.

Because no government agency can take the necessary actions needed to protect investors or help them recover financial losses, investors must take charge.

To do this, they need to:

- Critically question all investment recommendations and develop a realistic outlook about being able to create and preserve personal wealth, and;

- Shift the burden of disclosure back to financial professionals, mutual funds, and insurance companies, so they can demonstrate their activities are not based on conflicts-of-interests.

Many of the interpretations in this book do not represent mainstream thought. They are based on the observation that today's investment world has become extraordinary complex, expensive, and is often riddled with conflicts-of-interest. It is a situation in which the interests of investors have been subordinated to those in the financial services industry.

But there is an emerging movement to positively change investment sales practices. Some financial professionals, such as Registered Investment Advisors (RIAs), have adopted the fiduciary standard, meaning that the investment choices they make for clients should benefit clients more than themselves. This is a bright light for individual investors. It provides a clear alternative to less professional, self-serving sales practices.

Under the new DOL rules, 401(k) participants, at a minimum, can expect to see this information in the new disclosures: 1) The names of the plan service providers; 2) A description of services provided to the plan and an attachment of the service agreement; 3) A declaration of the provider's fiduciary status; and, 4) Fees charged to the client-plan (either a tiered fee schedule or flat dollar amount) and whether those fees are paid by the plan or the client. The burden of explaining these and other disclosures falls on the plan sponsor or employer. If a participant feels the disclosure is inadequate, they should push for more information concerning their plans and investments.

Investors must also discover who and what has worked to reduce or improve their portfolio returns. Finding those answers will be the first steps in an important journey of discovery, which may hopefully lead to a more secure financial future.

CHAPTER I

A BRIEF HISTORY OF RETIREMENT
AND THE FIDUCIARY STANDARD

Growing old is an imperceptible process. People work, marry, raise a family, live with a partner or alone, and watch the fruits of their labor mature. Quietly accompanying this inevitable evolution are hard realities concerning health, finances, and our ultimate finality. But when it comes to retirement, it is also no wonder people don't know about the overwhelming issues they will face 40 years into the future, especially when many of these questions cannot be answered.[8]

While people live their lives in many ways, the idea of old-age sustenance, or retirement programs in some form, has a long history. As early as 1597, local parishes in Great Britain established houses for people who could not care for themselves. The church assumed these responsibilities after the decline of feudalism, which had an established hierarchy of roles and responsibilities,

I

including one that made landed aristocracy (lords of the manor) responsible for the well-being of the surfs working their land. In the 1670s, the first organized pension scheme for Royal Navy officers was enacted; at the time, the life expectancy was 48.[9]

In 1889, an enlightened German statesman, Otto Von Bismarck, established a national insurance plan for his citizens. Using census data and mathematical advice, he arrived at a retirement age of 70, which also coincided with the nation's average age at death. Cold-hearted, but politically shrewd, he created an insurance program that half of Germany's citizens would not live to collect.

Von Bismarck's social insurance experiment was a practical political alternative to more radical socialist proposals, as well as an effort to prolong worker productivity. As such, it was clever national policy; it offered a great potential reward, even though the majority of citizens would never reap its benefits. This German national plan covered both old-age and disability benefits and was mandatory, with contributions coming from employees, employers, and the government. The net result, however, would be the same: part of an enlightened national effort to provide old-age income.

Caring for the elderly is a characteristic of an enlightened society. In England in 1690, astronomer Edmund Halley developed probability tables to determine the life expectancy of London's residents. His work eventually led to the creation of Lloyd's of London as the more formal structure for managing large pools of risk, whether they arose from individual mortality, shipping, or fires. What all these pools had in common was risk, or the uncertainty of the unknown future.

Halley and Von Bismarck were not liberal social policy advocates. They were practical men who faced a problem. Alms houses and excruciating poverty were intolerable for any nation that sought to advance itself politically, militarily, socially, and economically. Poverty was bad social policy and politically dangerous. So while social welfare programs did not exist for the able bodied, any hope of a pension-welfare system that could sustain the workforce and make it more aligned with state interests was viewed favorably.

Developing a national policy of caring for the elderly has definite economic results. It opens new opportunities in the labor market as older workers become more financially confident to leave their posts. Younger workers then have increased job mobility and salary increases, productivity improves, and companies can adopt more efficient production methods. In short, an intelligent retirement policy is essential for any effective job creation strategy.

Pensions in the U.S.

Retirement policy in the United States is intertwined with the nation's corporate and labor histories. As early as 1717, the Presbyterian Church had established its Fund for Pious Uses for retired ministers. This was followed in 1875 by the first corporate pension fund created by the American Express Company. In 1884, the Baltimore and Ohio Railroad established the first pension plan by a major employer. Employees who had worked for at least 10 years could retire at age 65 and receive benefits ranging from 20% to 35% of wages.[10] By 1900, the Pennsylvania Railroad, one of the largest railroads in the country, had a full-fledged pension plan for all employees when they reached age 70.

Due to their economic importance and large unionized workforce, railroad workers played an especially important role in the development of pensions, including a landmark Supreme Court decision in 1935 (U.S. Supreme Court in the ruling of Railroad Retirement Board v. Alton Railroad Co., 295 U.S. 330 (1935.) This case resulted from large scale pension plan failures among railroad plans, largely due to their aged workforce and poorly-designed plans. As a result, a group of independent railroad employees in 1931 formed the Railways Employees National Pension Association and petitioned Congress to form a national pension plan for railroad employees.

In 1933, under pressure from President Franklin Roosevelt, legislation was introduced to secure pension benefits for railroad workers in what became known as the Railroad Retirement Act. The Act gave workers higher pensions than they would have received under Social Security (enacted in 1935), as well as survivor and disability benefits. This was followed by the Railroad Retirement and Carrier Taxing Acts of 1937. These laws resulted in a federally administered pension plan providing old-age, disability, and survivor benefits based on lengths of service and earnings, and were similar to Social Security.

Meanwhile, the railroads benefited since they did not have to make any corporate contributions to the program, while they also reduced their taxes. While the court ruled against the Retirement Board as "an activity not connected to interstate commerce," the case focused attention on the issue of pensions.[11] Policy makers and those in the insurance industry took note of this form of group insurance policy to provide pension benefits at a lower cost than operating a private pension plan. This Act was considered important since it forced the attention of corporations on the role of government in providing individual pensions. This realization helped increase awareness about the importance of Social Security.

While not generally known, the idea of providing pensions in the U.S. was originally introduced and advanced by some of the nation's largest corporations in the 1920s and 1930s. Companies, such as Standard Oil of New Jersey, General Electric, and Metropolitan Life, advanced pensions as a way of building labor-management relationships and preventing strikes. According to Professor G. William Domhoff, moderate executives at corporations supported pensions from the 1930s to the 1970s as a means of attracting and maintaining motivated and engaged workers.[12]

The nation's most significant industrial leaders, such as John D. Rockefeller, Jr., began to see the importance of company-level old-age pension plans. To examine the issue, Rockefeller created the Industrial Relations Counselors, an organization to promote better labor relations, especially in the companies he controlled, and to prevent the formation of unions. This effort produced "employee representation plans" that relied on managers inside the plants to meet with employee representatives elected by plant workers. There, they could discuss work-related issues, although they were not allowed to discuss topics concerning unions and wages.

The popularity of pensions was accelerated by the introduction of accident insurance, or workman's compensation benefits, at the state level in the early-1900s. These plans relied on private insurance companies to provide the insurance, and corporate leaders thought insurance companies could also manage their pension plans. According to Professor Domhoff, Equitable Life and Metropolitan Life, which shared many directors in common with major banks and corporations, began conducting the analysis necessary to offer group life insurance programs and group old-age pension programs to corporations. Insurance companies soon realized they could do a better job with private pensions than individual corporations if contributions were made by both companies and their employees.[13]

The pension industry also adopted the use of actuaries, and in 1918 the president of the Carnegie Foundation for the Advancement of Teaching, an early incubator of corporate moderates in the policy-planning network, formed a pension plan for professors. The result was the Teachers Insurance and Annuity Association (TIAA), a life insurance company, which then fashioned the nation's first fully insured pension system.[14] But since the use of actuaries to design pension plans was limited, many privately funded pension plans were based on unsound data and policies. Many of these plans failed during the 1920s. This renewed calls for a federal pension system, especially among those who had lost their promised benefits.

In the 1920s, individual corporations expanded their pension plans, while insurance companies offered better designed and cheaper group programs by mandating employer and employee contributions. In the early 1920s, Metropolitan Life announced that its group pension plan was superior to ones corporations could offer. This advanced the role of insurance companies in providing corporate retirement plans, and included the adoption of certain insurance industry business practices, most notably, revenue sharing, which remains ingrained and controversial today.[15] (See "The Definition and Origins of Revenue Sharing" later in this chapter.)

Since pensions are so attractive to individuals, they have been a staple in the military since the Revolution. United States military service people receive pensions covered by the Servicemen's and Veterans' Survivors' Benefits Act (1957). When service personnel retire after 20 years of service, they receive 50% of their base pay at time of retirement, with automatic increases linked to the Consumer Price Index.

Pensions for federal employees were authorized in 1920. An exemption from World War II wage controls, followed by the growth of unions after the end of World War II, led to the expansion of these retirement benefits.

Old-age pension plans also were drawn up by cities for certain groups of public employees, such as firefighters, police officers, and teachers, which provided for compulsory contributions from employees. Most of these plans were the product of union bargaining.

While the idea of extending old-age benefit protections to all citizens developed earlier in Europe (notably Germany), many corporations and groups (such as labor unions, professional associations, and colleges) had made provisions for pensions before the Social Security Act was passed in 1935.

As a result, Social Security was never designed to be a sole source of retirement income. It was always referred to as "one leg of the three-legged stool," by New Dealers, with retirement income supplemented by private savings and pensions. These were traditionally considered the financial keys to a successful retirement.

At about this time (1933), due to the highly-publicized cases of Wall Street abuses related to the financial industry, President Roosevelt began addressing the need for the securities industry to adopt an industry professional standard, akin to doctors.

Following the Progressive philosophy, which saw the need for financial reform after the abuses that accompanied the 1929 stock market crash, Roosevelt met with Richard Whitney, president of the New York Stock Exchange, in 1933. During that meeting, Roosevelt told of the need for "moral reform of Wall Street," including the need for the New York Stock Exchange to adopt a code of ethics that could also be adopted by the nation's other stock exchanges.

"In essence, this would have amounted to a national standard for brokers in the securities industry. FDR's proposals for implementing his vision—fiduciary duties and a simple code of ethics—also speak to modern times."64 But Wall Street abhors reform. It would be another 41 years before anything approaching a partial national standard of investment conduct was even partially implemented.

The Passage of ERISA

On a steamy Labor Day in 1974, about 200 labor and business leaders convened in the White House Rose Garden to watch President Gerald Ford sign legislation that one observer called "the greatest single achievement since the enactment of Social Security."

The Employee Retirement Income Security Act of 1974 (ERISA) had spent seven years winding through Congress and was intended to protect workers who failed to receive pensions after their employers became insolvent. In the signing ceremony, President. Ford said ERISA would address pension abuses and "will probably give more benefits and rights and success in the area of labor-management than almost anything in the history of the country."

But 30 years after ERISA, many pension plans the law was designed to protect were being eliminated or curtailed to an extent that they could not deliver all they promised. Changes in the federal tax code, onerous regulations, accelerated vesting schedules, poor investment returns, high expenses, the decline of unions, the rise of financial engineering, and the misuse of pension assets have all been cited as reasons why pension plans have declined significantly.

But these were the most visible changes. While it rarely generated a headline, sometime during the past 30 years, a combination of poorly designed federal policies converged to allow pension plan sponsors to break the bond between worker and employer by not providing retirement benefits. This marked a fundamental change in worker-employer relationships and the start of a new 21st century workplace ethic.

While human resources departments and the business press cover the workplace and routinely report changes in employment, products, sales, and finances, many people also perform work for its emotional or spiritual benefits. So despite being dry and eso-teric, the idea of retirement and its financing, also have powerful emotional components.

This emotional factor played a role in ERISA's creation in 1974, and it was strong enough to be propelled by an event that occurred almost a decade earlier, the failure of the Studebaker-Packard car corporation. This corporate bankruptcy left thousands of workers without jobs and pensions, while others were left with only a frac-tion of the retirement income they expected. Like many other com-panies, Studebaker started by laying off younger workers first. By the time they got to the older employees, they were cutting workers with 30 to 40 years of service. This was happening in a town that had few other potential employers. Studebaker's failure trauma-tized South Bend, Indiana; some workers committed suicide.

While it sounds odd today, that inability to pay pensions had such "a catastrophic and cataclysmic" effect on the automaker's workforce and community that it singed the memory of a young attorney who some seven years later would become a primary author of ERISA legislation when he served as chief counsel on the Senate Labor Committee under then Senator Jacob Javits. Frank Cummings, an attorney with LeBoeuf, Lamb, Greene & MacRae, Washington, DC, said that without Studebaker there never would have been a federal law codifying and protecting retirement plans for their participants and beneficiaries.

However, passing the bill was another story. It's reform-orien-tation, scope and federal standards alienated many in Congress and industry. Most major retirement forces at the time, including those who today embrace all things retirement, originally opposed the bill, including the AFL-CIO, which sought an exemption for their union pension plans, which it contended were adequately supervised at the fund trustee level.

The bill wound its way through the legislative process without gaining any political momentum until impeachment proceedings against President Richard Nixon were announced. House leader-ship recognized that once impeachment proceeding began, any legislation not out of Committee before August 1, 1974 would be dead for the session. Despite the odds, and what Cummings said was some "begging," the Conference committee released the bill, which was passed.[16]

But while retirement is certainly an individual goal, we still don't have a national plan to get there. When ERISA went into effect in 1975, there were more than 100,000 traditional employer-paid pension plans; by 2003, there were less than 31,000, according to the Pension Benefit Guaranty Corporation.

When ERISA was signed on Labor Day 1973, it significantly professionalized and made accountable the people who were managing pension assets. Prior to ERISA, pension administrators thought they were doing a good job if they put assets into bond funds and rolled them over as they matured. In some states, it was illegal for pension funds to invest in the stock market. The era of modern investment management had not yet arrived.

ERISA's key provisions in the 248-page bill set new standards in seven key areas governing the granting, operation and administration of pensions. But its most significant contributions towards changing the way retirement benefits are offered to U.S. workers was in three areas, according to Cummings:

1. ERISA imposed standards of behavior. This included vesting, or the guaranteed right to receive a pension once the participant met the plan's requirements. Before ERISA, there was no vesting. If a worker lost their job one day before retirement, there was no remedy. "This was a huge change," Cummings said.

2. Imposing fiduciary standards. Before ERISA, only plan trustees had classic trustee powers and responsibilities, but ERISA expanded the definition of fiduciary to anyone who had a specific responsibility for the plan. This raised the level and involvement of more people who could be held accountable for plan administration.

3. Federalization of pension law. ERISA's most far-reaching and controversial provision nullified all state laws in the

pension area and replaced them with Federal law. Workers from anywhere in the U.S. could seek redress in federal court using the same laws, as opposed to using individual state law to claim pension benefits.

As to critics who say ERISA imposed a burdensome set of standards on the pension industry, Cummings noted that ERISA set professional standards, but it never compelled people to do anything. "ERISA does not provide for any damages. It only forced plan sponsors to deliver on their promises. That was the Studebaker problem: workers earned the pension, but there was no money to pay them."

Interestingly, in the 1970s, public support of pensions became unpopular with some political factions as a result of societal changes associated with the Vietnam anti-war protests, the impact of the civil rights movement, and the passage of ERISA. As corporations publicly moved away from their early support and advancement of pensions, organized labor filled the void by claiming credit for enacting pension protection benefits.

ERISA also advanced the application of formal investment theories related to funding and investing pension assets, such as Modern Portfolio Theory (MPT), and encouraged theories designed to better predict complex market behaviors, such as the efficient market hypothesis and the capital asset pricing model.

Many pension funds also developed a legal investment list, which specified acceptable investment classes and allocations. ERISA changed this by adopting some of the key concepts of MPT and formulating them into pension law and policy. This created a fundamental change in the way pension assets were invested by linking them to formal investment theory.

ERISA was the culmination of a decade of heated debate and negotiations, and represented a test of strength between the dominant political powerhouses of the day: labor unions, corporate management, and Congress. At the time, ERISA was coalescing into a law affecting both private and public sector workforce employees and non-union and union employees. (Public employees ended up being covered under a similar plan, the Public

Employees Retirement Income Security Act, PERISA, also enacted in 1974.) At the time ERISA was passed, labor unions represented some 22% of the U.S. workforce; 20 million out of a workforce of 93 million.[17]

During the early 1970s, this retirement bill was considered one of the most important legislative undertakings since Social Security passed in 1935. It was a major piece of legislation that required the sponsorship of two very different and experienced politicians: Senator Jacob Javits (R-NY) and Senator Harrison Williams (D-NJ). While Javits left Congress as a respected legislator, Williams was later snared in the ABSCAM scandal and indicted on Oct. 30, 1980, on nine counts, including bribery, receipt of an unlawful gratuity, conflict-of-interest, and conspiracy to defraud the United States. He was convicted of corruption by the U.S. Senate, but resigned before he could be expelled.

Creating a formalized private pension system in the U.S., with specific accountability for pension payments to qualified workers, was a huge undertaking and one its creators knew would change the nature of the employer-employee relationship. While controversial, the prevailing belief was that adopting pension plans would reduce worker turnover, increase motivation and productivity, and over time, improve the quality-of-life for retirees and make the U.S. more competitive in the global economy.

Formalized pension regulations covering such heated topics as time off, on-the-job death benefits, how pension contributions would be treated among employees transferring within the same industry, and survivor benefits, would have a far-reaching effect on employees, corporate management, board members, and human resources and treasury departments.

While ERISA had a profound effect in all these areas, as well in public policy, it also formally linked financial theory with retirement plan practices. Thematically, ERISA significantly professionalized pensions and made the people managing pension assets accountable. Some states, such as Indiana, had laws saying that state pension funds had to be invested entirely in fixed-income securities as recently as the 1970s. Many funds had a legal investment list, which specified acceptable investment classes and allocation.

ERISA changed this by adopting some key concepts of MPT and formulating them into pension law and policy. This created a fundamental change in the way pension assets were invested by linking them to MPT.

Among the concepts which Harry Markowitz, the developer of MPT, formalized in his 1952 work, *Portfolio Selection: Efficient Diversification of Investments*, was the quantification of diversification and how different elements of an investment portfolio correlate with one another.

From this statistical work came subsequent refinements, such as the concepts of diversifiable vs. non-diversifiable risk.[18] The resulting ERISA legislation provided institutions with regulatory guidance to manage employee retirement assets. In 1993, the DOL published its MPT-based investment interpretation bulletin, two years after verbally endorsing it at an American Bar Association conference. In 1995, the Uniform Prudent Investors Act further clarified Markowitz's investment principles into pension policy.

The Great Pension Shift

Beginning in the late-1970s and 1980s, the management of pension funds was challenged by four significant events that fundamentally altered the role of pensions as an employee benefit. These events were the lowest interest rates seen in decades, the impact of a punishing bear market, a weak economy, complicated funding requirements, and baffling accounting rules.

Separately, the impact of each event may have been manageable. But together, these factors threatened to derail the pension system, especially at companies with DB plans, which tend to be in traditional industries and heavily unionized. Taking the long view, some experts in the 1980s said that without a sudden improvement, the corporate DB industry would become almost non-existent by 2018.

By the early-1980s, the problems encountered by pension funds had become so overwhelming that funds were threatening to financially destabilize entire companies if their plans met actuarially determined funding requirements.

To stabilize the situation, companies reduced earnings to preserve their cash flows, causing widespread repercussions for the entire business. Company equity prices suffered. The gap between pension fund assets and liabilities had become a source of investor concern.

These problems did not result from the bear market alone. Several major, interacting influences drove the pension fund industry to make drastic changes. The first was lower interest rates.

Historically, yields on the 30-year Treasury bond were used to set the minimal funding required by pension funds. The reasoning behind this funding requirement was that the yield reflected current market rates for securities in which the company would invest the premium paid by the plan over the next 30 years. The lower the yield, the greater the plan sponsor's required contribution to finance future benefits because the money would earn less when invested.

Bond yields have been trending downward for about 20 years, steadily increasing minimum funding levels. In the early-1980s, the rate on the 30-year bond briefly exceeded 14% and then fell until it slid close to 5% in 1998. But, apart from occasional periods when some pension funds became underfunded, the declining rates did not pose a serious funding-related problem for most companies. During the equity bear market of the early-1980s, however, the problem assumed a new dimension as assets declined and rates fell sharply as the Federal Reserve eased the money supply aggressively.

The double threat of low interest rates increasing minimum-funding obligations, combined with low equity prices, hit pension plans hard.

But in October 2001, the Fed announced it would withdraw the 30-year Treasury bond, which was also a key benchmark for calculating fund contributions, lump-sum payments, and variable insurance premiums for the Pension Benefits Guaranty Corp.

The Bush Administration substituted a temporary replacement rate that allowed companies to use 120% of the rate at which the 30-year Treasury bonds, last issued in February 2001, had sold, even though they were then trading closer to 28-year bonds. That temporary situation lasted until the end of 2003. Companies feared that any permanent risk-free replacement based on lower rates, a suggestion made by the Treasury Department, would seriously harm DB plans.

A Declining Stock Market

The other major market event that eroded the financial stability of pension plans was declining stock prices. During the latter half of the 1990s, rapidly rising stock prices masked the effect of the steadily falling interest rates. But when the market correction began in 2000 and steepened in 2001, the problem became more serious.

While many funds were diversified and able to withstand much of the market's fall, the equity exposure of most companies' plans was around 65% or higher, with only about 35% in bonds. Had the market downturn not been so severe, this equity-heavy exposure could have enabled the pension funds to withstand the declining market. But from March 24, 2000, to March 24, 2003, the Russell 1000, an index of the 1,000 largest stocks, fell 44% in the most severe bear market in 30 years.

As fund assets and interest rates declined, plan sponsors used their profits or reserves, to continue funding their plans. The depressed economic conditions meant that pension funds, once considered a long-time source of surplus funds, were now a major drain on company resources.

The Weak U.S. Economy

The third serious factor affecting pension plans at this time was the weak U.S. economy. To meet pension obligations, some corporations had to dip into profits. Two industries suffered more than others as the economy dipped toward recession: the steel industry, which had been encountering increasingly tough times for two decades; and the airlines, which were hard-hit by the downturn in travel.

Some steel companies revoked retirees' pension plans, while America's eight largest airlines faced a combined deficit of more than $18 billion in 2003, according to estimates by the Fitch credit-rating agency. Only four years earlier, the airline industry had a pension plan surplus of $1 billion.

Hit by a combination of falling stock prices and lower inter-est rates, the pension funds of companies in the S&P 500 suf-fered their worst investment performance year ever, according to a 2002 study by Wilshire Associates. A group of 320 compa-nies suffered a pension deficit of $177 billion in 2002, according to Wilshire. The firm found that 89% of the companies' plans were underfunded (considered under ERISA to occur when the market value of a plan's assets falls below 90% of current liabilities).[19]

To meet their pension obligations, companies had to scramble. Ford Motor Company put $500 million into its pension fund in 2003 and 2004, according to Bloomberg News. The report added that SBC Communications would pay $1 billion to $2 billion into its pension and post-retirement health benefit funds in 2003. Georgia-Pacific Corp. said pension fund losses would require a charge to shareholder equity as high as $600 million in the fourth quarter of 2002.

In the first years of the new millennium, some companies had eliminated their established pension plans. Many others reduced pension benefits by restructuring their plans. General Motors issued bonds to raise $10 billion to buttress pension assets, while other corporations lobbied Congress for changes to reduce pen-sion contributions and make smaller retirement payments.

Due to the wave of plan terminations and bankruptcy filings, an increasing number of corporations sought relief from the PBGC, a federal agency that protects the pensions of nearly 44 million workers and retirees in over 27,500 private defined benefit pension plans.[20]

The increase in claims during 2002 caused the PBGC's single-employer insurance program to go from a surplus of $7.7 billion to a deficit of $3.6 billion, a loss of $11.3 billion in one year. This loss was more than five times greater than any previous one-year loss in the agency's history. By May 2003, the loss had grown to about $5.4 billion.

Complicated Accounting Rules

The fourth factor that contributed to the shift in pension plans was complicated pension accounting rules.

As if that were not enough to create the "perfect pension storm," companies had to contend with new and confusing accounting rules for pensions.

The rules in FASB (Financial Accounting Standards Board) rule No. 87, "Employers' Accounting for Pensions" were considered overly complicated and intentionally obtuse. For example, terms such as unrecognized gains and losses, service cost, prior service cost, projected benefit obligation, minimum pension liability, curtailment, and settlements were not specifically defined, some said. Rules from Section 412 of the Internal Revenue Code that determined when a company had to make pension plan contributions with unknown future cash flows added to the confusion.

One of the more complex accounting problems, which later had larger ramifications, was contained in the FASB rules used in preparing income statements. This rule said companies should include estimated gains, not actual gains or losses, from pension fund investments. This resulted in pension fund losses that were not reported on balance sheets. But in time, these liabilities caught up with companies and then presented an avalanche of losses.

This situation presented a problem for many companies that wanted to meet their pension obligations, while also balancing shareholder interests. Companies had to choose between meeting corporate needs versus the needs of their workforce. Unfortunately, these two interests were no longer aligned.

The conflicting battle for resources affected union negotiations where DB pension plans were often the center of attention. Traditionally, pensions were significant bargaining tools, considered as important as salaries and wages.

To meet these new financial demands, companies sought new sources of additional investment returns.

Some plans changed asset allocations to increase exposure to stocks. Other plan sponsors were advised to keep their traditional asset allocations. But it soon became apparent that there were no simple solutions. Some plan sponsors sought to diversify investment risk, while others began outsourcing their investment research and implementation by hiring dedicated money managers.

This confluence of events changed the way pensions were viewed and managed. Pensions also assumed a new role, largely due to changes in accounting rules. No longer were they dedicated long-term investment vehicles specifically designed to make regular distributions to a company's retirees; instead they became enticing pools of capital that could be diverted to meet other non-pension needs or whims.

The erosion of pensions continued, despite a number of significant lawsuits filed by abused pension recipients. This abuse did not go unnoticed by the federal regulators overseeing ERISA plans, the DOL, Justice Department, and U.S. Treasury. But the entrenched financial industry proved to be a formidable opponent, enough to steamroll the interests of retirees and other reformers.

By the 1980s, pension assets had become too enticing to resist. During this period, employers eliminated more than 2,000 pension plans, most of which were overfunded (with surplus assets of approximately $20 billion) and covered some two million workers.[21] These abuses caught the attention of Congress, which passed a 50% excise tax on companies that terminated their plans and looted their assets.

But if the corporation replaced the terminated plan with a "replacement plan," such as a 401(k) or new pension plan, it would pay only a 20% tax if it re-directed one quarter of the terminated plan's assets into the replacement plan.

As more companies closed their overfunded plans and used tax loopholes to re-direct pension assets to pay creditors or for takeovers, the role of 401(k)s became redefined. No longer were they the new sophisticated method of allowing employees to use self-directed accounts to accumulate retirement assets. Instead, they were really "the bastard stepchildren of dead pensions," according to author Ellen Schultz.[22]

Still, corporations continued to raid their pension plans by devising new schemes, such as the cash-balance plan. Developed in the early 1980s by actuaries, these plans slowed down the growth rate for individual pension awards. This reduced the contributions required per employee, and the pension plan would need to grow by a set amount annually versus the traditional formula that compounded based on salary times years of service. The cash-balance plan hurt employees, but benefited employers. Bank of America adopted a cash-balance plan to save money that had been lost on bad investments in South America. Instead of making pension contributions for its employees, Bank of America opted for the new plan, which it then mischaracterized to its own employees.

In 1986, new FASB 87 accounting standards went into effect. Among other things, the new standard required how corporations must state their pension obligations and how these changes affected quarterly income. This put more scrutiny on pensions contributed to, or detracted from, income and earnings volatility. By cutting pensions, corporations could create paper gains, which through the alchemy of corporate accounting, could be treated as income. This sleight of hand was used by IBM in 1999 when it cut its pensions by $450 million and then declared an increase of $200 million to its 1999 income, even though this money did not come from any new sales.

Most Employees Now Rely on 401(k)s, Not Pensions

The year 2012 marked the first time the majority of people will be relying more on 401(k) plans for retirement than on traditional pensions. This fundamental change makes it much more risky for individuals to plan their financial futures. It should cause a fundamental shift in the way people work, spend, save, and plan for retirement. The basic problem is how to determine what portfolio investments will deliver over time, a challenge even for dedicated investment professionals.

But turning the responsibility for making these difficult decisions over to amateur investors is dangerous. More optimistic investment professionals contend that employees will need more education and better guidance from plan sponsors, however, that guidance only helps those who have remained in their 401(k) plans.[23]

Many workers cash out of their 401(k) plans when they leave jobs, or they take out loans against them or make hardship withdrawals. The Government Accountability Office (GAO) reported that funds withdrawn for these purposes totaled $74 billion in 2006. While this represented only 3% of total retirement savings assets, these withdrawals posed "a nontrivial impact, to employees, who later regretted wasting their retirement savings," according to Brigitte Madrian, a public policy and corporate management professor at Harvard University's Kennedy School of Government.[24]

The decline of traditional pension plans, combined with the increased reliance on 401(k)s to provide some means of future retirement income, makes it imperative that investors know the fees and expenses they are paying in their 401(k) plans and how they harm returns.

As we will see in Chapter 2, fund expenses are crucial to building investment wealth. In an example provided by the DOL, a 1% difference in fees and expenses can mean a reduction in an investor's retirement account of 28%. That significant reduction is separate from any market returns, which will only decrease in a bear market.

The main difference between these variables–expenses, fees and market returns–is that investors can control fees and expenses, but this is only possible if they are known to investors. This basic fact explains the historic importance of the DOL fee and expense disclosure regulations.

CHAPTER 2

THE IMPACT OF MUTUAL FUND EXPENSES

When the average investor buys $10,000 of Class A shares in a load mutual fund, how much of that money actually gets invested in the market?

If you thought it would be $10,000, you are not even close.

The way load mutual funds operate, by the time the average investor writes their check to fund a $10,000 investment, only $9,450 will be invested in the market before they even leave the advisor's office. The other $550 gets eaten up by commissions and sales charges, which go to the selling broker-dealer and the fund distributor. In addition, another $50 typically is paid as an underwriting commission to the fund distributor.

That's just for starters. Every year, the shareholder pays about 25 basis points (bps), or one-quarter of 1%, in 12b-1 fees, a management fee of about 90 bps, plus a $20 administrative fee to the fund distributor.

Many mutual funds are so laden with special charges that the DOL has identified 17 distinct fees which can be paid by shareholders. While some costs are well-known (administrative fees, for example), there also are hidden costs, such as trading expenses, which can add up to 50% to shareholders' costs. While this may sound inconsequential, the fees can be devastating. Finance Professor Burton Malkiel estimates that over time, fees of just 3% can devour up to 50% of investment returns.[1]

Why Managing Fund Expenses is Critical

While the majority of investors focus on individual fund selection or asset mix, they miss the most critical and easily manageable variable in investment product selection: fund expenses and fees.

Investors buy mutual funds for a simple reason: they expect a positive return. But there is more to it than seeking a simple solution. "Just as people do not buy drills because they want drills, they buy drills because they want holes, people buy mutual funds either for return or as part of a diversified portfolio. It's true a fund can lose money when part of a portfolio, but it should behave as stated in its own investment goals." That is the obvious thing to expect.[2]

But less obvious is the fact that all mutual funds charge fees and expenses which are entirely paid by investors. This is justifiable and understandable. The problem is that most investors do not receive the full benefits of what they are paying for, nor do they know exactly how much they are paying for each individual service. This situation is unique to the 401(k) industry and represents a serious abuse of consumers, who are often investing hundreds of thousands of dollars accumulated over a lifetime of work. These are accumulated savings, which are uninsured and can never be replaced once they are lost.

Managing and manipulating fund expenses represents a main point of contention between investors and mutual fund companies. Every day, participants in 401(k) plans pay about $164 million in fees to the financial services industry.[3] While this is a stunning amount, the problem is that most investors do not even know they are paying anything. From the mutual fund industry's perspective this omission is beneficial since "the vast majority of the new funds added to 401 (k) plans are high-cost actively managed equity funds, as opposed to lower-cost equity index funds."[4] This means more unsuspecting investors are paying more for expensive products when less costly ones will suffice. Most investors fail to recognize that the main performance difference between funds is largely attributed to expenses.

This explains why Nobel Laureate William F. Sharpe asserts that the difference between market returns and a fund's actual return is simply due to costs. So in a practical situation, the difference between the returns of a particular 401 (k) plan and market returns is represented by the actual costs of the plan.

Fund costs and fees are off the radar screen for most 401 (k) plan participants and fund investors, and sadly, even 401 (k) plan administrators. But in today's higher risk, low-return environment, one of the few things investors can readily control is the fees they pay fund companies.

These fees come in a variety of forms and often are not broken down, specified or easily explained by fund companies and investment professionals. This is because fees, in all of their various formats, are used to support the administrative, sales and investment management departments common to fund companies, especially those which employ national sales forces and large investment staffs.

Fees have a direct impact on one of the most critical factors in selecting a mutual fund: the expense ratio. But according to one study, 401 (k) plans often offer funds that are cheaper-than-average, at least if they were offered to individual investors in their own accounts. A study by Deloitte and the Investment Company Institute found that in 2008, the average 401 (k) stock fund had an expense ratio of 0.72%, compared with an average of 0.84% for all stock funds. In fixed income, the average 401 (k) bond fund had an expense ratio of 0.52% compared with an average of 0.63% for all bond funds.[5] But this study did not include other related 401 (k) administrative fees or the use of ETFs that have lower expenses than mutual funds.

The expense ratio is a critical measure of the fund's total annual expenses expressed as a percentage of the fund's net assets. For example, an expense ratio of 1% represents the annual charge to the fund's assets, including your proportional interest in those assets of 1% every year. An extra 0.5% annual fee can cut an employee's savings by 10% by the time they are 65-years-old, according to Vanguard.[6]

The expense ratio includes management fees, marketing and distribution fees (12b-1 fees) and other ongoing fees that are deducted from a mutual fund's assets. These fees pay for the services of the mutual fund's investment advisor, the selling advisor or broker, transfer agent, and other expenses. Charges which are not included in the expense ratio are front-end sales charges and Contingent Deferred Sales Load (CDSC) because they are charged one time and directly to the investor.

Investors can see a fund's fee table in the front of a mutual fund prospectus, which includes the expense ratio, front-end sales charges, and CDSCs. However, the problem is that few investors ever read the prospectus. This fact is well-known in the industry, yet this document contains all the information which is required to be supplied to investors that can effectively absolve fund management and advisors of any claims made against them.

One veteran financial advisor said burying critically-important information in the prospectus is done by the fund industry "in an effort to protect its interests, [as a result] the industry created word games and a philosophical spin to define disclosure, leading fiduciaries to believe they acted responsibly in authorizing certain transactions, platforms, approaches, and fund types. Instead of disclosure meaning possession of facts coupled with understanding, it has evolved to mean legalese, or rarely understood, seldom-read prospectuses."[7]

How Fees Affect Investors

While there are many fees associated with mutual funds, their impact is not often recognized by investors. This is because fees are commonly deducted on an annual or quarterly basis and appear as line items on a fund statement.

Regardless of how they are named, fees have a definite drag on returns. Here is some of the simple arithmetic from the DOL that drives home the importance of fees in a 401(k) plan:

"Assume that you are an employee with 35 years until retirement and a current 401 (k) account balance of $25,000. If returns on investments in your account over the next 35 years average 7% and fees and expenses reduce your average returns by 0.5%, your account balance will grow to $227,000 at retirement, even if there are no further contributions to your account. If fees and expenses are 1.5%, however, your account balance will grow to only $163,000. The 1% difference in fees and expenses would reduce your account balance at retirement by 28%."[8]

In this example, the return is reduced by a staggering 28% over 35 years.

Even a very small fee has a significant impact. In another example, provided by the Center for Retirement Research, over a 30-year career, an annual fee of just 0.7% of assets reduces a participant's balance at the time of retirement by more than one-eighth (12.50%.)[9]

Another example illustrates the minimum return an investor needs to achieve just to cover their expenses. Assume that an investment advisor agrees to manage a $100,000 portfolio of stock funds for 1.5% management fee. If these stock funds also have annual expenses of 1.4%, which is about the average for domestic stock funds, then an investor effectively incurs a total of 2.9% in expenses each year, which are being deducted from their portfolio return before any of the gain accrues to the investor. In a low investment return environment, these fees can become significant. Warren Buffett has predicted that the next 20 to 30 years will be a low-yield investment environment, with fixed income yielding an average of 3% and equities 5%. In this example, over half of this hypothetical equity fund's return could be consumed by fees.[10]

To make matters worse, it is not exactly clear what investors receive for paying these fees over a 35-year-period, aside from receiving a quarterly newsletter. This DOL expense example cited earlier also assumes a constant 7% return over 35 years. That return is optimistic and certainly open to question; if it is lower, your return drops significantly. (The historical return for the S&P 500 Index over the past 35 years is 10% per year.) However, these average returns include returns from bull and bear markets occurring over shorter time frames, which can reduce returns significantly.[11]

Over a shorter time span, the average mutual fund lost 3% of its value in 2011, while the S&P 500 index lost a minuscule .003% during 2011, ending the year at about the same point as where it started. But during 2011, the indexes suffered considerably more volatility. On 40% of the trading days in 2011, the Dow Jones Industrial Index gyrated 100 points in a single day, while the S&P 500 suffered through more than 60 days when the index value rocked by about 2% or more. The low return and increasing volatility may help explain why investors redeemed over $250 billion in equity mutual fund assets in 2011.[12]

Another study of the popular target date funds by Towers Watson found that most target-date fund owners lose 30% or more of their potential retirement income to fees. This loss is equivalent to losing between five and 15 years' worth of retirement income from an employee's 401(k) account over a worker's lifetime.[13]

But again, investment returns are outside of your control, while one of the most important variables you can control is fees. In a 401(k) plan, managing the fee variables are the responsibility of your employer, who may, or may not, be acting in your best interests by monitoring overall fund and administrative expenses charged by the mutual fund record keeper, fund administrator, and mutual fund companies. The way the system is organized, employers have the responsibility for managing the fees that impact investors' net return over many years. When this responsibility is mismanaged, employees assume all the costs. When losses occur, they represent actual lost money for employees, but are often considered just an administrative error for management. There has to be more accountability built into this 401(k) system.

Fees Associated with Mutual Fund Purchases

The reality of mutual fund investing is that all investors pay fees, but sometimes the fees are not visible. All mutual fund share classes generate fees that are paid out of the fund's assets to the fund's portfolio managers. These fees are charged for in both "soft" and "hard" dollars. (Soft dollars are a means of paying brokerage firms for services through commission revenue, as opposed to through normal direct payments or hard dollar fees.)

Investment professionals who sell the mutual funds are compensated through 12b-1 fees and revenue sharing. These fees are controversial and are paid to the fund company distributor to increase sales. Revenue sharing payments are more difficult for investors to discover.

The other complicating factor is that fees and expenses vary widely between different funds and fund companies. These fees can range from less than .10% (often for index funds) to over 2% (often for emerging market equity funds), and are affected by the fund's investment style, market capitalization, assets under management, comparisons between other similar funds, the fund company and fund share class.

Many of these fees, (but not including the very important trading costs) are included in the expense ratio. This ratio is calculated by adding all fund expenses divided by the average net assets to derive a percentage figure. The SEC requires that all funds make this calculation the same way to facilitate comparisons between funds. A typical mutual fund expense ratio can range between 0.20% and 2.0% of fund assets.

The expense ratio can be broken down into three main categories: investment management, fund services, and 12b-1 fees.

Here is a list of the fees and expenses commonly charged to investors in mutual funds:[14]

Administrative Expense: A portion of a fund's expense ratio is allocated to overhead expenses, such as the cost of registering the mutual fund, mailings, maintaining a customer service call center, etc. Although these are all necessary costs, they vary in size from fund to fund. Typically, this fee ranges from 0.05% to 0.40% of invested assets.

Revenue Sharing: Easily one of the most controversial practices in the mutual fund industry, revenue sharing has been politely described as the "behind-the-scenes" transfer of revenue from investment funds to the 401(k) plan recordkeeper as an incentive to include the mutual funds on the plan's investment menu.[15] This fee usually consists of 12b-1 fees, shareholder servicing fees, sub-transfer agency fees, and commissions

These fees are so well hidden that professional plan administrators often do now know what they are paying or how they are managed. According to the Callan Associate's survey, 19% of plan sponsors did not know what proportion of their funds paid revenue sharing, and the 37% of respondents that had excess revenue sharing credited back to plan participants did not know how this happens.[16]

According to a 401(k) plan expert at the firm which conducted the survey, "The number of sponsors that are unclear about the status of their plan's fees is remarkable–especially in light of the DOL's new fee regulations."[17]

12b-1 Fees: Named after the 1980 SEC rule that created them, 12b-1 fees have been controversial since they were first introduced. These fees allow mutual funds to charge investors for sales and marketing costs and were originally rationalized to regulators and the public as an incentive to strengthen customer communications and provide more investor education. Over the years, as fund assets grew, this rationale was scrapped. Today, these fees are charged by some mutual funds, including no-load funds, to cover expenses associated with marketing and distributing mutual funds. These fees are generally paid to an intermediary, often called the broker of record, for placing clients' assets into a fund. They are also called "trailing" commissions paid to brokers when clients keep their money in certain share classes over time.

Additionally, these fees can be used to compensate a third-party administrator (TPA) for plan administration or recordkeeping services. Commonly, these fees generally range between 0.25% and 1.0% of invested assets. SEC Rule 12(b)-1 allows for two types of 12(b)-1 fees: (1) sales commission fees are paid to a registered representative for selling mutual funds for an individual or within a plan; and (2) servicing fees paid to a person or entity, who services an account after the sale of the fund. This rule is partially responsible for the proliferation of mutual funds in individual account plans because it pays a trail of commissions for as long as the investor owns the funds.

Critics contend these payments, which can become very significant over time, alter mutual fund relationships since they ultimately favor investment professionals and fund company salespeople more than individual investors. This is especially evident when fund asset levels increase and fund companies fail to reduce expense ratios to reflect a fund's improved cost efficiencies. Not surprisingly, as many fund companies gather more assets, they keep their expense ratios high to maintain profit margins.

As a result, cost savings often are not passed along to shareholders, while fund companies post significant profits. The fees have also been cited as fomenting agency problems. This has led one expert to comment: "The [agency] rule creates a conflict-of-interest between the brokerage firm and the mutual fund, thereby rendering each unable to devote their loyalties to the plan participants."[18]

Shareholder Servicing Fee: Shareholder servicing fees are similar to 12b-1 fees, but are typically used by no–load mutual fund products. Only service providers such as TPAs, and not brokers, can receive these fees, which can be used to compensate a TPA for recordkeeping, annual administration, and education services. No-load fund products can pay up to 0.25% of invested assets as a shareholder servicing fee without being required by SEC rules to call it a 12b-1 fee.

Sub-Transfer Agency Fees (sub-TA fees): Considered one of the most esoteric and unneeded of mutual fund fees, this is usually a payment to a TPA or record keeper who holds an omnibus account at the mutual fund company. Omnibus accounting eliminates the need for the mutual fund company to maintain individual participant accounts. Instead, participant accounts are maintained by the TPA or record keeper. Because this reduces the cost for the mutual fund company, they pay the TPA or record keeper a fee for this service. Typically, this fee ranges from 0.10% to 0.35% of invested assets.

Commissions: Commissions are usually paid from plan assets to a broker for servicing the retirement plan account. This fee typically ranges from 0.25% to 1% of invested assets.

Investment Management Fee: This fee is charged to pay for investment management; mainly the portfolio manager's time, internal research, support of the investment management organization, and other associated expenses related to deciding which securities the mutual fund will acquire or sell. Typically, this fee ranges from 0.25% to 1% of fund assets.

Sales Load: This is the commission funds pay to brokers. The SEC doesn't limit what a fund can charge, but the Financial Industry Regulatory Authority (formerly the NASD) limits its members to a maximum of 8.5%. Sales loads come in two types – front end and back end.

Sales Charge on Purchases: This is a front-end sales load and is paid by investors when they purchase shares. This fee is directly taken from the investor's amount.

Deferred Sales Charge: This is a back-end sales load and the fee is paid when investors redeem shares. Generally, the percentage is calculated on the lesser of the investment amount or the redemption amount. This means that if an investor's shares have appreciated, the fund will take a percentage of the initial invested amount. If the investor's shares fall in value, the fund company takes a percentage of the selling amount.

Contingent Deferred Sales Load: This is a sales load that decreases with time and is designed to entice investors to hold onto their investments. Generally, they're structured like this: Investors pay 4% if they redeem within one year; 2% if they sell within two years; and 0% if redeemed after two years.

Redemption Fee: This fee is charged when shareholders redeem shares, which sounds like a back-end sales load, but technically is not. It's not a sales load because the redemption fee is used to pay for the redemption and not paid to a broker for securing the sale. The SEC limits the redemption fee to 2%.

Still, funds love redemption fees because they are not paid to the fund company, but to the fund itself. This payment flow reimburses the fund for direct and indirect trading costs the fund pays to redeem shares that short-term traders exchange. (This fee was enacted by the SEC to help prevent market-timing trading.)

This fee can also be used to boost fund performance. "Fund companies love charging redemption fees because it helps fund returns. This is especially true when redemption fees exceed the actual cost of short-term investing in the fund."[32] Because the fees bolster fund returns, the improved performance figures make the fund more attractive by improving quoted returns, even though they were never derived from any actual investment strategy or manager talent.

Exchange Fee: Want to trade in your shares for another mutual fund in the same class? If so, then you may incur an exchange fee.

Account Fee: This is an account maintenance fee charged to keep an investor's account on the recordkeeper's electronic books.

Purchase Fee: This resembles a front-end sales load to the investor, but the money does not go to a broker, but to the fund.

Annual Fund Operating Expenses

These are fees the fund pays to its management. These fees are governed by SEC rules. Investors often see these values expressed as part of the fund's total expense ratio.

Management Fees: This is how much the investment advisor, managers, and their affiliates get paid, as well as any administrative fees that don't fall under "other expenses" section below.

Distribution and/or Service (12b-1) Fees: 12b-1 fees, also known as Distribution Fees, are especially controversial and have been the target of reform for over two decades. The reason: ""Every dollar collected in 12b-1 fees is a dollar deducted from a fund's return," according to SEC Commissioner Elisse Walter.[19]

Distribution fees are governed by the SEC's rule 12b-1 (hence the name) and are now used to pay commissions to brokers. The fee is controversial since it is essentially used to hide a sales load inside an otherwise innocuous looking marketing charge (distribution also covers the printing of prospectuses, purchasing promotional items, advertising, etc.). The total amount of 12b-1 fees a fund can charge is capped at 1% of assets. The 12b-1 fee is also used to pay shareholder service fees, which covers salaries for the call center staffs, who respond to shareholder inquiries. Some fund experts consider this another way to hide fees. FINRA limits the sales load to a maximum of 0.25%.[20]

Contingent Deferred Sales Charge (CDSC)

This fee is charged when you sell mutual fund shares. For example, if you redeem shares valued at $1,000, and the mutual fund imposes a CDSC of 1%, you would be charged $10 and receive $990. For B shares, CDSCs normally decline over time and, eventually are eliminated after six years from the purchase of those shares.

Front-End Sales Charge

This fee is charged when you purchase mutual fund shares. For example, you spend $1,000 to purchase Class A shares and the fund imposes a front-end sales charge of 5%. You are charged $50 on your purchase and receive shares with a market value of $950. Depending on the size of your purchase, a breakpoint discount can lower this sales charge.

Breakpoint Discounts

A mutual fund may offer you discounts, called breakpoint discounts, on the front-end sales charge if you:

- Make a large purchase.
- Already hold other mutual funds offered by the same fund family.
- Commit to regularly purchasing the mutual fund's shares.

Understanding Mutual Fund Share Classes

To keep things complicated, mutual funds offer a variety of share classes, which may have different voting rights, holding periods, minimum purchase amounts and commission structures paid to the selling broker. (For a description of fund share classes, see chart on page 49.)

Fees Embedded in Various Share Classes

Mutual fund investors commonly face a confusing set of choices when it comes to selecting a fund share class. While each class offers exposure to the same fund, the share classes provide distinct benefits to the fund's salespeople rather than shareholders.

This is because each share class is designed to have its own cost structure to provide different payments at different times to financial professionals, advisors and plan sponsors. Regardless of the share class, however, they are all based on the same mutual funds. Because of this common source of revenue-generating assets, the gross investment return (that is, before any fees are deducted) is the same for all shareholders in the fund. However, the net investment return (the gross return less expenses) varies depending on the share class' expense level.

A good analogy here involves a plane full of airline passengers flying to one city, yet each passenger is paying a dramatically different airfare, even though they are all going to the same destination on the same plane. In a mutual fund, the main difference between fund share classes is that the fund will charge different fees and expenses depending on the share class. In turn, the fund's net return is also affected by the choice of the share class, even though the portfolio manager follows the same strategy for the entire fund, regardless of share class.

However, as described in the airplane passenger example, the management fee charged by the fund management company often does not vary from share class to share class; they often are exactly the same for each.

How important is the choice of a share class to an investor? According to Drinker Biddle, if an investor makes a $10,000 investment and holds it for 10-years in the most expensive share class, the investor would incur $1,713 in expenses. However, an investment in a less expensive share class would have been charged about half that amount, or $847. In other words, on a $10,000 investment, the participant would have earned almost $900 more with the least expensive share class compared to the most expensive, yet the fund's performance would have been identical.

Even worse, Biddle said "fiduciaries have a duty to understand the range of possible payments to the broker-dealer and financial advisor and to evaluate any potential conflicts (for example, is there an incentive for the advisor to recommend a particular share class?). Unfortunately, as a practical matter, most fiduciaries are not aware of the existence of the multiple share classes or of the impact on participants of the selection of a particular share class. In fact, in some cases fiduciaries may not even know the share class owned by their plan."

Transaction, or Trading, Costs

Of all the expenses associated with administering a 401(k) plan, one of the most difficult to identify, yet most important, are expenses associated with buying and selling the fund's shares.

As the interpreter and enforcer of ERISA regulations, the DOL has asked fiduciaries "to identify all costs which are "return-reducing" and ensure these costs are reasonable and fully disclosed to participants," according to a Brightscope paper.[21]

The SEC has identified four major types of transactions costs which have a direct impact on investment returns:

Commissions are paid to a broker who acts as agent for customers while executing and clearing trades.

Spread costs are the price gaps between "asked" and "bid" prices. The difference between the bid price and the asked price is known as the "spread."

Market Impact Costs are incurred when an equity's price changes due to an increase or decrease in buyer or seller interest.

Opportunity Costs are the costs related to missed, incompleted, or "broken" trades.

These costs affect the trading of all investment instruments, but only commissions are directly measured and disclosed by investment funds subject to the Investment Company Act of 1940. The other costs are not disclosed since they are difficult to determine and more difficult to explain. Regardless, they have a definite impact on fund returns.

Industry studies on transaction costs indicate they are on the order of 1%-2% of a fund's net assets and are often as large, or larger, than fund expense ratios. This has prompted one leading firm in the transaction costs analysis business to call transaction costs "one of the largest erosions of investment value that investors face." The SEC said that transactions costs "can greatly exceed the explicit costs."[22]

While these expenses are difficult to calculate, they are important factors that reduce fund returns and trigger a fiduciary obligation. According to Greg Kasten, CEO of Unified Trust: "The fact that turnover costs are 'hard to find' does not give the plan fiduciary the leisure of deciding not to monitor them."

The DOL disclosure regulations also cover these important trading-related expenses that are not now readily available. Isolating trading expenses should have a negative impact on multi-manager funds, which are comprised of numerous independent, discretionary, active traders.

The Importance of Trading Expenses

Trading costs are associated with investment management, but they are not included in the expense ratio of a fund. Instead, they are paid by the actual shareholders out of the invested assets. In practical terms, this fee represents the cost of buying and selling securities, but it is a significant, hidden expenses. Investors who want to find their fund's trading costs have to obtain the Statement of Additional Information (SAI) report, which is issued separately from the fund prospectus. Even then, the expenses will be difficult to decipher and may not be complete.

Mutual Fund Share Classes and Expenses

	Class A Shares	Class B Shares	Class C Shares	Class I Shares
Charges front-end load	Yes, so dollar amount I invested is reduced by amount of sales charge.	No, so full dollar amount paid is invested.	No, so full dollar amount paid is invested.	No, so full dollar amount paid is invested.
Charges asset-based sales charge	Yes, often 0.25% annually.	Yes, often higher than A share charge.	Yes, often higher than A shares.	12b-1 fees and other loads do not apply.
Breakpoint discount effect	Eligible for break point discounts on large purchases.			No. Fees vary widely.
Other features	Often carries the lowest expense ratio of the three share classes.	Generate a CDSC if held less than a certain time, often 6 years. When CDSC expires, B shares convert to A shares. May generate a sales charge when sold.	Often charge 1% if shares are sold in less than one year. Do not convert to A shares. Have higher costs than A shares if held f or a long period.	Sold to large investors on a negotiated basis.

CDSC is a Contingent Deferred Sales Charge. I shares are sometimes known as Y Shares.

Source: FINRA, Financial Times

Trading costs have a direct impact on a fund's total return. Brokerage fees average 1.44% in expenses, according to financial advisor Ric Edelman.[28] High trading costs can significantly reduce returns, especially if a fund is actively traded. Studies have found that equity mutual funds with long track records generally fail to match the performance of market index funds, while actively managed mutual funds have very poor track records and underperform their benchmark indexes 99.4% of the time over the past 30 years.[23]

Trading costs also are very different between mutual funds and ETFs, due to how they trade and their composition. ETFs have very small cash positions compared to mutual funds because they do not have to liquidate securities when trades are made. In contrast, mutual funds keep about 3% cash on hand, which acts as a drag on performance since the fund is not fully invested. According to Darwin Abrahamson, mutual funds disregard trading costs and "best execution," (jargon for getting the best price), because they are more interested in soft dollars payments paid by their executing brokers. In practice, soft dollars mean that for every dollar spent on commissions, the broker (service provider) rebates 50 cents in expenses back to the mutual fund. This practice is not common in the ETF world, nor do ETFs pay revenue sharing to advisors.

Studies of actively managed equity mutual funds have found that, on average, trading costs (expressed as a component of total transaction costs) are about as large as the fees charged directly to participants and to a lesser degree, the plan sponsors. These are also known as "explicit fees."[24] The fees collected through the expense ratio account for about three-quarters of all explicit fees.[25]

Trading expenses can range from an average 0.27% for low turnover domestic equity funds to 1.65% for high turnover domestic equity funds. Some experts have noted that the true cost of trading is not in commissions, but in the spreads that exist between bids and offers. While important, this cost is totally outside of a 401(k) participant's access.

Another problem caused by trading costs is their disproportionate cost allocation among plan participants. In cases where there are active traders in a plan, less active traders can effectively subsidize the trading costs of more active participants. In an ideal situation, all investors in a plan would pay their trading costs on a proportional basis to reflect their investment balances in the pool.

However, if the pool has more frequent traders, who incur trading costs based on their average balances, these trading expenses are offset to passive investors. This situation is complicated when a plan offers different share classes that are also used by more active traders. In this situation, all participants are subject to lower returns since they are effectively subsidizing the costs of the more active traders.[26]

Another key component of trading costs is portfolio turnover, which measures buying and selling activities of fund holdings over a year. Technically, this measure includes the turnover rate for a mutual fund by dividing the lesser of purchases or sales of portfolio securities for the particular year, by the monthly average value of the portfolio securities owned by the fund during the past 13 months. In 2009, this rate increased slightly, placing it somewhat above the average experience of the past 36 years (the average for the years between 1974–2009 was 58%), according to a 2010 Investment Company Institute report.

In the case of multi-manager funds managed by Russell Investments, the turnover rate for the period ending Oct. 31, 2011 ranged from 29% for a tax-exempt bond fund to 339% for a short duration bond fund. Commissions are critical expenses and are affected by the investment strategy, manager turnover, market volatility and portfolio strategy changes. These costs are always outside of the control of shareholders, but are costs borne by them.

Understanding trading costs is a very arcane and politically sensitive area of institutional and retail mutual fund trading. This is because the institutionalization of the equities market requires the ability to trade huge blocks of shares instantly at the best possible price without moving the market.

The price displacement caused by trading large numbers of shares is called "market impact" and it is an important source of price risk. Market impact happens when buyers or sellers initiate large purchases or sales and effectively elicit interest in the stocks which can raise (or lower) the price to make it more expensive to trade. For example, this happens when large buy-orders push prices higher. While important, market impact is one of the key factors which comprise the "best price," along with identifying liquidity pools, high- and low-information traders, commissions, the use of soft dollars, timing, and the choice of electronic trading systems. Mutual funds are all subject to these trading factors, but not ETFs.

The Recordkeeping Industry

Managing the costs built into 401(k)s has evolved over the past 30 years, but their management has become the specialty of the recordkeeping industry. In 1974, the same year ERISA was passed, individual retirement accounts (IRAs) were created for individuals who could not participate in pension or 401(k) plans. IRA participants made tax deductible contributions and received a favorable tax treatment on their investment earnings. Since this was offered on a mass basis, it generated significant interest from individuals, as well as the brokerage and mutual fund businesses intent on managing these new asset pools. This built new business relationships between mutual funds, which offered their trading services, in exchange for accessing the brokerage firm's sales force. The new relationship enabled fund companies to push their products through new sales channels to more potential investors.

In 1981, Congress passed the Economic Recovery Tax Act (ERTA), which made IRAs more publicly available and increased the investment limit to $2,000 per year. The Revenue Act of 1978 created 401(k) plans. With their technology platforms is place to service IRAs, brokerage firms and fund companies could now handle the larger accounts, accompanied by expanded product offerings to make them all available to 401(k)s. This created renewed competition among providers, who pushed to add new services, and anything else which would differentiate their service packages.

Recordkeeping became important to provide daily, per share pricing for individual accounts. This repetitive, continuous business, operating with real-time prices, fostered a specialized business that required service providers to comply with its technology processing protocols. If a supplier could not format their system to meet the recordkeepers' demands, they were not invited to participate in the business.

To provide more specialized services, new businesses, such as third party administrators and fund administration, were added. The net effect was an increase in fees, which soon became too complicated to be enumerated to companies. By the 1990s, the industry streamlined their pitch by offering bundled services in exchange for managing all of a fund's assets. This simplified package had great appeal, but it masked individual costs. No one complained. As a result, that business model thrived.

In the interim, laws regarding the regulation of 401(k)s lagged the industry. IRAs were managed by individuals, while 401(k)s were trusts managed by employers. The legal evolution, however, made 401(k)s exempt from ERISA and all of its prudent man investment standards, including the prohibition against undisclosed fees, conflicts-of-interest, and offering restricted lists of approved investments. It was under these adverse conditions that average individual investors were given the mandate and authority to plan, manage and live with the end results of investing in an increasingly complex world. This was the same task that professional money managers had been struggling with for decades. In 2011, 79% of active, large-cap fund managers failed to beat the S&P 500 index, the worst showing since 1997, according to Morningstar. A main reason was fees. An analysis of the data found that yearly expenses for the large-cap funds averaged 1.3% compared to 0.69% for index funds.[27]

Examples of How High Fund Expenses Hurt Investors

The number of academic papers and authoritative actuarial examples on the importance of fees agree on the fact that the lower the fees, the higher an investor's investment returns. For this reason, many experts note that the optimum fund expense ratio is 0.5% or less annually or less.

While there are many complex issues in the investment management world, one of the easiest is to remember is this simple rule: The gap between the returns of a particular 401(k) plan and the market represents the 401(k) plan's actual costs.

The dramatic difference in reducing fees to an individual investor is illustrated in these examples:

- Assume a 30-year-old employee makes $50,000 per year and saves 6% of annual pay.

- This same employee gets a 50% 401(k) match, and earns 3% annual pay raises.

- At retirement, he would have $115,000 more in savings at retirement if his 401(k) plan had fees of 0.6% instead of 0.9%, (assuming an 8% annual return.)[28]

A study of target-date funds, the most common default 401(k) investment, found that most target-date fund owners lose 30% or more of their potential retirement income to fees. That works out to be between five and 15 years' worth of retirement income that is deducted from a 401(k) account over a worker's lifetime due to high fees (ranging from .5% to 1% annually), based on a Towers Watson analysis. This same analysis found that the perceived benefits from TDFs (asset allocation, diversification, risk management) were negated by the high fees charged to investors.[29]

In another example, switching to a target-based investment with a lower expense ratio could allow an investor to retire years earlier.

- Consider an employee with a starting salary of $45,000, who contributes 8% of his pay to a 401(k) each year between ages 25 and 62.

- If he invests his retirement savings in a target-date fund charging 1% annually, he will lose 13.9 years' worth of retirement income to fees.

- If he instead chose a target-date fund charging 0.5% in annual fees, he will spend 7.7 years' worth of retirement income on fees. An even more affordable target-date fund charging 0.2% in fees would deplete his savings by just 3.2 years' worth of retirement income.[30]

As John Bogle observes, "An obvious and documented inverse relationship . . . clearly links mutual fund costs and mutual fund returns."[31]

The Impact of Fees on Mutual Fund Returns

Savings rate: $10,000
Average rate of return: 7%
Expense Fee: Susan, 0.5%; George, 1.0%; Morgan, 1.50%

Fee #1--Susan   Fee #2--George   Fee #3--Morgan

Year	Savings	Fee #1	Balance $50,000	Savings
1	$10,000	$321	$63,879	$10,000
5	$10,000	$648	$128,967	$10,000
10	$10,000	$1,191	$236,981	$10,000
15	$10,000	$1,933	$384,726	$10,000
20	$10,000	$2,949	$586,817	$10,000
25	$10,000	$4,338	$863,245	$10,000
30	$10,000	$6,238	$1,241,354	$10,000

Year	Fee #2	Balance $50,000	Loss to Fee #1	Savings
1	$642	$635,558	($321)	$10,000
5	$1,276	$126,321	($2,646)	$10,000
10	$2,304	$228,119	($8,862)	$10,000
15	$3,676	$363,898	($20,828)	$10,000
20	$5,505	$545,002	($41,815)	$10,000
25	7945%	$786,561	($76,684)	$10,000
30	$11,200	$1,108,756	($132,598)	$10,000

Year	Fee #3	Balance $50,000	Loss to Fee #1	Loss to Fee #2
1	$963	$63,237	($642)	($321)
5	$1,884	$123,722	($5,246)	($2,599)
10	$3,344	$219,596	($17,385)	($8,523)
15	$5,243	$344,276	($40,450)	($19,622)
20	$7,712	$506,419	($80,398)	($38,583)
25	$10,923	$717,281	($145,964)	($69,281)
30	$15,099	$991,500	($249,853)	($117,256)

Source: Paychecks for Life, Charles D. Epstein, The 401(k) Coach, 2012, p. 128.

As this chart demonstrates, the impact of small changes in fees on long-term performance is significant. This chart shows how three individuals, who each save $10,000 annually and earn a 7% return, sustained very different end results (and losses) due to paying fees of 0.5%, 1% and 1.5% respectively over time periods ranging from one to 30 years. These significant losses are detailed in the headings, "Losses to Fees" for the three different fee levels.

CHAPTER 3

THE POWER OF DISCLOSURE:
THE DOL'S FEE AND EXPENSE REGULATIONS

After at least a decade of regulatory and industry debate, people who participate in 401(k) plans will finally be able to see what they are paying in fees and expenses thanks to the DOL. While fee and expense disclosure is taken for granted in many industries and has been an accepted element of consumer protection in the U.S. since the early 1900s, fee disclosure in the 401(k) industry is unprecedented in this format and on this scale until it was mandated in 2012.

On July 1, 2012, new transparency requirements took effect under rules §408(b)(2) and §404(a)(5) of ERISA. Additional disclosures are also required on revised DOL Form 5500 that plan sponsors must file with federal regulators.

While the regulations seem forbidding because of their legal language and technical titles (they are named for the sections of the ERISA legislation), they represent a major advance for individual investors. The reason: investors will finally be able to identify the fees and expenses they pay to participate in a 401(k) plan.

What most investors don't realize is that these fees are among the most important and easily managed investment variables to control. But this has not been possible simply because fees have been kept hidden because of the way 401(k) plans are designed and administered.

The new DOL regulations also must be examined in the context of the deteriorating quality of retirement in America. Consider these results from a 2011 survey commissioned by the city of New York and conducted by Deloitte Touche Tohmatsu Limited:[1]

- Compared to the 2010 survey, the average 401(k) participant's account balance was flat or had decreased slightly.

- Only 39% of plan sponsors indicated that they are very informed when it comes to their ability to deliver the disclosures. More than half (56%) say they are somewhat informed.

- More than one-third of New York City households headed by a person nearing retirement age (55-64) have less than $10,000 in savings. These households will either have to subsist almost entirely on Social Security or will have an elderly member who is unable to retire.[2]

- Between 2000 and 2009, the percentage of employees in New York City who had access to employer-sponsored retirement plans declined from 48% to 40%, which is below the U.S. average of 53%.[3]

The phasing out of pension plans, declines in home equity and savings, and flat-to-negative portfolio returns over the past decade make 401(k) participants reluctant to give up their steady wages and benefits to retire. But all this is not new.

What has changed—and has far more serious implications for America's policies related to job creation and its critical corollary, retirement—is the employer-employee relationship.

The demise, some call it looting, of the U.S. pension system was an intentional effort to use financial engineering, new accounting rules, and aggressive anti-employee policies to eliminate the long-term security of employees and divert billions in pension assets to other uses. As corporations re-directed employee pension money, it was used to artificially boost earnings, pay executive salaries and their retirement plans, and fund acquisitions and expansions.

And while some call the rise of 401(k) plans a distinct advantage over pension plans, that claim is misguided and untested.

While 401(k)s present the great benefit of portability, they were never intended to serve as primary sources of retirement income or even as retirement plans.[4] Instead, they were originally designed as tax-deferred profit-sharing plans to accommodate deferred compensation (as opposed to direct cash payments) for managers and executives. Their intended benefit was to provide a tax break on income received as deferred compensation. At the time 401(k) provisions were enacted as part of the Revenue Act of 1978, the 401(k) was considered a complement to pensions, not its replacement.

But as time passed, industries adopted new management standards; new tax laws were enacted, and employers positioned 401(k) s as the next new thing to replace the eroding pension system. This was done more for the benefit of corporations than employees. And it was certainly not suited to the original 401(k) design, which effectively transferred all the investment risk to the employee.

These risks are exaggerated in the design of many 401(k) plans, which often offer employees high-fee, actively-managed mutual funds; limited access to new low-cost passive funds and exchange traded funds (ETFs).

While the DOL regulations contain some of the most pro-investor provisions ever enacted by a federal agency, they are years overdue. Some would say they are too little, too late. They're certainly too late for the millions of people who have retired over the past three decades and were never told the exact costs of what they paid to participate in their own plans. More importantly, participants were not told how much they lost in retirement income because their investment choices were so limited.

In the investment world, there is a concept called "opportunity cost."[5] It is the monetary difference between the path that an investor took and an alternative path that the investor *could* have taken. For instance, investment decision A resulted in a $10,000 loss over a four-year period; investment decision B would have resulted in a $20,000 gain over that same period. The opportunity cost of making investment decision A is therefore $30,000.

The opportunity cost for millions of retirees who invested in higher-priced mutual funds versus cheaper ones is extraordinarily high, although it isn't possible to calculate an exact number. What can be determined is that millions of retirees have less to spend in retirement now as a result of poor management decisions made by many employers over a period of many years. This is a management failure that can never be corrected.

The Long-Awaited Investment Disclosures: What Took So Long?

The new disclosure requirements for fund fees, expenses and revenue sharing will be a rude awakening for many people in fund management and administration. For some, it will upset the way the 401(k) business is conducted. Disclosing 401(k) fees and expenses seems a straightforward task, but one industry authority said that most people in the industry "would agree that this (fee and expense disclosure) could create a crisis."[6]

The reason: Once fund-specific expense and fee data are collected, compiled and analyzed, plan participants and employers will finally be able to make intelligent cost comparisons between similar-sized plans, individual fund expenses, fund offerings, recordkeeping services, and the wide variety of associated activities needed to administer 401(k) plans. They will also be able to see the flow of payments between plan providers, administrators and employers that could indicate conflicts-of-interest.

With this comparative data, participants will see for the first time the labyrinth of indirect and direct costs associated with administering their funds. In many cases, these costs far outweigh the benefits participants receive and have dragged down investment performance for decades.

How important are fees and expenses in an investment portfolio?

In the case of disciplined investors who have made regular contributions over decades to their 401(k) plans, these costs can be very significant. And once these hidden expenses come out of individual investor accounts, they can never be recovered.

These overpayments went from unsuspecting employees to plan administrators, insurance and mutual fund companies. In many cases, 401(k)-related account losses represent overcharges for services that were not needed or never delivered to plan participants.

All told, these events represent a massive wealth transfer. This transfer affected millions of investors, but for most people, it will take years to recover, especially when accompanied by stagnant growth in real incomes and losses in home equities. This is the wealth destruction story this book seeks to address.

Focus on 401(k)s

Individuals have little recourse to the decline in home equity values resulting from the 2008 recession. But the new DOL disclosures offer better opportunities for participants to manage their 401(k)s.

The new DOL expense- and fee-related data is expected to show that some participants with smaller average 401(k) account balances end up paying proportionately more to participate in their own plans than others with smaller balances, even though they received the same levels of service.

A Deloitte study found this was the case because employees have to pay for more expensive products, such as annuities that have additional layers of fees. However, there are certain fixed and variable costs that all plans pay.[46] This practice has existed in the 401(k) industry for years, yet it has never been corrected. The new DOL data also should show that some plans and individuals have been paying for services they never received.

The DOL provision concerning fee disclosures, (408(b)(2), "is a rule that nobody will forget about because it's so important.

It very well might be the most important change in the 401(k) marketplace in its history," according to industry executive Mike Alfred, of BrightScope.[8]

The DOL's straightforward regulation to disclose investor fees and expenses has been debated and delayed for decades. While it has been criticized by powerful financial services and mutual fund industry trade groups, it is a modest beginning that could alter the balance of power between investors and the 401(k) industry.[9]

This point was made by industry expert, Louis Harvey, president of DALBAR, Inc., who said: "The impact of both of the (main DOL disclosure regulations) together is going to be huge," especially as they affect fees, employee relations, and how different industry salespeople and 401(k) providers interact with plan sponsors.[10]

The real impact of the DOL disclosure regulations is likely to be the revelation of fees and expenses that could shock many participants who assumed their employers were acting in their best interests.

Sadly, as too many employees will discover, this did not happen. Many 401(k) participants, who have been contributing regularly for decades and trusting their employers to do the right thing, may be shocked to discover these deficiencies. Those lost investment returns can never be recovered. In many cases, this will mean a significant decrease in retirement income and a diminished quality of life in retirement for thousands of investors.

Why Disclosure is Critical

High fees and expenses clearly benefit investment professionals and 401(k) plans administrators more than investors. This imbalance becomes more important due to the precarious financial position of plan participants.

One report found that about three-fifths of 401(k) plan participants had no investments in stocks, bonds, annuities, or mutual funds other than those in their employer's 401(k) plans.

It also showed that over 10% of participants "held no financial assets at all outside the plan, while roughly half had bank or thrift deposits but no outside investments in stocks, bonds, or mutual funds." This would make their employers' 401(k) plans the sole source of contact with the investment services industry and one of their very few ways to build wealth.

But in the vast majority of circumstances, these participants were offered a selection of 19 funds, many of them skewed toward more expensive, actively-managed funds.[11]

These participants also do not typically receive any formal investment education. A September 2011 Financial Engines study found that only 30% of 401(k) participants had access to professional investment assistance in their plans at the end of 2010. This was a low figure, but an increase from 25% in 2009.[12]

The impact of fees and hidden expenses is especially important to the ongoing national debate about efforts to privatize Social Security. If the billions in Social Security balances were put into play, the financial services industry would be the first and greatest beneficiary.

As described in the following chapters, the primary interest of mutual fund companies, 401(k) professionals, and the investment services industry is to benefit industry professionals first. In too many cases, individual investors are looked upon as fee- and commission-generating entities, rather than clients, who rely on professionals for unbiased, objective advice.

The Power of Disclosure

Why would the simple act of disclosing fees charged to investors be considered so disruptive to the 401(k) marketplace?

After all, American consumers must be informed about the contents of the food they eat and the cosmetics they use because of requirements from the Pure Food and Drug Act; the Beef Inspection Act (passed in 1906); the Food and Drug Administration (created in 1927); the Pure Food, Drug and Cosmetics Act (passed in 1938); the Fair Packaging Act (enacted in 1966); and the Food Quality Protection Act of 1996. Americans can also rely on the veracity of weights and measures because of the National Bureau of Standards, established in 1901.

U.S. consumer protection statutes are enforced at the federal level by the Fair Debt Collection Practices Act, the Fair Credit

Reporting Act, Truth in Lending Act, the Fair Credit Billing Act, and the Gramm-Leach-Bliley Act. Federal consumer protection laws are mainly enforced by the Federal Trade Commission and the U.S. Department of Justice. Consumers also have significant protections at the state level, mainly from the Uniform Deceptive Trade Practices Act.

Many of these consumer protection agencies and legislative acts date back to the early- and mid-1900s, when elected officials in the Progressive Era pushed for public safeguards and set quality standards to create more confidence in consumer products and commerce.

However, the financial services industry has escaped these large-scale, pro-investor initiatives. While the Securities and Exchange Commission (created in 1934) and the Financial Industry Regulation Authority (or FINRA, a private agency created in 2007) regulate the financial services industry, the pro-investor records of these agencies is debatably weak. In fact, FINRA's $1 billion budget comes directly from the financial services industry.

This makes the DOL's fee and expense disclosure regulations especially important. While it is a simple act to tell people what they are actually paying for, doing so has far-reaching implications for many financial service providers, in addition to millions of investors and those working in the 401(k) industry. The reason: This has never been done before in 401(k) plans.

What Are Investors Paying For?

What is so special about fees and expenses in a 401(k) plan?

The answer lies in the fact that the vast majority of the people who own the nation's 50 million 401(k) retirement accounts have no idea exactly what they are buying and what they are receiving in return for the thousands of dollars they pay in fees and expenses every year.[13]

It is hard to imagine any other situation in which company employees would be encouraged to participate in employer-sponsored, tax-deferred savings plans without knowing the details about what they were being charged.

Since their inception, 401(k) plans were positioned as being tax-deferred savings vehicles for employees, while employers contributed a percentage into the plan for each employee. In turn employers received a tax deduction for those contributions.

Yet like most extraordinary offers, the enticement of "free money" to employees came at a great price. When 401(k) plans were in their early development stage in the 1990s, most plans invested with trust companies, which disclosed their costs. Gradually, as recordkeepers were able to perform daily valuation services, the business model changed to one offering mutual funds and insurance company products. The underlying assets of mutual funds and insurance company products are not considered "plan assets" under ERISA, while a similar fund developed by a trust company would have to disclose its costs.

Mutual funds and insurance products have specialized terminology to describe most of their costs. Soon, funds dominated the 401(k) space because they appeared to offer a low-cost solution to employers. But instead of employers monitoring the plans' costs themselves, this duty was transferred to plan administrators. In the mid- to late-1990's, fees did not become a great concern since plan participants and sponsors were distracted by positive stock market returns.

This was a mistake. Employees soon realized their "free money" was accompanied by fees and expenses charged by an assortment of specialized mutual fund company managers, portfolio managers, fund recordkeepers, lawyers, and service personnel, many of whom were handsomely paid, yet contributed little to actual fund performance. Yet it is investment performance that matters most to plan participants, but in many cases this performance was severely reduced by the undisclosed expenses charged by all those associated with the 401(k) plan's administration.

The new DOL regulations change this. Employers now know what key facts they have to disclose and to whom and when. They must also supply any missing facts to plan participants. This new disclosure process will show that some employers were negligent in their duties. It will also test the results of a 2009 Transamerica study that found that 73% of 401(k) plan sponsors said they believed employees had a clear understanding of fees.[14] But more recent industry feedback indicates some dramatically different conclusions.

The DOL regulations may reveal that many plan sponsors have failed to monitor and police their own plan's expenses. This information will become available once DOL regulations allow intelligent cost comparisons between similar funds. In other cases, these same regulations will highlight better-managed company plans, which deserve credit for containing costs, so more of their investment net returns could accrue directly into their employee's 401(k) accounts.

Illuminating investment expenses is especially important to younger and mid-career employees since they can save more over their working careers as a result of the new regulations. But the greatest burden of paying high 401(k) fees and expenses has already been shouldered by the 79 million Americans, who comprise the Baby Boom, and started turning age 65 at the astounding rate of one every eight seconds. That translates into 10,000 persons a day, or four million people a year (based on January 2011 data.)

Yet despite these huge numbers and the various uncertainties associated with retirement, Americans do not seem to care about the costs associated with investing, including how much it costs to have their money invested in a simple mutual fund.

This is a costly mistake. Morningstar, the mutual fund rating firm, concluded that fees are the single most important factor affecting a fund's performance and are more important than a fund's Morningstar star rating.[15] Not surprisingly, the mutual fund industry makes it very difficult for investors to determine the complete cost of investing (including all fees, revenue sharing, and transaction costs) in a mutual fund.

If investors checked, they would discover that a mutual fund can charge investors with 17 separate fees. And based on the $3 trillion invested in 401(k) plans in 2011, a 1% fee produces about $30 billion in revenue annually for mutual fund companies.

That's real money. Worse, it all originally comes from investors. The problem is that the reality of mutual fund accounting demonstrates an ironclad link between fund expense ratios and a fund's return. The more an investor pays in fees, the lower their net investment return. Over time, a slight difference in fees can become disproportionate. For instance, one study found that over 20 years, fund expenses that differed by only 1% could reduce an investor's returns by 17%. Other studies have shown the reduction in net returns can be even larger.[48]

For these reasons, as early as November 2003, former Illinois Senator Peter Fitzgerald said, "[t]he mutual fund industry is now the world's largest skimming operation—a $7 trillion [now $12 trillion] trough from which fund managers, brokers, and other insiders are steadily siphoning off an excessive slice of the nation's household, college, and retirement savings."[16]

This has become possible because in the mutual fund industry hierarchy, a shareholder is the least important person and well behind top management, mutual fund salespeople (known as wholesalers), and other sales support staff.

Investors are encouraged to buy and hold funds through years of bear markets on the advice that a market turnaround can happen unexpectedly. But since employees are making contributions on a regular basis as part of their payroll cycle, they buy regardless of market fundamentals, or whether a stock or sector looks attractive. Since this is an automatic process, they constitute a captive audience, who is always buying.

This complements the mutual fund company's goal since it is compensated on its assets under management. The larger the asset base, the larger the fee income. As a result, investors pay fees and expenses in bull and bear markets. And most importantly, whether portfolio managers deliver gains or losses, investors always pay fees.

Fees and Expenses Are Critical

While fund expenses are important because they significantly and erode investment performance, reducing plan expenses can offer a risk-free avenue toward improving investment returns.[17]

Fees are one of the most important investment variables that can be managed. Numerous academic and real-world studies have shown that the best indicator of a fund's future performance is its low expenses. As more investors realize that active management is a zero-sum game, meaning that over time, active management produces the same gross returns as an index fund, investors will be prompted to look for alternatives.[18]

But when market impact, fees, expenses and taxes are factored into the results, it's no longer a zero-sum game—the net returns of actively managed mutual funds fall below zero. This explains why only 32% of equity mutual funds beat the S&P 500 index from 1989 to 2008. It is also the reason why 85% of all institutional money managers, such as the pension, endowment and fund professionals, who claim to be diviners of the future, fail to beat the market since they also succumb to the corrosive impact of trading costs.[53]

As noted, while the new disclosure regulations fail to fully disclose trading expenses, the investment industry itself has also not recognized the real impact of the "incremental value" of fund returns versus the expenses paid to professional fund managers. In an essay, Charles Ellis notes that while management fees look small (often 1% for individuals and half that for institutions), this number is deceptive since it neglects to acknowledge that investors already own the investment assets. As a result, when the fees are expressed as a percentage of portfolio returns, the expenses are significantly higher. For example, if management fees are 1% and a portfolio's return is 8% per year, the actual cost is over 12% for individuals and half that for institutions.

When compared to the much lower costs of index funds and ETFs (often in the range of 0.05%), the gap between active management fees and those of lower-cost alternatives become even greater. The negative impact of these incremental fee increases in a low-return environment. This has led Ellis to conclude that "investors should consider fees charged by active managers not as a percentage of total returns but as *incremental* fees versus risk-adjusted *incremental* returns above the market index."[54]

Most people, including institutional investors, find this concept difficult to grasp, which helps explain why about $102 billion, representing about 80% of all investment assets, is spent on active management.[19]

But since hope springs eternal and investors seem to relate well to portfolio manager stories about how they can beat the odds and deliver positive portfolio returns, investors continue to repeat the same mistakes.

This may help explain the current mindset of American investors. One somber snapshot of the status of retirement is offered here:

- The average balance in all 50 million 401(k) accounts is just over $60,000, according to the Employee Benefit Research Institute.

- Even people within 10 years of retirement have saved an average of only $78,000, and more than a third of them have less than $25,000.

- More than half of U.S. workers have no retirement plan at all. With Social Security payments averaging $14,780 a year for individuals and $22,000 for couples, many Americans will exhaust their savings in just a few years. Since millions of boomers are likely to live into their 70s and 80s, the country is headed toward a major retirement crisis. For these reasons, "it looks like most middle-class Americans will become poor or near-poor retirees," said Teresa Ghilarducci, a retirement specialist at the New School in New York.[20]

This is especially critical as investors enter a low-return investment environment, accompanied by low retirement account balances. This is occurring at the same time other traditionally available wealth engines, such as home equity, savings, and wage increases, have all misfired or become extinct.

The billions in lost wealth as a result of the 2008 recession have been staggering. An estimate by the Center for American Progress found that from June 2007 to March 2009 "wealth was vaporized at a breathtaking, eye-popping speed. American families lost a total of $19.4 trillion (in 2010 dollars) in household wealth." This lethal combination cost American families $6.4 trillion in lost home values during this period. Nor will these losses be recovered quickly. For example, a $250,000 house, which suffered a 20% price drop, would take 15.2 years to recover, according to Thompson. (See "Recovery Times Needed to Recoup a House Price Loss" chart on page 141.)

Worse, this lost home equity was followed by serious declines in the stock market.[21] These market losses during the recession were estimated at $1.6 trillion, or about one-third of the total value from the nation's 401(k) accounts.[22]

Home equity and portfolio investments are the two prime wealth-creation engines available to Americans. These severe shocks have made it critically important for investors to contain all threats to their remaining wealth. While the drop in housing prices is outside of any individual's control, the simple act of monitoring investment expenses in 401(k)s and non-tax-deferred accounts *is* something they can handle. Taking control of these accounts will positively affect an investor's bottom line.

The good news is that monitoring expenses and making any needed adjustments (shifting funds, firing an investment manager, choosing lower-cost investment alternatives) is easier today than ever before.

This is because lower-cost investments, such as ETFs, offer index exposures to hundreds of asset classes, industry sectors, market capitalizations, financial characteristics, and geographies, including many strategies not available through long-only mutual funds. As will be shown, the expense profile of ETFs and low-expense mutual funds can provide investors with needed portfolio exposures at a fraction of the cost of many bundled, actively-managed funds offered in 401(k) plans.

Yet, while ETFs offer distinct benefits, many 401(k) participants have limited investment choices inside their plans, including the lack of ETFs. One little-known reason for this is due to the technological limitations in the recordkeeping industry.

According to Darwin Abrahamson, CEO of Invest n' Retire, the software used to drive one of the nation's largest recordkeepers uses COBOL programming, a language first developed in 1959. As used by some of the nation's largest recordkeepers, this archaic software cannot hold ticker symbols or hours worked for plan participants. As a result, it also cannot handle the features needed for ETF trading, such as trading in whole dollars, as opposed to fractional shares used in mutual funds.

This technological impasse to adopting new investment products has happened before. In the 1970 and 1980s, employee benefit plans only offered annuities to employees. In 1982, Vanguard approached SunGard, a dominant recordkeeper, to change their software to accommodate mutual funds. SunGard refused, so two years later, Vanguard paid for eight of its employees to move to Birmingham, Alabama to develop the software needed to trade mutual funds on the SunGard system, according to Abrahamson. This system worked. Mutual funds quickly replaced annuities as the investment product of choice in 401(k) plans. This same situation exists today as the fund industry remains reluctant to adopt the new technology to accommodate ETFs on a mass basis.

Another impediment to the wider adoption of ETFs in 401(k)s is due to the special relationships many 401(k) third party administrators maintain with plan providers. This often forms the basis of a good business relationship for everyone in the 401(k) plan, except participants. The wider adoption of ETFs poses a fundamental threat to the mutual fund industry. Ric Edelman, who manages a large retail invest firm and is an ETF advocate, predicted "over the next five to 10 years, when ETFs become more commonplace in 401(k)s, workers will recognize that they're getting ripped off with their mutual funds, and they will sell their mutual funds and replace them with ETFs. And as that happens, the mutual fund industry will be gone." The reason is "retail mutual funds operate in a manner that is not in the best interests of investors" and "I'm not just talking about high expenses. I'm talking about outright fraud." [47]

The DOL disclosure regulations should reveal such practices and alter any favorable intra-industry relationships, many of them involving conflicts-of-interest. If this occurs, these favorable relationships will be scaled back and plans will feel pressured to offer participants more low-cost investment choices, including ETFs and low-expense funds.

Benefits of the New Expense Disclosure Information

It is important that investors concerned about their investment portfolios pay close attention to what these regulations uncover about their own plans, especially as they relate to fees, expenses and the variety of product offerings inside the plan.

While the DOL regulations are a significant positive advance for investors, they also come decades too late for millions of retirees who have lost untold billions to excessive fees, expenses, and menus of inappropriate investments. These are financial losses that can never be recovered.

They also indicate that employers who had responsibilities for managing these employee benefits failed to supervise and meet their principal duties. Some of these failures to manage 401(k) costs were intentional. Human resources and financial executives, especially at large corporations, have already been faced with eliminating or freezing pensions and re-directing those pension assets to other non-retiree uses.

This same misuse of pension assets may have simply been re-applied to 401(k) plans as a means of solidifying relationships and profitability with recordkeepers and investment firms at the expense of uninformed plan participants. If that is the case, it evaporates the argument that these fees were too complex because they were bundled or opaque, or that service providers did not want to reveal these costs to plan sponsors. What is more likely is that any overpayments were knowingly made for years. This is especially egregious if overpayments were made by large, sophisticated corporations.

Correcting a Serious Mistake

As these regulations evolve and data emerges to permit comparisons across similar-sized funds, some employers will be forced to pay for their mistakes. But their previous lack of accountability should not be considered an accident. Over the past few decades, the employer-employee compact has changed.

Taking personal control over 401(k) investments is critical because relationships between employers and employees have changed dramatically over the past 30 years. And while their public statements repeatedly say that employers consider their employees "their most important assets," the reality in terms of wages, benefits, and job security is that many employers consider their employees as expenses.

This change alters the vision of what it means to work and retire in America, including how millions of Americans interact with their employers. Unfortunately, too many in the retirement-investment industry have failed to publicly discuss these changes and how they affect the nation.

This includes taking public positions and actions regarding income disparity, unequal tax treatment, and workplace practices that affect the customer-investors in the retirement industry.

Instead, the retirement-investment industry, with too few exceptions, has run to the sidelines whenever it faced a challenge that would change the way business was conducted or would provide a new benefit to investors. This is understandable from the industry's perspective. But this void has contributed to the deterioration of employer-employee relationships, declines in consumer confidence, the rise in political friction, and the loss of direction and national purpose as it relates to the role of work and retirement. After all, what is the long-term goal of working if there is no sense of what to expect in retirement?

While "financial security" has significant rhetorical value, it has not produced the retirement account balances in dollars and cents to warrant widespread confidence. The main reasons for this (discussed in Chapter 4) include the inability of all wealth-building engines (home equity, portfolio returns, savings, inheritance, and wage growth) to produce the returns needed to re-build the money lost by U.S. households since the start of the 2008 recession. (Tax policies definitely affect wealth creation, but are outside the scope of this book.)

Another important impediment is that successful investing (defined as meeting a pre-determined return objective) is very difficult for professionals to achieve, let alone amateurs. The odds against being a successful amateur are even higher because they lack access to basic analytics and do not have the investment choices, ready access, and cheap commissions available to professional traders.

As discussed in Chapter 5, the investment business underwent a metamorphosis in the mid-1990s when member-owned exchanges realized that the new world of global, electronic, 24-hour, institutionalized trading had squeezed profit margins, imposed new regulations, created electronic audit trails, increased risk, multiplied the number of exotic, short-term strategies, and tightened spreads. The financialization of the U.S. economy had also been exponentially successful. Over the past 50 years, trading volumes have increased 2,000 times–from two million shares a day to four billion–while derivatives, (as measured in value traded), went from zero to more than the value of the underlying or "cash" market. Better financed and more sophisticated institutional activity on the stock exchanges went from less than 10% of trading volumes to over 90%.[55]

Despite their bravado and financial daring, less-capitalized individual floor traders were no match for the greater trading volatility, tighter spreads, and new strict compliance standards. This meant the golden days of being a floor member had ended. Exchange members then did what any smart trader would do: they cashed out. This gave new meaning to the saying, "When the going gets tough, the tough get going." This marked the time exchanges (the CME, NYSE) went public. Now, the risk of managing an exchange was passed to the investing public.

All this happened at about the same time more employers started to tell employees to begin managing their own money. Newly-empowered employees could now take all the investment risk, in an increasingly institutionalized, sophisticated, global computerized trading environment. Worse, individuals were now burdened with managing their money for decades until retirement. What they would end up with was anyone's guess. Given their limited investment knowledge and tools, combined with an inability to see the actual costs in their own 401(k) funds, the odds of investors being successful were seriously handicapped from the beginning.

This is what makes the enactment of the DOL's new fee disclosure regulations more important than they initially seem. Since sunlight increases visibility, the more investors see what they have paid, the greater their ability to manage expenses and investments. But employees in 401(k) plans should note that these regulations call for something that should have existed decades ago. The disclosure changes should not be considered a major advance, but rather something that rectifies a serious deficiency that never should have happened in the first place.

Aside from a home, a person's 401(k) is probably their second largest asset. No homeowner would ever buy a house without knowing its tax rate, insurance costs, projected annual maintenance expenses, and whether there were cheaper alternatives to cut these critical homeownership expenses. But when employees invested in their 401(k) plans, often over decades, they were never presented with the costs of managing their own plans. In some cases, investors' 401(k) balances may be worth more than their homes. Yet investors know vastly more about the costs of managing their homes than their 401(k) accounts.

It is now the responsibility of individual investors to investigate the expenses affecting their 401(k) accounts, including what fees are being charged, what they are receiving in return, and if their service charges are justified. These DOL regulations can help 401(k) investors determine those answers, but they should also foment more questions than answers.

Specifics of the New Regulations

Here are the specifics of the new DOL regulations and what they mean to investors in 401(k) plans:

When the Regulations Became Effective

The final 408(b)(2) fee disclosure regulations went into effect on two dates. The first regulation required 401(k) providers to give employers full fee disclosures starting July 1, 2012.

The second regulation required that calendar-year plans provide participants with their first set of investment fee disclosures by August 30, 2012. Other fees and expenses paid by participants should have appeared on Sept. 30, 2012 quarterly statements.

ERISA Section 404(a)(5)

Section 404(a)(5) of ERISA requires that each of the nation's 72 million plan participants receive information, expressed in dollars and cents in their quarterly statements, about how much they are paying every quarter for the administration of their 401(k) plan. This information began to appear on individual statements in November 2012.

ERISA Section 408(b)(2)

Under regulation 408(b)(2), covered service providers—essentially any professional who provides critical services to the 401(k) plan—are required to present clients with a written agreement of services, fees, compensation, and any conflicts-of-interest, including revenue sharing. Many of these services are often included in the service agreement provided to plan sponsors. But service providers who do not use a service agreement will have to specify the services they provide. After all, the goal of disclosure is to take the relevant information service providers disclosed to the plan sponsor fiduciary and translate it for individual participants.

If revenue sharing or any forms of indirect compensation are being paid, that must be disclosed. The issue of whether the advisor is serving as a fiduciary will also be addressed in these disclosures.

The 408(b)(2) and 404(a)(5) regulations, which have both been under repeated fire by broker-dealer and industry advocate groups, require investment advisors and money managers to base investment advice on objective computer models or to give advice on what's called a "level-fee basis." This means that compensation does not vary based on the investments in the account. All covered services providers are subject to 408(b)(2) regardless of whether the funding vehicle is a set of mutual funds, a group annuity, or a collective trust. It is important to note that plan sponsors must report non-compliant service providers to the DOL. If not, they are considered to have violated their fiduciary obligations by engaging in a prohibited transaction and can be penalized and fined.

Schedule C of Form 5500

This document, filed with federal regulators, is the primary tool used by the DOL and the Internal Revenue Service (IRS) to gather information about qualified retirement plans for compliance and research purposes. The form includes information about the plan's operation, funding, assets, and investments. Schedule C of Form 5500 is required only for plans where there are more than 100 participants. Even though about 85% of the 401(k) plans in the U.S. have less than 100 participants, the DOL is implying that large plans (in terms of assets and employees) can expect to see greater scrutiny as they comply with the new regulations.

Goals of the New Regulations

Given the reality that 401(k) plans have effectively come to replace traditional pension plans, accompanied by the well-recognized role of the destructive effect of excessive fees and expenses on participants' net returns, the DOL has acted to protect participants' interests. The DOL's publicly stated goal in implementing the new regulations (specifically 404(a)(5)) is to reduce fees and expenses paid by plan participants, which is expected to produce a savings of an astounding $15 billion to individual investors. The DOL also estimates that it will cost plan and 401(k) services providers about $2 billion to comply with the new regulations. As part of this unprecedented level of disclosure, the retirement plan industry is expected to suffer an estimated $16.9 billion in lost revenues and added expenses. However, any lost revenues from the fund industry will accrue to the benefit of its own customers, investors in the fund industry's own products.

However, while the financial services industry and some of their congressional supporters often demand a financial impact study of any new regulations on the industry, no one ever asks for a financial impact study to be conducted on behalf of the public—in this case, the millions of people who invest in 401(k)s. After all, these are the people who trust their employers to act in their best interests. The financial impact on participants of excessive fees, revenue sharing, and the myriad cash flows that flow from investor accounts through the 401(k) plan and back to the industry is incalculable, but my bet is that it easily dwarfs the $2 billion it will cost the financial services industry to comply with these long overdue regulations.

Follow the Lobbying Money

Just to keep this estimated $2 billion compliance cost in perspective, let's look at what the financial services industry spends on lobbying and campaign contributions to influence elected officials and regulators.

From 1998 to 2008, the financial services industry spent $1.7 billion on campaign contributions and $3.4 billion on lobbying expenses. The securities industry alone spent $500 million on campaign contributions and $600 million on lobbying. When these campaign contributions are compared to other industries during the period starting in 1989, contributions from the financial services industry alone are greater than the combined contributions from the energy, health care, defense, and telecommunications industries.[23]

This is an extraordinary amount. Accordingly, anyone with common political sense would ask why the financial services industry would go to such great lengths to lobby elected officials and delay all types of financial reform and regulation if the expected revenues from the status quo were not worth defending. One main reason is to protect profitability. For the five years ending in 2009, the nine largest publicly-traded fund companies earned an average net profit margin of 14%, while the return on equity in the same period was 19%.[88] As a result, many firms have expressed an interest in starting their own fund companies or acquiring fund managers.

Given this backdrop, it is extraordinary that the DOL managed to navigate the financial services industry's lethal lobbying minefield to get these regulations passed at all. But by defying the serious career-killing odds, the people at the DOL have done millions of investing Americans and their children a tremendous, incalculable favor. They have accomplished something the SEC would never even have attempted, even though it is commonly considered acting in the tepid interests of individual investors.

With this valuable new information, the burden now falls on individual investors and companies to determine where the con- flicts-of-interest lie and whether investors have been overpaying for services. The main driver of this unprecedented shift in rev- enues from the retirement industry back to plan participants (in the form of lower expenses) is that plan participants must actively question their employers and 401(k) plan providers about the fees they are paying.[24] Accordingly, 401(k) participants should not take anything for granted and assume their company's 401(k) plan administrator is working to reduce the expenses that will improve the investors' bottom line. In short, employees should not assume their interests and those of the 401(k) administrator are always aligned.

Specific Provisions Related to 401(k) Plans and Mutual Funds

As with all covered service providers, plan providers will be required to show both the direct and indirect compensation they receive from their vendors. This will include all investment products included in the plan (mutual funds and annuities), as well as any indirect compensation paid to the plan sponsor, such as sub-transfer agent fees. But for the first time, participants will be able to see the itemized list of expenses that have been deducted from their accounts. This will be expressed as a dollar cost per $1,000 of the annual expenses of their investments (commonly known to mutual fund investors as the expense ratio) and will be shown in the disclosure, but not as an itemized expense line on the statement.

In the opinion of one industry professional, Rule 408(b)(2) "will only tell plan sponsors what they should already know, but it will be 404(a)(5) that will really rattle some cages because, according to an American Association of Retired Persons (AARP) study, 71% of plan participants either don't know what they pay or think the plan is free. As scary as that should sound, imagine the sound of a gang of them knocking on HR's door the day after Q2 statements go out."[25]

Specific Provisions Related to Group Annuities

All covered service providers (CSPs) must disclose all fees. This includes annuity providers that may actually be CSPs under several umbrellas (fiduciary, recordkeeper, receiver of offsets.) That said, two things will make this disclosure effort challenging: CSPs can use formulas to disclose how fees are calculated, but they do not need to disclose fixed annuity product fees, which may be where a large percentage of fees are hidden. On an optimistic note, an industry benchmarking report should disclose fees clearly in both dollars and basis points.

Rule 408(b)(2) applies to variable investment accounts within the annuity contracts used to fund 403(b), 401(k) and other 401(a) plans. The rules apply differently to registered variable annuity separate accounts often found in 403(b) plans, and to non-registered variable annuity separate accounts commonly used in 401(k) plans.

According to attorney Robert Toth, registered variable annuity separate accounts cannot be publicly traded outside the annuity, under which their assets are not treated as plan assets.[26] Because of this, the insurance company is not considered a fiduciary with regard to the management of those assets. This applies to group and individually owned contracts.

The "securities" are held in an annuity contract platform, under which the insurance company has a direct contractual relationship with the responsible plan fiduciary, and under which the insurer provides both recordkeeping and other services to the plan. It will receive direct compensation for these services, through its M&E (mortality and expense) charge, but it is also possible that it will receive indirect compensation as well from managers of those separate accounts.

Non-registered variable annuity separate accounts, often found in 401(k) plans, resemble trust arrangements rather than annuity contracts. According to Toth, the assets in these non-registered separate accounts constitute plan assets, which-means the insurance company serves as a fiduciary with regard to the management of those assets.

Because these accounts are held in insurance company accounts, the assets may be actively managed, under which an investment manager is often delegated the fiduciary obligation to manage the assets; or they may be passively managed by holding specific mutual funds. The mutual fund may pay 12b-1 fees or sub-transfer agent fees to the insurance company.

Since the insurer has a direct contractual relationship with the plan, under which it will also provide recordkeeping services, it typically gets a contract charge levied on assets under the contract. This makes it a fiduciary because it provides recordkeeping and/or administrative services and/or receives 12b-1 and sub-transfer agency fees, according to Toth.

History of the DOL Rule Changes

Significant federal reform takes years to emerge and in most cases, it never docs. That's why the simple requirement to disclose costs to financial product customers deserves more attention.

The push to disclose more information to 401(k) participants began around 2005 with complaints Congressman George Miller (D-Calif.) was hearing from his constituents about 401(k) plan fees. Miller listened and asked the GAO to investigate.

In 2006, the GAO found participants had no idea what they were paying, plan sponsors did not know if the investment they were offering were appropriate and both were most likely paying too much. Motivated by the results, Miller introduced a bill in 2007, as George Bush was leaving office that would push plans to disclose fees. Miller found that high 401(k) fees over the life of plan participants could reduce their savings by about 25% due to high fees.

Miller's bill was then side tracked by the health care reform bill and was re-introduced in the Senate in 2010, where it died. But

Miller's legislative momentum was then picked up by the DOL, which proposed fee disclosure rule changes in July 2010. Final rules were announced in February 2011, but financial industry lobbyists then spent two years trying to have the rules delayed or killed.[56] But as more news about the Wall Street abuses that contributed to the 2008 recession and other mass fiduciary violations emerged, the political climate changed and the DOL's efforts finally succeeded. The effective date for disclosure rule implementation was then changed to July 1, 2012.

TIMELINE OF THE NEW DOL REGULATIONS

ERISA Section 408(b)(2)

1978: The Revenue Act of 1978 allows for the development of 401(k) plans through Internal Revenue Code (IRC) Section 401(k). The first 401(k) plans contain only annuity products as the investment option. Front-end loads for these products range as high as 40%. Due to the generous compensation, the insurance industry claims there is no demand for any additional investment products, especially lower cost mutual funds. As a result, no one begins developing any technology to make mutual funds available in 401(k) plans.[33]

1996: Mutual funds become the largest segment of the 401(k) investment segment, as measured by assets.[34]

Feb. 2005: In an article, in the *ERISA Controversy* newsletter, attorney Joe Faucher wrote "[w]ith plan fiduciaries facing greater scrutiny than ever in the wake of the employer stock cases, what is the next ERISA litigation trap for corporate officers and directors that preside over their companies' retirement plans? The answer may be claims relating to payment of excessive fees and expenses."[35]

Sept. 11, 2006: Class action lawsuits are filed against companies, such as International Paper, Lockheed Martin, Bechtel, and Caterpillar, charging their 401(k) plans entered into agreements with third parties that allowed the plans to pay unreasonable, excessive fees; while they failed to inform themselves of, and understand, the various methods by which vendors in the 401(k), financial and retirement industry collect payments and other revenue from 401(k) plans. They are also charged with failing to monitor fees and expenses in their plans.

Dec. 12, 2007: DOL announces a proposed rule (as yet unnamed) "that will enhance disclosure to fiduciaries of 401(k) and other employee benefit plans to assist them in determining the reasonableness of compensation paid to plan service providers and conflicts-of-interest that may affect a service provider's performance under a service contract or arrangement."

March 31, 2008 and April 1, 2008: DOL conducts public hearings on proposed rule.

July 23, 2008: DOL proposes rule for greater fee disclosure in 401(k) plans. The goal of the proposed rule is to give 401(k) participants more information about the costs of their programs, a move that could help boost savings. The DOL estimates that the disclosures would save participants $6 billion over 10 years, including $2.3 billion from lower fees as investment providers compete more on cost. The rest will come from the time participants save tracking down the fees, which are currently found in a range of separate documents.

September 2009: President Barack Obama announces new steps to make it easier for American families to save for retirement, including expanded opportunities for automatic enrollment in 401(k)s and other retirement savings plans and improved ways to save tax refunds.

2009: DOL Schedule C disclosure requirements go into effect.

March 3, 2010: DOL sends the rule to the Office of Management and Budget.

July 16, 2010: Rule 408b-2 is published in the *Federal Register* (75 Fed. Reg. 41600).

October 14, 2010: DOL issues final regulations on what fee disclosure information must be provided to plan participants, beneficiaries, and any employee eligible to participate in a plan allowing participants to direct their own investments.

February 11, 2011: DOL announces intent to extend the effective date for the new disclosure rules of ERISA to Jan. 1, 2012.

June 1, 2011: DOL's Employee Benefit Security Administration (EBSA) publishes a notice in the *Federal Register* that proposes to officially extend the applicability date for the fiduciary-level fee disclosure regulations to Jan. 1, 2012.

July 13, 2011: EBSA publishes final rule to extend the applicability date for the fiduciary-level fee disclosure regulations under ERISA Section 408(b)(2) to April 1, 2012.

July 16, 2011: DOL publishes "Reasonable Contract or Arrangement Under Section 408(b)(2)–Fee Disclosure" in the *Federal Register,* (vol. 75, number 136). This was the Rule's original effective date, but the DOL initially proposed an extension to Jan. 1, 2012.

July 1, 2012: DOL Rule 408(b) (2) becomes effective.

Who Will Receive the New DOL Disclosure Information?

The term "participant" includes persons who have an account balance in the 401(k) plan, as well as those who are eligible but are not currently participating in the plan. This includes employees who have not enrolled or those who have opted out of a plan with auto-enrollment. Plan administrators should be addressing their communications to anyone in this group of employees.

The service provider regulation requires covered service providers to disclose information to assist plan fiduciaries in assessing the reasonableness of the service provider's compensation and whether there are potential conflicts-of-interest. The regulation applies to pension, 401(k), 403(b), and other retirement plans.

The rule defines "covered service providers" as any service provider that enters into a contract or arrangement with a covered plan and reasonably expects to receive at least $1,000 (paid to the provider, its affiliates, or a subcontractor) in direct or indirect compensation in connection with providing one or more of the following:

- Services provided by fiduciaries;

- Recordkeeping or brokerage services involving participant-directed plans;

- Certain other services, such as accounting, auditing, actuarial, appraisal, banking, consulting, custodial, insurance, investment advisory, legal, recordkeeping, securities or other investment brokerage, third-party administration or valuation services. These are services for which the service provider expects to receive either "indirect compensation." This is defined as compensation received from any source other than the plan, the plan sponsor, the service provider, an affiliate, or a subcontractor, or "compensation received among related parties," such as transaction-based compensation or charges against the net value of a plan's investments as part of a bundled service arrangement.

Covered service providers must provide plans with a description of the services provided to the plan, a description of direct compensation and indirect compensation that the service provider reasonably expects to receive, a description of compensation paid among related parties (including bundled service arrangements) and a reasonable estimate of unbundled stand-alone recordkeeping services.

The participant regulation requires plan administrators to make significant disclosures to individuals participating in 401(k), 403(b) and other defined contribution plans that have participant-directed investments.

Participants, as well as employees who are eligible to participate, must receive two major categories of information: "plan-related information" and "investment-related information."

Plan–related information includes:

- General information, including an explanation of the circumstances under which participants may give investment instructions; identification of the investment options under the plan; an explanation of any limitations on investment rights, including transfer restrictions; a description of any voting, tender, or similar rights associated with investment options under the plan; identification of any designated investment managers; and a description of any self-directed brokerage accounts available under the plan.

- Administrative expense information includes a description of any general fees or expenses that will be charged against an individual's account during the plan year, which are not otherwise reflected in the investment option operating expenses.

- Individual expense information includes a description of any individualized fees or expenses for plan loan processing or other services that may be charged against an individual's account during the plan year.[27]

What's New About the DOL Regulations

ERISA allowed plan sponsors of pension and 401(k) plans to delegate their supervisory duties to outside experts, such as pension plan and investment consultants, recordkeepers, and investment managers.

But the new 408(b)(2) regulations are historic because they require that plan sponsors take action themselves to discover, determine, and monitor plan expenses. If they fail to do so, they will be exposed to a fiduciary breach, which opens them to penalties and possible lawsuits.

This is a significant change. Having fiduciary status triggers new responsibilities that link to a long history of cases that resulted in significant penalties, fines, and public notoriety. No longer will plan sponsors be able to defend themselves against possible suits because they relied on the expertise of outside experts. This puts a new burden on the company's department that sponsors and oversees the 401(k) plan (human resources, finance, or benefits) to ensure that the plan's expenses are "reasonable" compared to those charged to similarly-sized plans. If plan sponsors determine that the costs of administering their plans are excessive, they also have the responsibility to fire and replace expensive plan providers or report them to the DOL.

Another new benefit of the regulations is that for the first time, sponsors and participants will be able to see the "indirect costs" associated with administering their plan. "Indirect costs" occur when a third party (such as an investment manager or recordkeeper) pays another provider (such as trustees, third-party administrators, or custodians.) The new regulations require that both recipients and payers from the plan disclose what they received in compensation (over $1,000 as filed on Schedule C), as well as any conflicts-of-interest that exist that adversely affect the plan sponsor.

The net effect of this will expose the scope and extent of a plan's indirect costs, including the questionable role of some providers. This is a new provision which has teeth. Under Rule 408, plan sponsors (fiduciaries) have 90 days to show that plan providers gave them all pertinent fee disclosure and revenue sharing information. If they do not provide information within the time frame, the new regulations state that the plan sponsor has to fire the offending provider.

And despite the forbidding legalese and regulatory jargon, these new rules will fundamentally change the way the 401(k) business is conducted simply because fees and expenses have to be disclosed to the people buying investment services.

This simple act—allowing buyers to see what they are buying and receiving—has been disputed, delayed, and thwarted for at least a decade by the investment industry and others associated with providing services to 401(k) plans.

The delays, calls for hearings, comment periods, revisions, and lobbying have cost the industry millions. But more important, it has cost investors in 401(k) plans much more, perhaps billions, in lost net returns while they overpaid for services that were not needed or did not contribute anything that could ever increase their net investment returns.

There are four groups who share varying degrees of responsibility for this gross abuse of investors:

First, the employers of the 401(k) plans themselves, known as plan sponsors, had a responsibility to buy the best possible services from the best-qualified providers at the best possible price. Employees would rightfully think this is the normal way their employers would conduct business. But when it comes to procuring 401(k) services, very little can be assumed. As these new DOL regulations will reveal over time, many employers did not manage the cost and quality of these services diligently.

Unfortunately, the data may show that many employers did not know the exact costs they were paying providers, or whether those same services could be obtained at a lower cost elsewhere. This constitutes a violation of the employer-employee compact and created an abuse of trust with their workers. Blame should fall directly on the human resources, benefits, or financial departments of companies that had direct responsibilities for their plan's oversight.

The second group is outside plan service providers. These are highly paid professionals who provide investment advice, plan design, investment strategy, and portfolio management, as well as specialists who provide individual oversight over plan participant accounts and their ongoing investment activities.

These individual account administrators, known in the business as recordkeepers, work as independent contractors or as part of the investment management company itself. When they provide services in conjunction with an investment management firm, their services are provided on a "bundled" basis, which makes it more difficult to isolate costs of individual services.

In most cases, bundled providers intentionally make it difficult or impossible to untangle these expenses in order to mask costs. Some plan sponsors have been complaining about this for years, but nothing changed. The service providers proved to be more powerful than their customers. These new DOL regulations may begin to alter that balance of power.

The third group includes federal regulators, who, as early as 1980, had become aware that the fiduciary standards imposed by ERISA were being trampled in the 401(k) industry. At that time, the majority of employees were covered by pension plans. But as those plans were phased out or closed to new employees, the industry shift to 401(k) plans should have made it obvious that the promised retirement benefits to employees were being eroded by conflicts-of-interest and high expenses. But those fiduciary protections from ERISA were not extended to 401(k) plans. This set the stage for a serious erosion of retirement benefits and a wealth transfer from employees to the investment industry.

Lastly, individual investors in 401(k) plans must assume responsibility for naively trusting that their employers and service providers would elevate the participants' interests above those provided by professionals. While this was a quiet battle between self-interests, the interests of the better-informed, more politically powerful professionals and recordkeepers triumphed over their customers. For their part, employers now have to face the sad reality that they were willing, silent participants in the abuse of their own employees. In the process, these abuses cost individual investors a huge amount in lost returns, easily into the hundreds of billions of dollars. Those losses will certainly decrease the standard of living for many future retirees.

What The New DOL Regulations Mean to Individual Investors

A decade of flat equity investment returns, combined with a decline in home equity values and the worst economy since the Great Depression, have focused attention on the power of full disclosure in financial transactions. If this simple practice was followed during the creation of exotic mortgage derivatives, some observers say the mortgage and related housing crises could have been avoided.

But that was not the case. As a result, the economic stress placed on millions of Americans comes at a time when the Baby Boomer generation is entering retirement and funding for Social Security is a source of great concern. This has raised the issue of retirement, and indeed the nature of work itself, to a significant social and political issue affecting all Americans.

The demographics involved in this wealth management situation are unparalleled. Starting in January 2012, the 79 million Americans of the Baby Boom generation began turning 65 at the rate of one every eight seconds. This translates into a rate of 10,000 people per day, or four million per year until 2030.[36]

The new regulations come at an important time because most investors are woefully ignorant about the impact of the myriad fees cutting into their investment returns. Studies from AARP found that 80% of the public does not know what they're paying in 401(k) fees.

In fact, the studies showed that 71% of people enrolled in 401(k) plans were not aware that they pay any fees at all to participate in their plans. When told that fees exist, 62% had no idea what they paid. This situation is not surprising given that plan sponsors previously never had to release complete fee information.[37]

Uninformed investors often become victims and in a 401(k) plan with high expenses, the toll can be devastating. For example, an employee who has been working for 35 years and contributes $5,000 annually into a 401(k) account would earn about $469,000 over that period (assuming a 7% annual return and no fees). But an annual fee of just 1.5% of the account balance would reduce the return to $345,000 over the 35-year period, a loss of $124,000.[38]

Another factor is that the 2008 recession destroyed billions of dollars in net worth for millions of Americans. According to economist Gary Shilling, the investment losses suffered by individuals in the 2000-2002 dot.com-led stock collapse and the 2007-2009 subprime mortgage-driven market collapse means "investors have suffered through two of the five stock-market declines of more than 40% since 1900. Furthermore, the S&P 500 index was flat in 2011 and has experienced 13 years of drought since 1998."[39]

The good news for participants is that they will see a more refined and screened list of investment alternatives in their 401(k) plans if they have a diligent plan sponsor who adheres to the new regulations. The menu of new offerings to plan participants should include low-cost investments (such as ETFs, collective trusts, and mutual funds with low expense ratios), and mutual funds with limited share classes (often those offered only at net asset value, or NAV), without any hidden costs.

This should be welcome news because much of the mutual fund industry contains redundant, look-alike funds that do not consistently offer any consistent valuable attributes. This is demonstrated by the fact that 85% of bond mutual funds[41] and two-thirds of actively managed funds[40] fail to beat their benchmarks. Another serious problem is that one-third of all mutual fund assets are invested in funds that secretly track an index (called "closet index funds"), even though their managers claim their funds are being actively managed. This means investors are paying for active management even though the fund is being passively managed.[42]

The bad news is that these changes should have come many years earlier. It is hard to accept that responsible plan sponsors, who have a significant agent responsibility in performing this crucial service of managing retirement assets for their own employees, did not police these critical expenses more closely. As early as December 2001, a consulting group noted that "there is no standard against which a trust fiduciary can determine 'reasonable' versus 'excessive' costs. There is no grid, literally or figuratively, for comparing 'like' services provided by 'like' enterprises under 'like' circumstances."[43] The industry's inability to make intelligent cost comparisons cannot be dismissed as an oversight. In many cases, it was an intentional effort to conceal costs from service customers and investors, and it lasted for decades. Clearly, there were a few groups that benefited from this information disparity, but there were millions of people who did not.

The enactment of the DOL regulations also exposes conflicts, some of them deep-seated, between plan sponsors and the employees enrolled in their 401(k) plans. These problems expose a fundamental shift in the relationships between employers and their employees. These will become more evident as the actual costs and expenses of administering employer-designed savings plans reveal that employers (plan sponsors) have failed to monitor these critical costs as diligently as the same company's purchasing agent would have monitored and assumed responsibility for buying a case of pencils.

This situation reveals an "agency problem," an economic term for a mismatch of incentives in a transaction between the principal (in this case, the 401(k) investor) and the agent (in this case, the employer.) The agency problem in 401(k)s arises when the employer (the agent) profits at the principal's expense. In some 401(k) situations, the plan sponsor's overhead expenses can be reduced as a result of revenue sharing agreements with service providers (most commonly recordkeepers), who make payments to reduce administrative costs.

Increased Odds of Becoming a Victim

Given the proliferation of investment abuses since the 2007 recession began, consumers can quickly become victims given the right circumstances. Unfortunately, managing large 401(k) plans, with undisclosed pricing, is fertile ground for abuse. This is difficult to accept, but it represents the inherent tension in the way some business is conducted, especially when it is possible to over-charge tenths or hundredths of a per cent through a continuous stream of financial transactions on a mass basis.

In practice, the 401(k) system often works like this: The average investor pays 0.83% of their 401(k) assets annually in fees. In small plans, fees can run as high as 3%; while in large plans, they are slightly less. In addition, some plans charge administrative or "wrap fees" of up to 1% of investor assets as an extra management fee. This wrap fee often does not provide any tangible service to those who pay for it.

In addition, fund companies or plan providers charge additional fees to manage the mutual funds inside the 401(k)s. Many plans also limit their selections to only offer funds that charge fees of 1.5% or more. This is much higher than the 0.77% median fee for stock funds. As a result, an ordinary American household with two working adults participating in a 401(k) plan with large balances can spend almost $155,000 in fees over a lifetime.[57]

The Old Testament teaches, "You shall not curse the deaf nor place a stumbling block before the blind …." (Leviticus 19:14). In a metaphorical context, a biblical scholar has interpreted the verse to apply to "any person or group that is unaware, unsuspecting, ignorant, or morally blind, and individuals are prohibited from taking advantage of them or tempting them to do wrong." This certainly applies to those who lack the knowledge to make a good decision. He extended the verse to apply to one that "prohibits one from giving bad advice to another person." Perhaps these

DOL regulations can awaken the meaning behind this ancient admonition.[28]

What the New Regulations Mean to Plan Sponsors and What Plans Are Affected

The final rule applies to ERISA-covered defined benefit (pension) and defined contribution (401(k)) pension plans. It does not apply to simplified employee pension plans (SEPs), SIMPLE retirement accounts, IRAs, and certain annuity contracts and custodial accounts described in Internal Revenue Code Section 403(b). The final rule does *not* apply to employee welfare benefit plans. The final rule *does* apply to covered service providers who expect to receive at least $1,000 in compensation for services to a covered plan.

The regulations state that all participants receive fee disclosures, regardless of their plan's size.

The final rule applies to the following covered service providers:

ERISA fiduciary service providers to a covered plan, or "plan asset" vehicle in which such plan invests; investment advisors registered under federal or state law; recordkeepers or brokers who make designated investment alternatives available to the covered plan (e.g., a "platform provider"); providers of one or more of the following services to the covered plan, who also receive "indirect compensation" in connection with such services: accounting, auditing, actuarial, banking, consulting, custodial, insurance, investment advisory, legal, recordkeeping, securities brokerage, third-party administration, or valuation services.[29]

Responsibilities of 401(k) Plans Under DOL Rule 404(c)

The DOL has established rules about plans that permit participants to direct their own investments. Under these rules, if, and only if, you truly exercise independent control in making your investment choices, plan officials will be excused from their fiduciary responsibility and will not be held liable for the consequences of a plan participant's investment decisions.

A plan where participants exercise independent control over the investments in their individual accounts is called a 404(c) plan (after section 404(c) of ERISA). If an investor participates in a 404(c) plan, they are responsible for the results of their investment decisions and cannot sue the plan's officials for investment losses resulting from their decisions. In short, participants in a 404(c) plan take all the responsibility for their investment decisions, including any and all profits and losses.

Participants in these plans are entitled to receive a broad range of information about investment choices. As part of this informational presentation, the plan sponsor must inform participants it no longer has any fiduciary responsibilities over the investment decisions of plan participants. The 404(c) plan must give participants sufficient information about investment options so they can make informed decisions. This includes information about the fees, and pertinent information about the funds, their management, managers, investment philosophies and goals.

What the Rule Covers

The final rule requires 401(k) plan sponsors (also known as "covered service providers," or CSPs) to provide responsible fiduciaries with information they need to:

- Assess whether the total compensation, both direct and indirect, received by the CSP, its affiliates, and/or subcontractors is reasonable;

- Identify potential conflicts-of-interest;

- Satisfy reporting and disclosure requirements under Title I of ERISA.

Schedule C Disclosure Provisions

Schedule C went into effect in 2009 and contained an important provision that requires plan sponsors to disclose "indirect compensation" paid to plan providers. "Indirect compensation" is

CHAPTER 3

a euphemism for revenue sharing commonly paid to some brokers, third-party administrators, and recordkeepers. Revenue sharing is the process of re-directing money back to salespeople as a hidden commission. It is often cited as a primary source of causing conflicts-of-interest between people who provide financial advice and their clients.

Unfortunately, DOL rules do not require that revenue sharing be disclosed to participants at the fund level. This is an unfortunate omission because it can reveal whether salespeople or investment firms could have an ulterior motive in making specific fund recommendations. As a result, 401(k) participants must take it upon themselves to become aware about revenue sharing practices in their plans, unless specifically told by employers that it is not allowed or being conducted. Investors also must understand that revenue sharing taints the quality of "objective" advice and in some cases, can make this advice worthless.

The rules also require that investments be compared against a benchmark, or a broad-based market index or combination of indexes. This applies to target-date funds that do not have readily comparable indexes to compare their performance.

Expenses also must be presented to investors as both expense ratios and in dollar terms (per thousand dollars of an investment.) This was designed to be a more understandable expression of actual investment costs. (A lower expense ratio translates into less expensive funds, which often out-perform more expensive funds, according to Morningstar.)

For the first time, plan participants will be able to see management expenses, conflict-of-interest costs, such as the "pay-to-play" payments, which earlier scandalized the municipal bond sales industry. Unfortunately, trading and related fund transaction costs (also known as turnover costs) will not be part of participant disclosure. Trading costs are a critical factor in determining an investment's overall expenses and are not included in the expense ratio. If this data were disclosed, it would fill a critical information gap because trading cost disclosures cover investments in mutual funds, collective trusts, separate accounts, and other non-registered investments. Trading costs are an integral factor in determining investor returns.

Still, Schedule C mandates that service providers release more information. This rule, Rule 408(b)(2), includes all direct and indirect compensation that service providers (including mutual funds) receive for providing services. A vendor is required to provide information to the plan sponsor if the vendor expects to receive at least $1,000. A related source of information comes from Schedule H, which contains the balance sheet and income statement portion of the Form 5500. In many instances, Schedule H also includes a list of investments in the plan. If the plan has a large dollar amount in an investment that could create high investment costs that could exceed $1,000, the vendor should have provided a disclosure.

Sponsors have seen this information before, but one expert said it was not clear how the DOL identified vendors that did not provide expense information, especially because the 408(b)(2) disclosure has not been officially implemented. However, changes to the Form 5500 Schedule C have been in place since 2009. The DOL has taken the position that if the investment vendor receives significant compensation, even if indirect, it should be disclosed. To determine the amount of compensation, a plan participant should multiply the amount of the investment times the basis points (hundredths of a percent) for that investment. If the result exceeds $1,000, it should be disclosed.

Participant Disclosure Rule (ERISA 404(a)(5))

This DOL rule provides that initial disclosures to participants under ERISA Rule 404(a) must be furnished no later than either 60 days after the plan's applicability date or 60 days after the effective date of the 408(b)(2) regulation. The rule covers both existing and newly eligible participants in the 401(k) plans.

Specific Provisions of 404(a)(5)

Under Rule 404(a)(5), which is governed by fiduciary standards, plan sponsors have 60 days from the effective date of the 408(b)(2) plan provider disclosure rules to provide fee information to participants. If plan sponsors failed to distribute fee disclosure information to participants by August 30, 2012, and then participants suffer losses from their investments, they may have recourse against their plan sponsors. According to ERISA attorney Fred Reish, if participants suffered losses because plan sponsors did not follow the rule, the DOL can impose a penalty, as well as the inability to use ERISA 404(c) as a defense, Reish said.[30]

Rule 404(a)(5) and Revenue Sharing

This rule has attracted the attention of plan sponsors because it has been used in class action lawsuits related to revenue sharing. Attorney Reish said that in a decision issued by the U.S. District Court for the Western District of Missouri on March 31, 2012 (*Tussey v. ABB* (W.D. Mo., No. 2:06-CV-04305)), the court found that ABB, Inc. and Fidelity had breached some fiduciary duties owed to participants in ABB's retirement plans.

The judge stated that ABB had violated its fiduciary duties when it failed to monitor recordkeeping costs, did not negotiate rebates for the plan from either Fidelity or other investment companies servicing their plans, chose more expensive share classes for the investment platform when less expensive share classes were available, and replaced Vanguard's Wellington Fund in the list of available funds with Fidelity's Freedom Funds.

In this case, the judge ruled that ABB had violated its fiduciary duties because it failed to comply with the plans' investment policy statement. The statement said, "at all times, [Alliance], rebates will be used to offset or reduce the cost of providing administrative services to plan participants." These lower costs would have benefited plan participants, but instead they were used to enrich the plan's service providers.

The judge also said she was not convinced that ABB had monitored the recordkeeping fees charged by Fidelity Trust to determine whether they were reasonable, nor had it monitored the expense ratios of the retail investments chosen for the participants. Not surprisingly, the court also found that ABB, Inc. and its Employee Benefits Committee violated their fiduciary duties when they agreed to overpay Fidelity an amount that exceeded market costs for plan services. Given the convoluted accounting that can occur in some benefits plans due to revenue sharing, these overpayments were made to subsidize the corporate services provided to ABB by Fidelity. These included ABB's payroll and recordkeeping for ABB's health, welfare and defined benefit plans.[31] This case sent shockwaves through the plan sponsor community. It put employers on notice that the new DOL regulations would force a change from doing business as usual.

Specific Provisions of 408(b)(2)

Regulation 408(b)(2), referred to as the service provider fee disclosure rule (29 CFR §2550.408b-2), requires initial disclosures of potential administrative and investment-related fees applicable to all plan participants. Disclosing these fees is required before a 401(k) plan participant is able to first direct investments under the plan. This rule has some very important potential benefits of investors because it provides data on investment expenses that had never been available previously. As noted by many investment professionals and academics, investment expenses directly affect an investor's all-important goal of increasing their net investment return.

This rule requires fiduciaries, recordkeepers, and brokers who have direct responsibilities for the plan's operations to disclose the fees they charge. This includes legal, accounting, and recordkeeping fees. It also specifies that any fees be broken down by whether they are charged on a pro-rata or per capita basis. This is an important distinction because it could reveal whether investors with large 401(k) balances were charged more for the same services than others with small account balances, even though they all received the same services. The results of these disclosures are expected to create significant problems for some plan sponsors.

For fiduciaries, this section has some other important provisions to increase the plan's disclosure of investment expenses, such as disclosing the plan's total annual operating expenses, including the very important expense ratios of an investment. (This is called a "designated investment alternative," or DIA in DOL jargon.) These total operating expenses have to be expressed as a percentage of the plan's total expenses and have to be disclosed to the plan's individual participants. Any other "investment-related information" must also be disclosed to participants (see 29 CFR §2550.404a-5(d)(1).

While disclosing the plan's total operating expenses is a major benefit, it is not ideal because it is expressed as a percentage, rather than being broken down into specific dollar expenses and categorized. This is a shortcoming, but not unexpected considering the antagonism toward full disclosure in the first place.

For recordkeepers and brokers, this section (Para.(c)(1)(iv)(F)) mandates that participants receive investment-related disclosures, such as prospectuses. This section affects registered investment companies (such as mutual funds), insurance companies, issuers of publicly traded securities; or registered financial institutions. The main benefit to participants in this section is that the plan sponsor should prevent the distribution of materials it knows are incomplete or inaccurate. But given that studies have shown that most investors do not read prospectuses, this section could be considered one that protects recordkeepers and brokers.

Because any changes to a plan's investment must be communicated quickly, this section (Para. (c)(1)(v)(B)(2)) covers the frequency of disclosure communications. Specifically, "all investment-related information must be distributed to participants at least once a year." If there is a change to information that has previously been disclosed, the plan sponsor has to notify participants within 60 days of finding out about the change.

In addition, the plan must issue a quarterly statement of actual fees charged against a participant's accounts in the prior quarter.

Rule 408(b)(2) Effective Date

This rule went into effect July 1, 2012 (see Para.(c)(1)(xii)) for covered service providers that must be in compliance by disclosing information about fees and services to plan sponsors of ERISA plans.

Which Investment Products Will Be Affected Most by Fee Disclosure?

Exposing the actual costs and expenses for individual categories of investments will produce winners and losers. Some casualties of the new regulations could be target-date funds and multi-manager funds.

Multi-Manager Funds

While many multi-manager funds display an expense ratio comparable to single-manager funds, they often incur significantly higher transaction and administrative costs. For example, one multi-manager fund lists eight managers in its large-cap growth fund. Because each manager acts independently in pursuit of a sub-index, or variation of the fund's target benchmark, trades generally occur more frequently in multi-manager funds than in a single-manager fund counterpart.

But what does this multi-manager approach actually do for investors? Does the use of multiple managers, with at least one manager from outside the fund family's investment management group, actually produce better investment returns than funds that use a team of in-house advisors?

The answer depends on whom you ask.

Multi-manager (aka multi-advisor) funds have existed since October 1958, when Vanguard's Windsor I Fund employed a team approach of in-house managers to handle investment responsibilities. The Windsor II Fund was started in June 24, 1985, with four in-house managers and was then combined with the Windsor I fund.

Multi-manager funds hire separate, outside fund companies to manage a specific fund. The fund company that hires outside managers claims they bring different resources, experience, and expertise to the fund advisor. When these different managers are combined to manage a specific fund, the goal is that their combined expertise will be greater than the sum of the individual parts. That's the theory.

But this does not make a definitive case that more manager talent will consistently catapult a fund into the top quartile on a consistent basis. One of the biggest criticisms of multi-manager funds is that they can identify the "best" managers in their respective categories, but the results are very different.

For example, one investment officer of a top multi-manager fund company emphasized that "our insight [is] in distinguishing managers who, we believe, have a better-than-average chance of outperforming [which] can be used to the investor's advantage."

However, people who have criticized multi-manager funds contend that it is too difficult to consistently identify and monitor manager performance to assure shareholders that they have hired the best and brightest managers.

Many have noted that multi-manager funds often are too slow to fire underperforming managers, while others have said that too many managers in a single fund (one multi-manager fund has 11 managers for its core equity fund alone) promotes closet indexing. Then, there is the critical issue of trading expenses, which grow significantly with more managers, yet are almost impossible for investors to discover.

Origins of the Multi-Manager Strategy

Mutual funds have evolved as the investment industry has become more complex, larger, and global. Funds managed by an individual manager are less common, and today many funds employ a team approach to fund management.

But the idea of using multiple managers to provide day-to-day investing expertise for a single fund was prompted more by regulation than the pursuit of alpha (the value that manager expertise adds). ERISA, considered the most complex piece of legislation since the New Deal, created new responsibilities for pension plan sponsors, including the mandate that they hire qualified, professional investment managers to obtain the best risk-adjusted return for their pension plans.

But how does a pension plan sponsor find the best qualified investment manager? This was the great question that reinvigorated the institutional investment consulting world in its expensive and unending quests to find the most deserving managers in the land. At one time, in the salad days of institutional money management, pension funds conducted Cinderella-like searches for the most attractive investment managers.

By the late-1970s, it became apparent that while continuous manager searches were profitable for consultants, it was a difficult task because each quarter produced hard data showing there was a near-continuous rotation among the "best" managers. This problem led to the idea of hiring a team of external managers selected from the screened manager universe. The Frank Russell Company takes credit for developing the multi-manager concept for mutual funds in the late-1970s. While this may have been prompted more by the pension fund board's need to meet their fiduciary duties under ERISA than the pursuit of exceptional fund performance, the idea gained traction.

Yet, while this was a novel idea, it was not universally accepted among some respected investment managers of the time. In a 1983 article, Dean LeBaron of Batterymarch Financial Management, wrote:

"Agents often behave in ways that may be uneconomic to beneficiaries. Take for example, the growing use by pension sponsors of multiple managers, with its corollary of having sharply rising costs. There is little evidence that aggregate results improve enough to justify the expense. This phenomenon may be best explained in terms of the sponsor's desired to minimize short-term career risk from volatility by diversifying across many managers."

Today, the multi-manager "phenomenon" continues, but it remain unclear whether the net investment results justify the hidden expenses for this entire category of funds, or whether they are appropriate for individual investors.

Target-Date Funds (TDFs)

Since the DOL endorsed TDFs in the Pension Protection Act of 2006 as "qualified default investment alternatives" for all 401(k) plans, TDFs have garnered an impressive amount of assets under management. Statistics from the September 2010 ICI Fact Book show that $340 billion was invested in target-date funds being offered by some 40 fund families, according to Morningstar.[44]

TDFs have also become more popular in 401(k) plans and accounted for $380 billion in assets at year-end 2011, and are expected to hit $1.1 trillion by 2016, according to Cerulli Associates.

These funds are usually offered in five-year increments to match an investor's planned retirement date. The main attraction of these funds is their built-in portfolio diversification, not their performance. This is because numerous academic studies have found that asset allocation is responsible for more than 90% of a portfolio's performance variability over time.[45]

Shortcomings of Target-Date Funds

Yet while the built-in diversification argument is powerful, it does not trump the fact that almost all target-date funds are composed of funds from a single fund family that are cleverly packaged into the target-date format. Individually, these funds would not be able to attract investor interest, often due to their mediocre returns, but their packaging attraction overcomes their individual performance deficiencies.

But as any expert baker will attest, it is difficult to bake a superior cake using mediocre ingredients. The same is true for target-date funds. However, long-term performance results are not yet available to make a definitive case that target-date funds deserve to be the default provision for millions of 401(k) investors.

TDFs also often suffer from high expenses, poor components, and untested "glide paths," or the management of asset class exposures, especially fixed income, over time. A survey by Janus Capital Group in November 2011, found that half of the plan sponsors surveyed did not know the glide path of the TDFs they were offering, but 70% said they were certain their employees understood the asset allocation in the fund over time.

With over $380 billion in assets (as of December 2011), TDFs continue to be the most popular investment choice in 401(k) plans. According to Cerulli Associates, by 2016, the amount invested in

TDFs is expected to reach $1.1 trillion. The future for TDFs is especially bright.

According to a study by Brightscope/Target Date Analytics, TDFs account for 10% of total invested assets in retirement plans. This number is expected to exceed 28% by 2020. In the 401(k) space, Vanguard Funds reported that 79% of the 401(k) plans it administers offered TDFs last year, an increase of 13% from 2004. Vanguard also said that 42% of its Vanguard plan participants used TDFs last year, up from just 2% in 2004.[49]

But with this exceptional popularity comes more responsibility. Joe C. Nagengast, co-founder of Target Date Analytics, said TDF managers "like other managers of qualified default investment alternatives, [should] serve as ERISA fiduciaries, by pointing out that the allocation and glide path decisions have even more impact on the outcome than on the selection of the underlying funds."

In an article, "Recovery in Target Date Funds," Nagengast also wrote:

"The evidence clearly supports our contention that target-date fund managers should stick to their core mandate, prudently managing participant assets during the accumulation phase, and give up the unsupportable claim that they must manage to participant death. That claim is becoming increasingly transparent as a thinly disguised justification for trying to hold on to participant assets."

Risk management was another significant problem often neglected by managers, he added.

"These [target-date-fund] aggressive managers have highjacked participants accounts by refusing to adhere to a basic tenet of target date investing, the need to substantially and rapidly reduce risk as the target date approaches. For many investors this change had the effect of a bait-and-switch, which promised a target retirement date strategy, but provided something entirely different.

"The aggressive managers justify their actions by claiming they address 'longevity risk,' but all they really do is add market risk to longevity risk. Participants (especially those hoping to retire in 2008 and 2009) were badly burned by this strategy. The managers decided to avoid the need for principle preservation at the target date in favor of a simplistic, long-term, risky portfolio strategy."

Nagengast, an expert in analyzing TDFs, has compiled a series of indexes to measure associations, risk and performance, as well as company management, fees, strategy, risk and performance. The 2011 TDF study of 34 fund families, covering some 400 individual TDF funds, noted that Vanguard had introduced 100% passive, low-cost TDF funds.

Fee competition has also prompted a few other fund companies, such as TIAA-CREF and Fidelity, to launch TDF funds with average expense ratios of 19 basis points. This brings the total to three TDF series which have average expense ratios under 19 basis points, the study found.[50] However, these fees could go even lower, to 12 basis points, if ETF providers were pressured, according to other industry sources.

While that is good news on fees, it is not shared by the vast majority of TDFs. Some TDFs charge an overlay fee on top of the average weighted expense ratios of the underlying funds in the TDF. This overlay fee is similar to a management, or wrap fee, to handle the individual fund allocations over time. According to Nagengast, charging for an overlay fee is "never justified," because it constitutes a double fee on TDF participants. Making TDFs expensive does not serve investors, plus since the TDFs glide path should not change over time, investors should question why a high management fee is needed.

The study also noted that most fund companies are "sacrificing returns" by adhering to 100% active management. As a result, "the cost for this preference in the face of contrary evidence is borne by individual investors in target date funds." This may explain why TDF fees remain high, with the average expense ratio of TDF I shares priced at 75 basis points. The study found that this expense "is far too high."[51]

The analysis also found other significant problems in these areas:

Risk management. The study found many TDF families "continue to pay too little attention to risk, [are] too aggressive, especially just prior to, and at, the target date." This helps explain why

TDF investors were "brutally punished" by investment losses since November 2007 by strategies that were too aggressive.

Not enough asset classes. TDFs do not include enough different asset classes, and while the industry touts the number of "approved asset classes" or "target allocations," the reality is that that "fund companies only pay lip service to diversification."

More passive management needed. The analysis found that the industry "continues sacrificing returns in their superstitious preference for active over passive management." The investment losses due to pursuing active strategies are borne by investors.[52]

WHY SOME FINANCIAL SERVICE PROVIDERS RESIST THE FIDUCIARY STANDARD

At this point, we switch from characteristics of some investments to what governs the actual daily behavior of investment advisors. Previous chapters have discussed the fiduciary standard and why it has remained the basis of ERISA since 1974. But the adoption of the fiduciary standard is dealing with ERISA-covered accounts poses a glaring problem since this standard has never been extended to the brokerage industry, including financial advisors, and the related vendors that supply services to 401(k) plans.

Because the fiduciary standard covers relationships between employees enrolled in registered pension plans and the professionals hired to manage the funds and provide specific investment advice, it's logical to ask why brokers and vendors would not be covered by this same standard.

The answer lies in the higher level of business conduct practices mandated by ERISA versus those performed on a wider basis by investment salespeople (brokers) working in a highly transactional environment.

One explanation is that the brokerage industry does not want brokers to be accountable for their recommendations or responsible for providing ongoing fiduciary duties that are in the consumer's long-term best interests. This is only aggravated by the large number of uninformed consumer-investors, who feed the vicious cycle because "the providers (financial service professionals) continue to obfuscate costs and benefits of products by providing dissimilar comparisons of product features. [As a result, the] information power continues to favor the sales representative; [since] the majority of financial services consumers do not have the access or inclination to master the information necessary to match that of the sales representative, making the decision of who to use as a financial advisor a critical decision for the consumer." [62]

Under the current business model, the brokerage industry maintains that brokers do not provide advice. In most firms, it is considered a violation of internal compliance protocol for brokers to acknowledge that they render advice and owe their clients the fiduciary duty of care and loyalty.

If they adopted this position, it would require brokers to act in their clients' best interests, according to Steven Winks, senior consultant at PCT Research and Consulting, "The industry's principal defense against the fiduciary liability of tens of thousands of brokers, who are independently rendering advice, has been to simply maintain that brokers do not render advice, which according to the brokerage industry way of thinking, effectively absolves brokers from any responsibility for their recommendations," Winks said.

This industry sleight-of-hand has shaped the role of the broker as a licensed professional, who simply makes an investor aware of their investment alternatives. Then, it is up to less-informed investors to make their own decisions, regardless of their investment knowledge. So in practice, what the investor thinks is advice simply becomes "a sales story," where no advice was implied or presented. In this scenario, the broker has no ongoing accountability for the investment results that occur.

Another side effect of this intentionally confusing practice is the semantic ploy of what to call financial professionals. Over the years, the industry has referred to people who sell financial products and services to individuals as "brokers," "customer men," "agents," "registered investment advisors," "registered advisors," "registered representatives," "investment advisors," and "sales consultants." One reason for the various professional titles is that not all licensed salespeople are licensed to sell all products (stocks, bonds, futures, options, limited partnerships, annuities and insurance).

But another reason is the attempt to avoid responsibility for actually selling a product that fails to perform as promised or best-suited to meet clients' needs. If there is no promise or specific recommendation, explicit or implied ("past performance is no guarantee of future results"), then there is also no accountability since the sales person is only providing advice. It is certainly intentional that this job description slight-of-hand has evolved over the years, and never been corrected.

Because the adoption of a fiduciary standard entails adherence to professional and financial responsibility, it is understandable that large sections of the industry would vigorously resist these serious changes in business practices. (Under SEC rules, only Registered Investment Advisors must adhere to the fiduciary standard.) If the fiduciary role was broadly adopted, these higher standards would mean a fundamental shift in the assumption of risk from customers to professional advisors and their supervisory firms.

While brokers may evade responsibility for their recommendations, mutual fund companies have encouraged sales of specific products by offering to pay larger commissions. According to Kasina, an investment research firm, fund companies "seek to drive sales of profitable products by varying basis point payouts according to product profitability."

For example, a firm specializing in annuities products pays wholesalers up to three times more basis points for its variable products than its fixed annuities. These extra incentives create suitability problems for brokers, who are being rewarded for selling investors inappropriate products. One broker surveyed by Kasina rhetorically asked, "What if the best product for a given advisor client is one of our lower-margin offerings? Will wholesalers feel inclined to recommend it, knowing the impact it would have on his or her variable compensation?"

Aside from money, the actual objective of adopting the full fiduciary standard has changed from its original intent. Under English common law, the fiduciary duty of directors is to the company itself, not the shareholders. This change in emphasis focuses on the benefits of the company's ongoing activities and the impact of transactions on the company itself. In the U.S., the goal of exercising the fiduciary duty is to maximize the value of company shares if the company is sold. This primarily benefits the company's largest shareholders and management, not its employees and small investors.

At this point, it may be appropriate to discuss this divergence in how the fiduciary standard is applied in different sectors of the financial services industry.

CONFLICTS-OF-INTEREST VS. THE DUTY OF LOYALTY OR EXCLUSIVE BENEFIT RULE

A reality of the way many investment professionals conduct business today is that often their interests are not the same as their customers. This disparity is evident in many actions, ranging from the quality of supposedly "objective" advice provided to unsuspecting investors to the overall business goal of keeping an investor's money invested with the same firm for as long as possible, regardless of the level of investment returns or quality of service.

These misaligned interests should not exist, but they have a long history that is philosophically linked to the concept of trust, which is unique to the Anglo-American legal tradition. This concept evolved slowly, beginning around 700 AD, and took several centuries to appear in a form we would recognize today.

To foster trust, however, history shows that some abuses occurred that catalyzed change. In the 11th century, for example, Crusaders leaving on the First Crusade commonly entrusted their lands and families to the safekeeping of a friend. Upon returning home, some Crusaders discovered that the "trustee" had evicted their families and expropriated the property for their own use.

Legally, these knights had no recourse in common law because title had been transferred. But upon appeal to the king, the knights were able to assert that a moral obligation existed to safeguard the property on their behalf. It took several centuries for the moral obligations of trustees to be enforced by the courts of common law. This move from a moral to legal responsibility started in 1536 with the passage of the Statute of Uses by the English Parliament.

In its broad modern interpretation, ERISA embodies many of these common law concepts and states that the goal of securing participants' retirement income should be the objective of all retirement plans under its rules (supported in *Donovan v. Cunningham,* 716 F.2d 1455, 1467 (5th Cir. 1983). According to attorney Fred Reish of Drinker Biddle, ERISA requires that "fiduciaries act for the exclusive purpose of providing retirement benefits. A reasonable interpretation of the language would mean that fiduciaries must focus on the actual benefits being produced by [retirement] plans, as opposed to the current culture of looking at a plan's features and services."

The "prudent man rule" requires that fiduciaries act as a knowledgeable investor (or "prudent expert") would in accomplishing the "aims" of the plan. If the aim of a plan is to provide adequate retirement income, the prudent fiduciaries should focus first and foremost on whether or not the plan actually is accomplishing that goal. If it is not, then the prudent man rule would require that fiduciaries determine why the plan is not working and take prudent steps to improve its performance.[61]

This highlights the serious issue of whether a plan meets its goal of providing adequate retirement income, which can be determined by the all-important measure of fund performance. Because it is well known that high fees degrade fund performance, a prudent-man standard requires a plan to take this key variable into account. A 2010 Morningstar study found for the five years ending 2010, low-cost funds in all asset classes posted, on average, better returns than the most expensive funds. [89]

Another study conducted by State Street Global Advisors found that while 85 % of equity managers in the study underperformed the market in nearly all relevant time periods, the global total of fees extracted for this and other financial-intermediation services is in the range of $1.5 trillion annually, according to Suzanne Duncan, global head of research for State Street's Center for Applied Research.[63]

In a presentation before the CFA Institute, panelists addressed the issue of compensation in the investment management business, specifically the need to define and institute "more credible, long-term-focused compensation that rewards performance, not just asset accumulation by managers."

The panel noted that investors pay performance fees to management on an annual basis for any short-term gains in their portfolios, even though their ultimate goal is to generate positive returns over decades.

This raises the issue of compensating managers at a different level for long- and short-term performance, but according to a *Chartered Financial Analyst Journal* article on this panel discussion, "the notion of asset managers paying a negative performance fee for poor results...and [p]aying money back to clients from fees collected, when you as manager do not beat your benchmark, sent an air of unease across the audience of mainly investment professionals."[64]

That "air of unease" was undoubtedly an understatement. When I addressed the issue of underperformance and compensation with a major money manager in Chicago, whose fund had produced a gain of $24 for 2011, the manager replied (through an intermediary) that while his annual performance was "hardly a glorious time for the fund," the manager ended the year in the middle of the pack, according to Lipper, and near the 40th percentile according to Morningstar.[65]

This use of percentiles certainly cannot justify an investor's assumption of all the risk, while the manager continued to receive his full management fees. When a fund fails to beat its benchmark, an investor can either stay or leave. Because mutual fund managers have refused to consider tying their compensation to performance, except in the rare use of fulcrum fees offered by a handful of funds, investors are invited to redeem their shares and go elsewhere. This pay-for-performance inertia in the fund industry persists since there is no consumer pressure for change.

However, a 2005 CFA study found "that a significant portion of incentive pay for asset managers should be measured by long-term (three to five years) metrics similar to those used at the companies in which they invest. To confirm this longer-term focus, asset management firms should provide investors with more information about their incentive structures."[66]

Low investment returns and the volatile environment help explain the $135 billion in redemptions from equity mutual funds in 2011 that were accompanied by inflows of more than $119 billion into ETFs in 2011, according to Index Universe.[67] The amount flowing into ETFs contrasts with the $58.5 billion in net new money that went into traditional mutual funds in that period, according to Morningstar.[68]

Another key issue concerns the role of fiduciaries in 401(k) plans. This has been overlooked by many corporate plan sponsors and participants, who have neglected the problem that many 401(k) plan administrators do not have exact cost figures for the expenses being charged in their plans.

This is because the plan administrators, often insurance companies, have mastered the art of intermingling fees, rebates, extra charges, and other a la carte items, so only a few people can actually determine the true costs for each plan participant.

This raises the issue of the fiduciary duty of protecting plan participants from the negative impacts of high expenses paid from participant assets.

The traditional fiduciary language associated with these situations calls for plan sponsors to act "solely in the interest of plan participants and their beneficiaries, with the exclusive purpose of providing benefits to them. This is the Duty of Loyalty, also known as the Exclusive Benefit Rule. These concepts link the fiduciary duty to pay only plan expenses that are reasonable relative to services provided. The plan sponsor also must document that these services and expenses are reasonable."[69]

The Exclusive-Benefit Rule in Practice

The American understanding of fiduciary duty in a sale of a corporation is that management is duty-bound to represent the interests of the stockholders in the transaction. This duty is usually interpreted as maximizing the share value of the company's stock. In the United Kingdom, by comparison, the directors owe their fiduciary duty not to the shareholders, but to the company as a whole. That means that their primary focus is on the interests of the company and the effect of any transaction on the company.[70]

In practice, failing to adhere to the fiduciary standard can carry stiff penalties. For instance, during the late 1980s, when the DOL was prosecuting labor unions, it routinely brought criminal charges for violations of the fiduciary standard.

The Michigan Conference of Teamsters Health & Welfare Funds discovered this when it saw some of its assets evaporate after a DOL investigation found examples of improper expenditures at the Fund from 1989 to 1994.

These expenses included:

- $99,000 for "golf outings, bowling, and other entertainment, including 'adult entertainment' featuring nude or topless female dancers;"

- $145,000 spent predominantly at local restaurants for luncheons and dinners whose purpose was "primarily social in nature;"

- $36,000 for "retirement parties, receptions, and liquor;"

- $94,000 for "flowers, donuts, milk, coffee and other refreshments for Plan staff;"

- $87,000 for "travel and entertainment expenses related to the participation in, or the Plan's sponsorship of golf events. These expenses included the cost of awards, including cash prizes, and golf equipment and supplies, such as, $217.27 for 'Golf balls for England trip,' or $145 for 5,000 imprinted golf tees."

While this makes for interesting reading, it shows the double standard that exists between critiquing labor union and corporate practices, as well as the changing standards of ERISA enforcement.

This disparity centers around institutions governed by the fiduciary standard (such as labor union pension funds covered by ERISA) and non-pension related corporate business practices. The public perception of unions has been tainted by stereotypes, when in reality the corruption statistics between unions and corporations are dramatically tilted against corporations. In 1978, estimates by the U.S. Attorney General's office found that 300 union locals had serious corruption problems. There are 65,000 union locals, however, so the 300 locals that had serious corruption problems represent less than 1 % of the total union locals.

Compare that to a 1980 survey in *Fortune* magazine of corrupt acts at 1,043 large U.S. corporations. The magazine defined corporate corruption as "bribery, fraud, illegal political contributions, tax evasion and criminal anti-trust." The *Fortune* survey found that 117 corporations, or 11 % of the total, had at least one serious violation in the period and that some had been cited more than once. In total, there were 188 citations. Because the study excluded bribes and kickbacks made outside the U.S., it underestimated the possible violations.

Had the study been extended to include smaller corporations, *Fortune* noted that the violation rate would have been higher because "bribing of purchasing agents by small manufacturers and the skimming of receipts by cash-laden small retail businesses are commonplace in commercial life."

Any mutual fund company that has a national wholesaler network could easily make expenditures for annual sales events and entertaining its wholesalers that are similar to the ones for which the Michigan Conference of Teamsters Health & Welfare Funds was punished.

In one case, the national sales manager of a large mutual fund company had $2,000 worth of wine delivered to his room for personal use. The fund company's special events manager signed off on the purchase because she was afraid of losing her job. If that exact scenario played out under the fiduciary standard, it could become a criminal prosecution. Instead, it was just tallied up as a miscellaneous entertainment expense.

Meanwhile, Back at 401(k) Plans

Similarly, some 401(k) plan vendors have been able to mask their fees to plan sponsors, evade responsibility, and cherry-pick the disclosures they want to make to both plan sponsors and their employees.

100

This practice has shaped the way brokers and vendors sell investment and service products. But the gap between the way business is conducted for pension funds and 401(k) plans has not gone unnoticed by the DOL over the past 30 years. In the more polite language of the DOL, this has produced an "information gap" between plan sponsors and their vendors.

According to Roland-Criss, a fiduciary service provider, "due to the esoteric nature of the investment vendors' processes and offerings, vendors are able to rely certain types of information to plan sponsors and make investment decisions that do not necessarily align with plan sponsors' best interests." [71]

For its part, the DOL cited the "information advantage" 401(k) service providers have over their customers, including the "strong incentive" salespeople have "to distort market outcomes in their own favor." The DOL also said plan sponsors are responsible for making responsible buying decisions under ERISA, even though they are often at a disadvantage to professional salespeople. This explains why "vendors can reap excess profit by concealing indirect compensation (and attendant conflicts-of-interest) from clients, thereby making their prices appear lower and their product quality higher." [72]

All this is in stark contrast to the policy and enforcement practices adopted by the SEC, which also has a regulatory role in the ways funds are sold to investors. For its part, over the past 80 or so years, the SEC has, with only a few exceptions, adopted a pro-investor stance on investor protections and prosecuting industry abuses.

While this has been the accepted business practice in the 401(k) industry for the 30 years that 12b-1 fees have existed, it should be a surprise to plan participants that their employers have not been diligently screening for the highest-quality providers to help them secure their collective financial futures. On the contrary, according to Roland-Criss, 401(k) administrators have been blinded by marketing and brand hype "to make investment and plan management decisions on their (and their participants') behalf—under the presumption that their vendors' reports contain all the information they need to properly oversee this process." [73]

The net impact of DOL fee disclosure rule 408(b)(2) should turn this naive "assumption on its head" by demonstrating that "their vendors may not be acting in their best interests and may be using certain reporting tactics to conceal excessive fees."

This creates a significant problem for the 401(k) plan administrators because they are ultimately responsible for "monitoring and determining the acceptableness of their vendors' behavior."[74]

Here is a good example: ETFs are an established, popular, low-expense investment option. But while low-expense products serve the needs of investors, they do not necessarily do the same for brokers. The reason is that some brokers seek to maximize trade executions because they are a profit center and serve their firms' best interests, although other advisors are more mindful of trading costs and their client's net gains. ETFs are also sold without using revenue sharing, which is a dollar incentive to brokers to stimulate sales in the mutual fund industry.

According to Steven Winks, brokers, who are also acting as salespeople, often double-dip when they charge an advisory fee plus commission, without a cap on compensation. When this occurs, usual and customary fees for services are typically not recognized, resulting in excessive compensation or inadequate service. Often, all of this is much greater than the consulting fees brokers are charging the 401(k) plan.

These sales activities can easily go against the broker's fiduciary role. They also create fiduciary problems for the plan sponsor because these extra costs are passed on to participants, not the plan sponsor.

"There are many salespeople who mistakenly think they are advisors. This is being clarified in part by the new 401(k) disclosure requirements, documentation of services rendered and the role and responsibility of the advisor," Winks said.

The other main problem is liability. The financial services industry has shaped the role of the broker as one who simply makes investors aware of their investment alternatives, but then guides their investor-customer to make investment decisions, regardless of how limited their investment knowledge and experience may be. Thus, what the investor thinks is advice is simply a sales story where no advice was implied or rendered and no ongoing accountability for whatever result may occur.

"The brokerage industry would like to continue to be absolved from any accountability or responsibility, which has resulted in a loss of trust and confidence of the investing public. Without the brokerage industry voluntarily acknowledging or supporting the fiduciary duty of the broker in the consumer's best interest, an Act of Congress was required that now makes it a regulatory imperative that the broker acts in the consumer's best interest," Winks said.

How to Hide Costs

Other esoteric features of the financial services business are ideally designed to hide costs. The compensation of recordkeepers provides a good example of how soft dollars are used to pay for expensive services, while effectively masking actual dollar amounts. This is done through soft-dollar transactions, which work like this: Because of their important role, recordkeepers establish a good relationship with plan sponsors. In turn, the recordkeeper is assigned the responsibility of selecting fund managers and other investment providers that rebate a portion of their fees back to the recordkeeper. The plan sponsor never sees a bill from the recordkeeper.

But acting as gatekeeper, the recordkeeper determines who can sell and which investment products are offered to the captive group of 401(k) plan participants. As a result, investment products may not be selected based specifically on their benefits, fees, and performance, but rather on the willingness of these product executives to rebate a large portion of their fees back to the recordkeeper.

Under the DOL's covered service provider and participant fee disclosure regulations, this cozy practice will expose plan sponsors to new penalties and responsibilities. But as in other examples, illuminating these cozy relationships is coming decades too late for millions of participants, many of whom are now retired.

All this should not make plan participants feel confident that their employers have been acting diligently on their behalf. Just the opposite. While many 401(k) plan industry publications and providers correctly note that the new DOL fee disclosure regulations will illuminate the cozy relationships between plan providers and their vendors, they fail to note the impact on the millions of plan participants.

This was the case when the DOL was asked to extend its rule enactment date, so a cost impact study could be conducted to determine how the new rules would impact the costs of a few hundred service providers.[75] But the congressman requesting the extension on behalf of the recordkeeper industry never considered whether the delay would increase the lost net returns of millions of plan participants.

Evading Responsibility

Can the average American investor trust their financial professional?

While polite people would unquestionably consider the question impertinent, the reality is very different.

Whether investors are dealing with stock brokers or planners, none of these titles carry any legal responsibilities to act in the exclusive best interests of their clients. The one exception is the Registered Investment Advisor (RIA) who is legally bound by fiduciary standards. As for dealing with investment pros, who carry other titles with different compensation arrangements, caveat emptor.

By lobbying against the adoption of the fiduciary standard for the nation's 600,000 brokers, the brokerage industry would like to continue to be absolved from any accountability or responsibility. Under the current regulations, brokers and planners only have to suggest a "suitable product." That is an intentionally broad definition and one which suits the industry better than its customers. The big difference is working with the higher fiduciary standard. This will change the way brokers (who are commission-based) and RIAs (many of whom work on hourly fees, and no commissions) are compensated, so it has become a contentious issue.

Understandably, the impetus for this change did not come from the industry itself, but from the Dodd-Frank Wall Street Reform and Consumer Protection Act signed into law by President Obama on July 21, 2010. A provision in the bill (Section 913) required the SEC to study the need for a uniform fiduciary standard covering stockbrokers and financial advisors who provide personalized financial advice. Since this affects the compensation of this lucrative business, it has become a very sensitive political issue.

When investors sustain significant losses on a mass basis in an adverse economic environment, however, they will logically turn back to the people who provided the advice. If the brokerage industry does not recognize that the broker has a fiduciary duty to act in the consumer's best interest, it will lead to a further loss of trust and confidence by the investing public.

Large brokerage firm have resisted the fiduciary standard because of their focus on gathering and retaining assets under management. Large brokerage firms, or wirehouses, have traditionally focused on the lucrative 401(k) and IRA rollover business. Adopting the fiduciary standard would limit, if not prevent, brokers (who are now considered non-fiduciaries) from rolling over plan accounts and assets to create a much larger revenue stream. Insurance companies, recordkeepers, and fund companies are focused on asset retention, and adopting the fiduciary standard would impair that objective, according to an industry expert.

To adopt the fiduciary standard, the brokerage industry has to essentially change the way it conducts business. This would include the use of advanced technology to provide the ongoing advice and transparency required for fiduciary standing. It would also include a process to manage conflicts-of-interest, so that objective advice could be provided. More painfully, it would include full disclosure or the elimination of the revenue sharing and 12b-1 fees that have provided a lucrative revenue stream for brokers, while simultaneously working against the best interest of customers. This could be an insurmountable sacrifice for brokers.

Essentially, the brokerage industry does not have any political inclination to share its self-interests with its own customers. If the brokerage industry fails to acknowledge these conflicts-of-interests, investors should assume they are victims and should act accordingly.

Informed investors should now rightfully assume that their own interests are secondary to their broker's self-interests. This creates a new balance of power. Investors, whether they are in a company's 401(k) or their own independent portfolio, should question every recommendation and fee and press their financial professional about all sources of revenues that person is receiving as a result of their investments.[76]

As to how plan sponsors should manage the new DOL rule, some simple advice came from Dr. Ron A. Rhoades, Assistant Professor and Program Chair for the Financial Planning Program at, said, "Plan sponsors should not wait for the DOL to act. The DOL's rules do not necessarily provide "safe harbors" for plan sponsors. Hence, I would advise plan sponsors to avoid any revenue sharing arrangements, of any type, between the advisors and other vendors of the plan. This includes not only payment for shelf space, but also soft-dollar compensation and other 'back-channel' payments."

A Variety of Arrangements May Be Used to Compensate 401(k) Service Providers

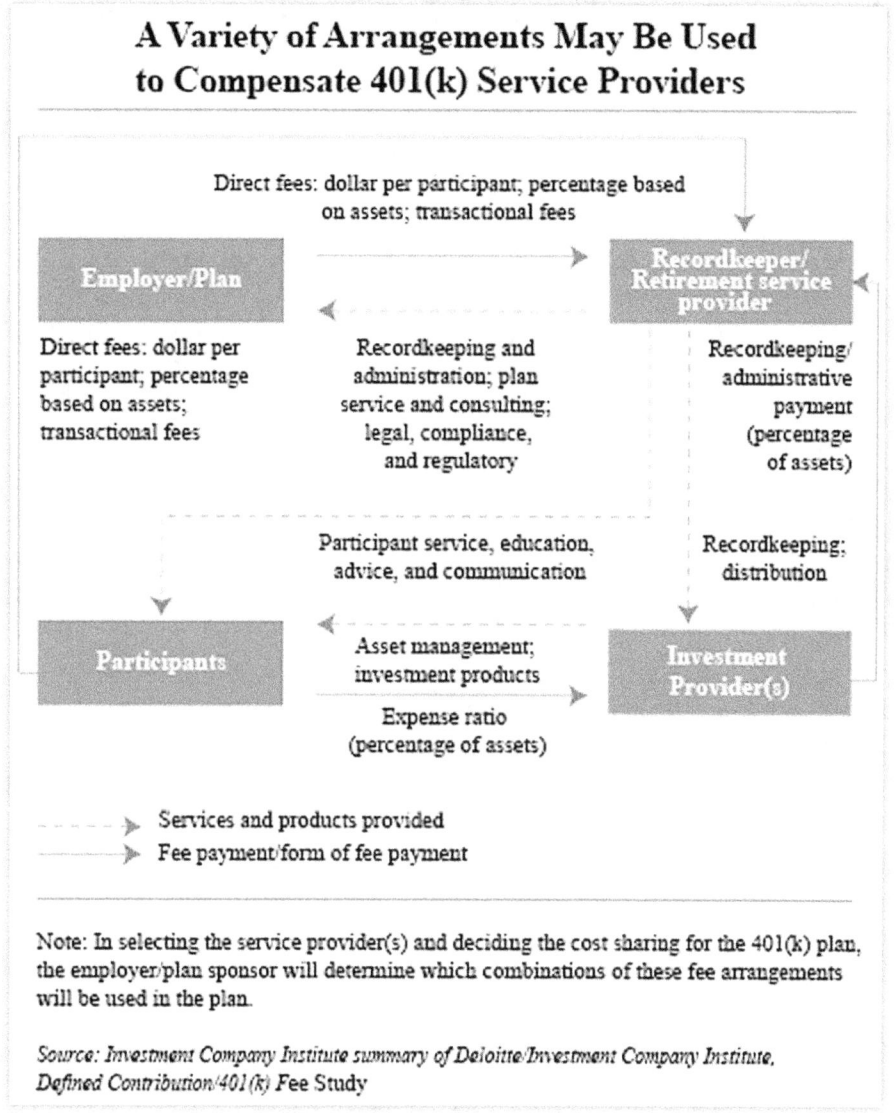

Note: In selecting the service provider(s) and deciding the cost sharing for the 401(k) plan, the employer/plan sponsor will determine which combinations of these fee arrangements will be used in the plan.

Source: Investment Company Institute summary of Deloitte/Investment Company Institute, Defined Contribution/401(k) Fee Study

Rhoades then said plan sponsors should "establish the compensation of the investment advisor in advance—before any investment recommendations are made—either as a flat fee, hourly fee, or percentage of assets (or some combination thereof). If revenue sharing payments are in place, demand that they be credited, in full, against any fees paid to the broker-dealer firm acting as the fiduciary to the plan."[77]

How Fees Benefit Financial Firms and Salespeople

While the industry presents the various share classes as vehicles that benefit investors, they actually were designed to benefit mutual fund salespeople. Each share class has a different payout profile for commissions to salespeople. The payouts can be immediate or deferred over the life of the account.

When revenue sharing is added to the payout mix, it creates a conflict-of-interest because the investment professional has a beneficial interest in receiving both the revenue sharing, plus the 12b-1 fees, for as long as the investor owns the specific fund and share class.

In real life, if the financial professional is presented with a better-performing or more suitable fund that meets the needs of a specific investor, the competing cash payments may cloud the advisor's objectivity. As a result, a financial professional with a low ethical profile has little or no interest in presenting a better-performing or more suitable fund to an unsuspecting client. This is the argument used by financial professionals, who advocate the adoption of a fiduciary standard in the brokerage industry.

The other driving force is money. Salaries in the financial services industry are among the highest in the United States. Almost everyone connected with the sale and administration of mutual funds and services to all forms of retirement plans, as well as individuals, are very well paid. This includes fund portfolio managers, consultants, actuaries, mutual fund wholesalers, ERISA lawyers, marketing people, and fund administrative staffs.

With all these people on the payroll, it is no wonder investors who buy funds through fund companies employing large sales forces pay more in expenses. Take the case of the LargeCap S&P 500 Index Fund sold by Principal Financial, a huge insurance company with a large national sales force. Investors in this fund are hit with fees totaling 1.50%, which is about ten times more than a similar fund sold by Vanguard.[78]

Moreover, fund and insurance companies with large national sales forces often develop cultures that elevate the needs and expense accounts of the sales force, comprised of internal, external sales people, management and key accounts staffs, over the needs of their own shareholders. When revenue sharing is mixed into this formula, it creates another stream of payments to financial advisors that reduces the status of shareholders even further.

Mutual Fund Wholesaler Salaries

Comparing Mutual Fund Wholesaler Salaries

Nuclear Engineer	$78,104
Lawyer	$117,988
Dentist	$82,100 A
irline Pilot	$128,648
Pharmacist	$88,816
Physician	$145,704
Physicist	$90,324
Anesthesiologist	$174,250
Econ Teacher	$95,836
Surgeon	$181,610
Financial Services Wholesaler:	$200,000+

Source: U.S. Department of Labor (2004)

Through the alchemy of the investment industry, the revenue streams generated by a simple mutual fund sale can produce an extraordinary amount of revenue for everyone except the actual investors in the fund. A great demonstration of this is the salaries of one of the least recognized professions in the financial services industry: mutual fund external wholesalers.

Fund wholesalers (people who sell mutual funds) are among the most highly compensated professionals in the U.S., including specialty physicians, engineers, and airline pilots. According to Kasina Research, "external [mutual fund wholesalers] typically receive an average annual base salary that ranges from $65,000 to

$98,000, with an average of $83,000.[79] Relative to hybrid and internal wholesalers, externals receive the highest base salary, though it generally represents a smaller portion of their total target compensation. Total target compensation can range broadly from $225,000 for an average-performing wholesaler to over $500,000 annually for top performers." But that only includes base salary.

In addition, external wholesalers receive compensation that can range from $100,000 to over $350,000 annually, depending on how much sales exceed the target. The wholesaler might also receive individual commissions calculated as a small percentage of gross sales or asset retention. Another perk is that all wholesaler expenses (travel, food, entertainment) are borne by their employers.

External wholesalers are commonly employed by large mutual fund and insurance companies as part of their national sales force. They are commonly assigned a territory to sell the mutual funds offered by a specific fund family. In the course of their daily work, they meet with financial advisors, brokers, and financial planners—anyone who has actual contact with end-investors and has the actual authority to sell a specific mutual fund.

While the training, educations, and talents of mutual fund wholesalers vary greatly, they share significant problems, as well as benefits. One problem is that wholesalers are often selling mutual funds that are very similar to the funds their competitors are selling. Performance gains and losses over time are common, so a typical fund will have both exceptional and lower-than-average performance. This is a given over the life of any fund (often evidenced by the volatility of quarterly performance over a five-year period, information that is readily available through Morningstar or Lipper).

The other significant problem wholesalers face is that because they are selling nearly identical products, often traded in very similar ways and burdened with the same high cost structures needed to sustain corporate profitability and the built-in overheads of their national sales networks, "[i]n order to compete, new 'bells and whistles' were (and are) created to entice plan sponsors to choose one vendor's 401(k) platform over another."[80] As Scott Adams has observed, "[t]echnological innovations will cause most companies to produce identical products and services. For companies to survive, they will have to become experts at confusing the public into thinking their generic products are better than their competitors' generic products."[81]

The biggest benefit, solely from the wholesaler's point of view, is that most mutual funds are sold using revenue sharing, which serves as an added commission paid to an advisor for as long as their client owns the fund. Basically, this is salesmanship on steroids because the sales talents of the wholesaler are diminished by the dollar amount of the revenue payments.

Revenue Sharing Defined

Revenue sharing, as defined by the SEC, occurs when the investment advisor to a fund makes payments to a broker-dealer. In some cases, the investment advisor may describe those payments as reimbursing the broker-dealer for expenses it incurs in selling the shares. Those payments, regardless of whether they are labelled as reimbursements, give the broker-dealer or advisor a greater incentive to sell the shares of one fund versus another which does not pay revenue sharing.

Revenue sharing can take many forms, including the use of 12(b)-1 fees. Revenue sharing fees are based as a percentage of the money invested or as a stated dollar amount for as long as an investor owns the fund. As a result, revenue sharing provides an incentive for a financial advisor to promote some funds over others, regardless of performance or investor suitability.

Revenue sharing remains the mutual fund industry's secret weapon to sell its commoditized, look-alike products. One reason for the vast commoditization of mutual funds is that there are too many funds covering the same limited number of traditional asset classes and market capitalizations. Technology has further focused development of similar products and services and only added to the commoditization problem.[82]

Revenue sharing has been a controversial practice in the fund industry for decades. "Revenue sharing is the 'big secret' of the retirement industry; a practice that makes it hard for employers and employees to understand the true cost of their retirement plan's services. Gross inequities can exist for both plan sponsors and participants."[83] Hutcheson has called revenue sharing "a euphemism for kickbacks from one financial service firm to another and is a common economic driver of conflicts-of-interest."[84]

This viewpoint has been cited by others as being the financial incentive for recommending ill-suited funds to investors on a mass scale. While the definition of revenue sharing is contained in the prospectuses from fund companies that engage in the practice (nearly all of them, although no official industry statistics are available), the reality is that few individual investors read prospectuses. Similarly, few investment advisors can actually find the revenue sharing language in the prospectus either.

As editor for a broker-dealer quarterly newsletter for a fund company that made extensive use of revenue sharing, I asked about 100 financial advisors, who received significant revenue sharing payments from the fund company, whether they actually ever explained the practice to investors in their face-to-face meetings. Not a single one had done so.

Revenue sharing is such an ingrained, sacred industry practice that it is rarely publicly discussed. This may explain why the recent DOL disclosure regulations were subjected to a barrage of industry lobbying to protect the essential role of revenue sharing in the fund sales process.

Phyllis Borzi, Assistant Secretary of Labor for the DOL's Employee Benefits Security Administration and the person widely cited as providing the impetus for making 401(k) plans more transparent about fees and expenses, said the agency was subjected to "a wholesale assault from broker-dealers" about the changes because the new regulations "prohibit advisors who accept a fee for providing investment advice to retirement plans from giving advice that represents a conflict-of-interest."[85]

Fund wholesalers make their large salaries largely as a result of free-riding on the revenue sharing payments that stimulate and support sales and repeat commission business. Because large fund companies are essentially sales organizations and the revenue sharing generates bonuses for many layers of management and sales staff, the practice cannot be curtailed without significantly altering the entire fund sales business model. This may explain why suggestions that deducting the revenue sharing sales incentive from wholesaler compensation packages has been vehemently resisted.

This practice is very lucrative to certain people. Revenue sharing payments have been known to amount to as much as 150 basis points (1.5%) in additional commissions paid to investment professionals, on top of 12b-1 fees. When revenue sharing, 12b-1, and other fees associated with mutual fund share classes are tallied, they present a formidable commission package to a financial representative, who wants to sell mutual funds based on commission income, rather than offering a more suitable and cost-effective investment product to customers.

According to fiduciary expert Dr. Ron A. Rhoades, "There is no reason to pay 12b-1 fees to a mutual fund, (since) 12b-1 fees were originally designed to assist in the retail marketing of a fund, where there is no benefit to the plan sponsor."[86] Over the years, 12b-1 fees have been hijacked to supplement marketing budgets.

Hiding Revenue Sharing Payments

One of the more insidious traits of revenue sharing is that most plan participants do not even know it is affecting their investment product selection and, more important, the impact it has on their net investment returns. While there are no industry statistics available on revenue sharing (for good reason), it is estimated that "most" small- and middle-sized 401(k) plans rely on service providers who accept revenue sharing payments to offset some of the plan administration service costs they provide. While this can help defray some of the costs of plan administration, plan sponsors have not fully investigated or calculated their short- and long-term negative impacts on their own employees.

In almost all cases, it is difficult to see how revenue sharing benefits investors over the long-term in any way aside from reduced plan expenses that are not passed along to individual plan participants.

Since there are 40 million participants in 401(k) plans, revenue sharing is used against a large number of investors.[87]

Another major problem is that the generous compensation is justified from the use of 12b-1 fees. When they were originally imposed in the 1970s, 12b-1 fees were intended to strengthen the communications between investors and their financial professionals. The intent was that as mutual fund assets grew, total operating expenses would decrease as funds achieved a more efficient scale of economy. Gathering more assets via improved sales and asset retention would then benefit investors, who would reap the benefits of lower expense ratios and, thus, higher net portfolio returns. More money into investors' pockets and more assets under management would be the proverbial win-win. But as fund assets under management have grown, expense ratios have not declined for the largest and most efficient fund complexes.

Revenue Sharing in Practice

Selling mutual funds is a complicated business.

Every day, financial advisors can choose from about 8,000 publicly available mutual funds in a variety of share classes, to select ones that best match investors' needs. To make their selections, advisors can then use at least 22 selection criteria and characteristics, ranging from fund rankings and tax efficiency to fund risk and manager tenure, to make their selections.

But what if these objective criteria were compromised by a fund company which made cash payments to advisors who sold their funds? How common is this and how does it change the relationship between an advisor and their client?

These are serious questions which affect thousands of shareholders. But these questions involve a practice called revenue sharing that is largely unknown to investors.

While it is a common industry practice, revenue sharing, and related fees, such as 12(b)-1 fees, are difficult to understand, and commonly not explained by investment advisors or plan sponsors.

While these fees are not well-understood by the public, they have been controversial in the industry for years. The simple reason is due to the competing interests of plan participants and the 401(k) industry. "The profitability of the 401(k) industry depends upon the magnitude of the fees it can extract from plan assets and plan sponsors—not on how well it protects and enhances the retirement income security of plan participants."[58]

These fees have also been the subject of numerous lawsuits.

For example, in 2007 the brokerage firm of Edward Jones settled a charge filed against them in 2004 by the SEC. In the 2007 settlement, Jones agreed to pay a $37.5 million fine, and return $37.5 million in "ill-gotten gains and interest" after the SEC said Jones failed to disclose revenue sharing agreements it entered into with seven mutual funds. Instead of disclosing these fee arrangements, Jones told customers the funds were chosen because of their exceptional performance and investment objectives.

Conflicts-of-Interest: How Revenue Sharing Taints 401(k) Plans

While the 401(k) movement has become the nation's dominant retirement financing program over the past 30 years, it now looks like some investment managers who were administering the funds and providing the advice have been engaged in a conflict-of-interest with their company plan counterparts. At least that is what the GAO charged.

In one study,[59] "401(k) Plans Improved Regulation Could Better Protect Participants from Conflicts of Interest," the GAO said the financial services industry's typical way of doing business involving revenue sharing to the plan administrator, record keeper, fund managers, custodians and anyone else getting a cash from the plan—all create a conflict-of-interest.

According to the GAO study, "If left unchecked, conflicts-of-interest could lead plan sponsors or participants to select investment options with higher fees or mediocre performance, which, while beneficial to the service provider, could amount to a significant reduction in retirement savings over a worker's career."

For 401(k) plan administrators, this report poses a large problem. Unfortunately for millions of plan participants, this has been going on for years. The report also wants to understandably avoid making any estimate of the amount of money flowing between fund companies and their clients, but pension and 401(k) plan experts can secretly estimate that this figure could easily hit many billions of dollars. That is money which should have gone to 401(k) plan participants.

The Importance of Revenue Sharing in the 401(k) Business

Revenue sharing also can be used to reduce plan expenses or pay for the "education" of plan participants or the people who sit on the 401(k) board. In all cases, however, the payments prevent the free interchange of objective advice. This is not a legal event, but one tied to human nature. Everyone knows it is hard to fire someone you like personally.

Applied to the 401(k) world, revenue sharing deals make it harder to fire a manager, record keeper or ascertain a plan's actual costs.

It is also difficult for plan sponsors and individual investors to decipher any language describing revenue sharing. Here is a section from an American Fund prospectus, which describes their revenue sharing program:

"[An affiliate of the investment manager] at its expense, currently provides additional compensation to investment dealers. These payments may be made . . . to the top 75 dealers (or their affiliates) that have sold shares of the . . . Funds. The level of payments made to a qualifying firm in any given year will vary and in no case would exceed the sum of (a) .10% of the previous year's . . . Funds sales by that dealer and (b) .02% of . . . Funds assets attributable to that dealer. For calendar year 2006, aggregate payments made by . . . to dealers were less than .02% of the assets of the . . . Funds. A number of factors will be considered in determining payments, including the qualifying dealer's sales, assets and redemption rates, and the quality of the dealer's relationship with . . . [the distributor]. . . makes these payments to help defray the costs incurred by qualifying dealers in connection with efforts to educate financial advisors about the . . . Funds so that they can make recommendations and provide services that

are suitable and meet shareholder needs. . . will, on an annual basis, determine the advisability of continuing these payments. . . may also pay expenses associated with meetings conducted by dealers outside the top 75 firms to facilitate educating financial advisors and shareholders about the American Funds."

According to the fiduciary advisory firm Drinker Biddle, "even if these (revenue sharing) payments were not a cost consideration, they would be a conflict-of-interest which plan fiduciaries need to be aware of and to evaluate. In other words, if the broker-dealer, which supervises the financial advisor, receives additional payments from certain mutual fund complexes, but not from others, does the broker-dealer have an incentive to encourage the financial advisor to sell investments from the higher paying fund families?"

As noted by many in the financial service industry, the answer is clearly "Yes." This conflict must now be disclosed under DOL regulation under ERISA section 408(b)(2).

Ethical Issues Related to Revenue Sharing

While revenue sharing and 12b-1 fees have a role in the sale of mutual funds, many professionals say they teeter on the borderline of violating ethical disclosure practices.

In a client-broker relationship, "the act of withholding information from a client, even if it is not intentional, still raises the flag of why it is not being disclosed in the first place, "according to Julie Anne Ragatz, a fellow at the American College Center for Ethics in Financial Services. When compensation is involved, the burden of proof is on the person (in this case, the advisor) who is not disclosing their relationship with a mutual fund company which is providing monetary compensation, she added.

Ms. Ragatz said the issue of fees is part of the larger issue of conflicts-of-interest which exist within the financial services industry. Yet while these conflicts are common, Ms. Ragatz said they do not have to be "vicious," or manifest themselves in ways which are self-serving and ethically wrong.

The compensation arrangements between advisors and their clients raise three key issues:

- The complex compensation schemes that exist between an advisor, their broker-dealer, and a fund distribution company;

- The lack of transparency which exists to discover these compensation arrangements;

- The difficulty of explaining compensation arrangements to clients in an understandable way.

Pending SEC Proposals

Debates about mutual fund fees have being going on for decades, but as part of the recent financial reform legislation, the SEC is finally acting on some key issues.

First, the SEC is slated to announce a new plan which would cap 12b-1 fees at 0.25% of assets. This fee is the amount funds can charge on a continuing basis to cover marketing and administration costs. In 2009, shareholders paid over $9.5 billion in 12(b)-1 fees to financial representatives and fund companies.[60]

Second, SEC Chairwoman Mary Schapiro has stressed that broker-dealers and investment advisors should adhere to the same fiduciary standards which exist in the institutional world, especially with respect to services provided to retail investors. If this standard is enacted, it means advisors would have to fully disclose their revenue sharing and other fee arrangements with their clients. But there is significant ongoing opposition to adopting this standard, and its future implementation cannot be assured.

CHAPTER 4

THE GREAT WEALTH TRANSFER AND WEALTH DESTRUCTION

Sometime over the past 30 years, American businesses have consciously adopted a new attitude towards their own employees. Shaped by changes in the tax laws, the rise of financial engineering, global competition, new accounting regulations, a myopic focus on earnings, and raw opportunity, large corporations started to raid their pension funds to fund executive pensions and their expansions.

Among the changes that allowed these changes were:

The Adoption of New Accounting Rules in the 1990s Pending SEC Proposals

These rules allowed corporations to book investment income into company profits to raise earnings. Prior to this change, pension fund portfolios were comprised of bonds that paid a steady interest rate to fund future retirement obligations. The accounting change was accompanied by a rule provision which allowed investment managers to assume a rate of return on pension plan assets, regardless of their quality or ability to generate a return. Since funds could assume more risk and fantasize a return, the equity exposures of pension funds rose to 60% by 1999 from 35% of assets in the early-1990s.[1]

Applying Aggressive Financial Engineering Practice

Financial engineering, combined with new tax laws, made pension investment more volatile to pension plan assets. In the 1990's, the investment policies of many pension plan began to include more equities (versus bonds), so earnings would increase as investment returns boosted profits. This flow through from higher investment profits to earnings was only possible if investment managers increased their risk levels. The softened accounting rules also let pensions assume a rate of return, not one they actually achieved, that could be used to determine how the pension plan's performance contributed to company earnings. This meant an investment manager could assign a return to any type of investment and apply that return to the pension plan.

As author Ellen Schultz explained: "Those rules gave pension managers a false sense of security because they delay the impact of the investment losses."[2] If this sounds like voodoo accounting, you are correct: It is the same approach used by Enron when then-Commodity Futures Trading Commission Chairwoman Wendy Gramm, (wife of Senator Phil Gramm (R-Texas) allowed energy companies to assign a future hypothetical price to energy commodities. This led to widespread price misrepresentations and fraud on a scale never seen before.

In the pension world, the net effect of allowing pension funds to assume a high rate of return translated into greater equity exposures. From the early-1990s to 1999, the equity exposures of pension funds increased, with the expected increase in portfolio volatility.[3] But it did not stop there. With their higher risk appetites, pension funds have become huge investors in hedge funds, venture capital, private equity, real estate and the most avant garde investments available.

A Fundamental Shift in Employer-Employee Relationships

One indication of this new relationship comes from the new ways pensions are considered. At one time, pension plan assets were intended for the exclusive benefit of the participants. But that way of thinking is dead, a victim of financial engineering. In the 1980s and 1990s, corporations began to consider pension plan assets, many of which were over-funded, as underutilized pools of capital which could be freely used for acquisitions and market speculation.

"With perfectly legal loopholes that enable companies to tap pension plans like piggy banks, and accounting rules that rewarded employers for cutting benefits, retiree benefits plans soon morphed into profit centers. Populations of retirees eventually were transformed into portfolios of assets and debts, which passed from company to company in swirls of mergers, spin-offs, and acquisitions. With each of these restructuring deals, the subsequent owner aimed to squeeze a profit from the portfolio, always at the expense of the retirees."4 The other beneficiaries of pension plan looting were executive compensation and retirement plans. This represents one of the greatest and under-reported transfers of wealth in U.S. history.

This grievous discrepancy is illustrated by a pension given to John W. Snow, former CEO of CSX Corporation. When Snow was nominated to become U.S. Secretary of the Treasury by President George Bush in 2002, he was awarded pension credit for working 44 years at CSX, when in reality he had only worked there 25 years. Snow was given this windfall based on his salary and bonus, but also because of the value of 250,000 shares of stock the CSX board gave him.

Snow received the pension credits for the years that he did not work, but instead had those pension credits based on almost all of his compensation. This is part of a trend available to top executives only and, as noted by Judith Fischer, managing director of Executive Compensation Advisory Services. The new pension formula gave Snow $2.47 million a year from CSX until he dies, according to company disclosures.[5]

The Least Sophisticated Now Carry the Most Financial Risk

If the average person is being bombarded by the news media with reports about the new dangers of retirement, it is no accident. Factors which were once professionally identified and managed by dedicated pension fund or employee benefit staffs have been shifted to average individuals. If news about these new dangers seems overwhelming, it should not be a surprise.

First, since the early days of the insurance industry, professionals have identified that risk is better assumed when risks are shared by large groups. This is called the "Law of Large Numbers" and it is based on the statistical observation that when a large number of people face a low-probability event, the proportion of people who experience the event will be close to the expected proportion.

As an example, if there is a pool of 100,000 people, who each face a 1% risk, the law of large numbers says that 1,100 people or more will have losses only one time in one thousand. This spreads the risk among a wider pool and it is an essential mathematical outcome which makes it possible for insurance companies to be profitable. But when it comes to an individual, that risk is impossible to displace, unless the risk can be diversified. But that is not possible with a 401(k).

Second, managing risk in 2012 is possible to some degree, but it requires sophisticated and expensive computer programs, which are certainly not available to individuals. When the financial media begins carrying stories about "outliving your retirement income," "longevity risk," or the need to conduct Monte Carlo simulations to determine an individual's personal exposure to financial or health dangers, it should be regarded as going to the modern-day version of the Oracle at Delphi. These simulations only give you certain probabilities, not definite answers.

The reason why investors are understandably confused is that employers have intentionally dumped these risks on individuals who are least able to manage them. This is nothing personal, since few people have the ability to be professional money managers and foresee their own future. Evidence shows that "lump sums also shift longevity risk to retirees, as well as investment risk, interest rate risk, and inflation risk."[6] All of these risks are outside of anyone's control, but they were better managed by pension plans, not amateur investors, who have limited resources and are working inside the strict confines of a 401(k).

All of these changes have made employees and retirees more responsible for making the complex choices affecting their own health care and investment income. In the process, both groups have also assumed the risk that was once assumed by their employers. The problem is that the majority of Americans are ill-equipped to make the complex decisions to provide themselves with financial security over a lifetime, especially in a more volatile, low-return marketplace.

This should not be considered a slight on most American's investment knowledge. On the contrary, the two-thirds of mutual funds, which are managed by professionals, who are paid significant salaries and have specialized training, fail to beat their own market benchmarks, according to Morningstar.[48]

So if trained, full-time professionals cannot consistently deliver above-average returns, what makes an average non-professional think they can?

In the case of pension plans, employers used to manage those assets with the assistance of teams of specialists, make regular contributions, and burden the responsibility of meeting their pension obligations. New accounting rules and the aggressive use of loopholes helped pension funds divert assets and allowed them to freeze plans entirely. In an increasing number of cases, corporations closed their plans altogether and let the PBGC, a taxpayer-funded federal agency, handle the mess. When that happens, many retirees receive smaller pensions than they would if their corporations had fulfilled their fiduciary obligation.

While it's common to think of wealth transfers in the abstract, this transfer of the long-term financial risks needed to fund retirement are more common. Take the case of a group of employees at the Stella D'Oro baking plant in the Bronx. When a private equity firm bought the bakery in 2006, it immediately informed workers that it was cutting pay and benefits. A strike ensued in August 2008. The workers eventually won their strike demands, but the equity firm then closed the plant and re-sold it to another private equity firm, Brynwood Partners, which moved the baking operations to a non-union plant in Ashland, Ohio. All this was done to save money by the acquiring private equity firms, but increasing wages and benefits was never part of the plan. At each step in the private equity transfer process, employees received less.

What makes this case notable is that it shows the disparity in pay between people who had steady jobs, good benefits, wages and a secure work environment, to the goal of private equity firms: extract higher rates of return. Too often, as shown in this example, it includes everything from skimping on ingredients to cutting overhead, salaries, and benefits.

While the story of the fired Stella D'Oro workers was playing itself out in the Bronx, a more positive story for some people was happening in downtown Manhattan. "In the second week of October, just days after the factory (Stella D'Oro) closed, Goldman Sachs announced that it would pay out twenty-three billion dollars in holiday bonuses to its executives and staff. The amount was the largest bonus pool in the hundred-and-forty-year history of Goldman Sachs. At the highest average salary Brynwood (the private equity firm which bought Stella D'Oro) had offered–about seven hundred and eight dollars a week–the hundred and thirty-four Stella D'Oro workers together would have had to work forty-hour weeks for about forty-two-hundred years to earn twenty-three billion dollars."[7]

How Taxes Benefit Pension Fund Plan Sponsors

Tax policies are a complicated topic outside the discussion of disclosures involving 401(k) plans. However, the favorable tax treatments, engineered loopholes and customized tax regulations that benefit corporate plan sponsors have been used to derail pension plans and re-direct those pension assets to other uses. The tax area is fertile ground for pension abuses since tax treatment is the single most powerful engine behind pension fund closures and the re-allocation of those cash assets.

This topic is covered in great detail in the excellent book *Retirement Heist,* by Ellen Schultz,[61] who describes how accounting standards designed by corporate plan sponsors, in conjunction with the Financial Accounting Standards Board, created the ideal condition to phase out pension plans, curtail benefits, and re-direct assets towards non-pension corporate goals.

In one example, Schultz notes that corporations often use their pension funds as scapegoats by claiming they are an undue financial burden, even when they are overfunded. In reality, corporations benefit from fund contributions because they are tax-deductible and earn tax-free gains, and any positive investment returns can be applied to increase profits.

These are all special benefits that were specifically demanded by the large corporations that offer pension plans. If these investments were not made under the umbrella of the pension plan, they would not be able to be posted as income unless they were sold. If they were sold, the sale would trigger a tax on the gains. Any amount remaining would be booked as income,

Corporations can also park surplus money in pension funds tax free. Because this topic is so arcane and complex, most reporters and policy makers succumb to the terrorized calls that an "underfunded" pension will drag down a corporation, state, or entire nation, when in reality the underfunding may not exist at all or, in the case of corporations, may include pensions from top executives or persons working overseas whose pension costs are often unfunded altogether. In these cases, the unfunded pensions (common in top CEO compensation packages) actually are a drain on the fund, but they are not being used for the benefit of average working employees.[63]

Re-Thinking Employer-Employee Relations

The shift in financial risk and reduced retirement security represents a major change in the employer-employee relationship.

While public pronouncements have continued to talk about how much businesses value their employees as extensions of their brands or as valuable assets, these pronouncements frequently have been accompanied by layoffs, stagnant wages, and the transfer of investment risk to less sophisticated people. As more people assume these risks and pay for more of their own health benefits, the net effect is a transfer of wealth from employees (who comprise the body of the middle class) to employers.

Wealth transfers can come in many forms. One study found that the average CEO's incentive compensation increased to 400 times their salary the same year a pension cut was made from about 300 times the year before. If the pension plan remained the same (in terms of benefits offered), so did CEO compensation. The study's lead author said "you could have real economic wealth transfers away from employees" as a result of pension cuts.[8]

In these instances, employees had become victims, not beneficiaries, of their pension plans, thanks to changes in accounting rules, financial engineering, and manipulative employee benefits consultants and lawyers.

These wealth transfers occurred because businesses have begun to make their employees pay a continuously larger share of both health care and retirement costs. In both instances, this has also meant that businesses had shifted many risks and costs associated with managing these programs to their employees.

Employees: Worth More Dead Than Alive

Another stark example about the change in employee-employer relationships concerns insurance policies taken out on employees in whom the firm has no demonstrable insurable interest. While this practice is not known by many employees, their employers have been taking out life insurance policies on them, which will be paid to companies when their employee dies. While state insurance commissioners, who regulate the insurance industry, as well as employers, claim they have no figures on this practice, an estimated one-third of all insurance cash-value life insurance sold in the U.S. is made on employees by their employers acting as sole beneficiaries.[9]

As part of this ghoulish practice, the money is paid when current and former employees die through Corporate Owned Life Insurance (COLI.) (When companies buying this same type of insurance are banks, the policies are called "bank-owned life insurance" or BOLI). COLI is straightforward: a company buys the life insurance with the employee's written permission, pays the premiums, receives the cash surrender value or death benefit. The employee does not pay any premiums, nor do they or their heirs receive a penny when they die. When an employee leaves the company (voluntarily or involuntarily), or retires, the COLI remains with the company as the beneficiary.

If companies create COLI pools using variable universal life insurance (VUL) policies, they can be managed using different asset mixes. Specialized insurance companies then keep track of when people die by scanning Social Security system death records. When the Social Security numbers match, the insurance company notifies the beneficiary (the deceased employee's former company) and the benefits are collected.

These programs date back to the 1980s when companies used the insurance to finance their employee benefits. There are millions of employees who have life insurance policies issued on them, including retirees, low-level workers, and ex-employees, who have no benefits due to them from their former employer. But thanks to favorable tax treatments, the practice became more popular.

When a company or bank buys insurance on its employees, such as COLI, it creates an "obligation" for the company that includes: Supplemental Executive Retirement Plans (SERPs), deferred compensation plans, Employee Stock Ownership Plans (ESOPs), buy-out obligations, group life, disability, medical and other basic insurance coverage. These COLI policies also became popular since they were attractive off-balance-sheet assets. Companies could take out loans against COLI policies and deduct the interest on their taxes. (This applied to COLI policies issued before 1996.) Companies also are not required to reveal how the proceeds are used once the death benefit has been disbursed.

When employees died, life insurance benefits went untaxed. This produced large cash streams for employers when an employee died. Companies could also borrow against the policies, and then deduct the interest they paid as legitimate business expenses.

But in the mid-1990s, the IRS identified this practice as a major tax loophole and began denying deductions and forcing corporations to re-evaluate their COLI policy practices. Congress then passed the COLI Best Practices provision of the Pension Protection Act of 2006 to make the practice less attractive for corporations who wanted to take out policies on their non-management workers, including janitors. (Some companies took out policies covering janitors and hourly workers, which helped COLI earn the names, "janitor insurance" and "dead peasants insurance.)[10] The practice proved popular and soon Disney, AT&T, Nestle, Procter & Gamble, Dow Chemical, Pitney Bowes, Wal-Mart, and Enron had become significant owners of COLI policies.

The heightened visibility of COLI policies attracted the attention of both non-management employees and lawyers. In the 1980s, families of deceased employees went to court to sue for misrepresentation, while some corporations sued their insurers for misrepresentation about the benefits of COLI policies. Many cases were settled out of court, including two class action lawsuits against WalMart: one in 2004 that settled for $10.3 million and another in 2006 that settled for $5 million. In the course of investigating events leading to the suit, investigators found that Wal-Mart had taken out COLI policies on 350,000 employees in Texas alone.[11]

While this practice spans all industries, it is particularly popular with banks that buy it for their employees at all levels. At the end of 2008, banks held $122 billion in life insurance on their employees which was twice what the $65 billion they held in 2004. The bank which held the largest amount of life insurance on employees was Bank of America with $17 billion.

The cover story for holding insurance on employees is that the proceeds are used to defray benefits expenses. But an analysis by *Wall Street Journal* reporter Ellen Schultz found that it is commonly used to defray the unfunded executive compensation costs of top executives. In many cases, these unfunded executive benefits (which appear on the balance sheet as supplemental executive pension obligations exceed those of all their employees.

COLI insurance programs exist because companies offer various types of benefit plans for employees and top management. These qualified plans, which meet specific IRS requirements and must be operated for the exclusive benefit of employees or their beneficiaries, are required by law to be funded. In contrast, non-qualified plans are commonly offered to executives and are "unfunded." Among the unfunded benefits offered to top executives are retirement, bonuses, golden parachutes, and severance. These are paid for on an as-needed, pay-as-you-go basis. COLI, complete with their tax benefits, was an ideal tool to meet these funding needs.

While employees do not have any input into this practice, the company becomes their beneficiary, so they are not entitled to receive any of the policy's death benefits. All death benefits, as well as the cash surrender value and any tax benefits, go to the company. One COLI insurance provider said that the death benefits paid by COLI policies help "to meet the company's obligations [and are] critical to the successful execution of these plans."[12]

Company-Owned Life Insurance: No Benefit to Employees

COLI is frequently used by companies as an affordable and efficient method of financing non-qualified plans. It is the only alternative that provides tax-free dollars precisely at the time they are needed in the event of a death, as well as cash values that can be borrowed against a policy to fund other pre-death obligations.[1]

But while accountants and managers accept the use of this insurance, others have raised questions about the morality of a corporation financially benefiting from the death of non-related, non-essential employees and retirees.[13]

According to John H. Biggs, the former chairman and CEO of TIAA-CREFF, the huge teacher's pension fund, among the key moral issues raised by this type of insurance concern the "reciprocity and fairness, the deception of employees, the generation of mistrust, and the use of the employee's life as a means to profit. No compensating social good is served by the sale of these policies." Biggs also called COLI "a form of insurance that's always been revolting to me." Another author noted that, in some cases, employees covered by COLI would be worth more dead than alive.[14]

The Transfer of Health Care Costs

According to an industry publication "almost every state that has dealt with public workforce issues in 2011 has made substantial reductions to the health care package employees will be getting in the future."[15] This trend of assigning employees more of their health care costs for both individual and family coverage is affecting private and public sector employees alike.

In 2011, the top five largest for-profit health insurance companies posted earnings of $12.2 billion, while dropping coverage for 2.7 million Americans.[16] Not only do the health insurance companies not have to specify why they are dropping an individual's coverage, but their health care rate increases are done without any public hearings. Utility companies, auto and homeowners insurance have more public accountability and must hold public hearing, but health care insurers have successfully lobbied against any modicum of transparency.

For example, in California, family health insurance premiums increased 153% since 2002, which is over five times the rate of inflation. This occurred even though Blue Shield of California had $3.1 billion in excess surplus, 1,400% more than the state required, yet it still sought to raise rates on more than 200,000 policyholders.[17] To reduce any free-market competition, about 71% of all the health care coverage in California is underwritten by only four insurance companies and their rate-setting process is secret, done without any public input, according to Justify Rates. org.

The net effect of this constitutes a wealth transfer from employers and health care providers to employees.

In the private sector, employees are paying more for health care than ever before. According to a Kaiser Family Foundation 2011 survey, the cost of the average family health plan rose 9% in

2011 to $15,073. On average, workers paid $4,129 and employers pay $10,944 toward those annual premiums.

But these payments alone are deceptive. Premiums have increased significantly faster than workers' wages (2%) and general inflation (3 %). Since 2001, family premiums have increased 113%, compared with 34% for workers' wages and 27% for inflation. The study also found that 31% of covered workers are in high-deductible health plans, facing deductibles for single coverage of at least $1,000, including 12% facing deductibles of at least $2,000. Covered workers in smaller firms (3-199 workers) are more likely to face high deductibles, with half of workers in smaller firms facing deductibles of at least $1,000, including 28% facing deductibles of $2,000 or more.[18]

Worse, employees have opted for higher deductibles that increase their own out-of-pocket expenses. The Kaiser 2010 survey found that 27% of employees were enrolled in plans with deductibles of $1,000 or more, as opposed to 22% of employees in 2009 and only 10% of employees in 2005.[19]

Since the Kaiser Foundation began conducting the survey in 1998, it has noted a steady increase in the premium amounts paid by workers. During the period 2000 to 2010, the total cost of average health insurance premiums for a family plan have risen 114%, from $6,438 to $13,770. But the share paid by employees has increased significantly, from $1,619 to $3,997, or a 147% increase. In a news story, Foundation President Drew Altman said "What workers pay for health insurance continues to go up much faster than their wages. You have to look over time to really see it, but from the perspective of working people, they're just getting less for more."

While there may be little or no connection with how companies evaluate and monitor their 401(k) providers, the Kaiser health plan survey also found that relatively few companies reviewed quality or performance data when choosing a health insurer. Only 34% of large firms and 5% of small firms considered that data, and only 49% of those reported that it was "somewhat influential" or "very influential" in their decision.

For federal employees, the news is the same. In 2011, federal employees saw their health insurance premiums increase at a faster rate than their pay, but less than many private sector workers. The average health care premium increase for participants in the Federal Employee Health Benefits Program will be 7%, according to the Office of Personnel Management (OPM). That is substantially more than their average pay raise, which is slated to be 1.4% in 2011. In dollar terms, federal workers will pay, on average, $5.53 more each pay period for self-only coverage and $11.45 more for a family.

In 2009, the average premium increase was 8.8%. The OPM said that based on estimates by consultants other large, employer-sponsored insurance plans will see premium increases between 8.9% and 10.5%.[20]

As the nation's largest private employer, WalMart set the tone in reducing health care benefits by significantly reducing its coverage for part-time workers, while significantly increasing premiums paid by many full-time staff personnel. Wal-Mart said it increased premiums and reduced coverage due to rising health care costs. The company also said that part-time employees, who work less than 24 hours a week on average, many of who are paid minimum wages, will not qualify for any of the health insurance plans offered by the company. Spousal benefits will also be eliminated for new employees who do not work full time, but the company will still allow the children of part-time workers to be covered.[21] "Paying more for less" may become the new motto for WalMart's employees, as well as others, who are shouldering rising health care and pension plan costs.

Transferring Pension Costs to Taxpayers and Individuals

Companies entering bankruptcy have conspicuously used their pension fund obligations as an excuse to offload retiree payments and secure more favorable debt re-payment plans from creditors. This has been used by hundreds of companies to dump their pension funds, even when the plans were financially stable, viable and able to continue to pay full pensions.

What would make a company terminate a viable pension plan?

In November 2011, American Airlines sought bankruptcy protection and announced it had only paid $6.5 million of a required contribution of nearly $100 million toward its pension plans. AMR, American's parent company, said it was planning to freeze or terminate pensions that cover about 130,000 employees and retirees. If it did, the company would shift its pension obligations to the federal agency which assumes pension payment from bankrupt companies, the PBGC. American's four traditional pension plans have assets worth about $8 billion and obligations that the PBGC estimated at $18 billion. If the pensions are off-loaded to the PBGC at taxpayer expense, American estimates that 10% of retirees would see their benefits cut.[22]

But AMR's plea that it had to cut pension benefits did not ring true. In 2007, AMR went to Congress to seek relief for its pension plans and got exemptions which saved the company about $1 billion. The PBGC estimated that at the time AMR filed for bankruptcy, it had about $4 billion in cash, including about $1 billion it had saved as a result of asking Congress for a special exemption to fund its pension plans.

According to the head of the PBGC, Joshua Gotbaum, the "one billion dollars didn't go into American's pension plans. Instead, that $1 billion is 25% of their entire bankruptcy war chest."

Gotbaum also said other airlines had entered bankruptcy, but have continued their pension plans. AMR employees and their unions also noted that American Eagle, an AMR subsidiary, hired Bain, a consulting firm, at a fee of $525,000 a month for the task of cutting jobs at the regional airline. The unions said Bain's job was to provide "strategic consulting services."[23]

Wealth Destruction From the Housing Crisis

For Baby Boomers planning to retire, housing wealth accounts for a majority of total net worth. While this figure is skewed according to demographics (education, race, age within the Baby Boomer segment, marital status, sex), home equity accounts for one-third of net worth at the mean and 50% at the median.[24] This makes Baby Boomers especially susceptible to housing price shocks, both positive and negative, which can significantly affect retirement planning and consumption patterns.

The financial losses caused by the housing crisis have produced $6 trillion in lost wealth and additional losses of $2 trillion are expected.[25] [26] These losses translated into declines in household wealth, but due to existing income disparities, the impact of these losses were especially hard on American families whose incomes were in the bottom four-fifths of the population. From 2007 to 2009, average annualized household declines in wealth were 16% for the richest fifth of Americans and 25% for the remaining four-fifths.[27]

According to a 2004 University of Michigan Health and Retirement Study of individuals between the ages of 51 and 61 in 1992, 80% of early Baby Boomers (people born between 1948 and 1953) indicated they owned houses, while only 30% indicated they owned stocks. This stock wealth accounted for only 13% of their net worth. As a result, most people in this study were highly vulnerable to housing price shocks. Among the least educated group in this study, housing wealth accounted for an even greater share of their total net worth. As a result, housing price shocks among early Baby Boomers could cause "substantial wealth losses."[28]

Recovery Times To
Recoup A House Price Loss

Amount of Loss	Dollar Amount of Loss	Time Period to Recover in Years	Time Period to Recover in Months
10% of $250,000	$25,000	10.3	123
20% of $250,000	$50,000	15.2	182
30% of $250,000	$75,000	19.2	230

Assumptions:

- S&P 500 Composite Total Return: $6,000 initial amount on 12/31/1975. Transfers to maintain allocation at 60.00% will be made every twelve months. Fees attributable to any transfers made were waived. The effects of income and capital gains taxes are not demonstrated.

Lehman Brothers Aggregate Bond: $4,000 initial amount on 12/31/1975. Transfers to maintain allocation at 40.00% will be made every twelve months. Fees attributable to any transfers made were waived. The effects of income and capital gains taxes are not demonstrated.

-Initial sales charge of 5.5%

Source: Thompson

This is why a February 2012 report by Federal Reserve Board Chairman Ben Bernanke should cause concern. According to Bernanke, "In a typical [economic] recovery, a rebound in housing fuels hiring and income gains, but that has not been the case this time," but the staggering declines in home prices have slashed household wealth by as much as $7 trillion, he said.[29] That is $7 trillion in lost household wealth.

This may also explain why in 2009, approximately one in four U.S. households had zero or negative net worth, up from 18.6% in 2007. For black households the figure was about 40%.[30] While no one keeps track of wealth destruction data, this could be the greatest amount of lost wealth ever recorded in U.S. history.

Home ownership comprises such an essential part of an individual's overall wealth that it affects many key life decisions, including whether people will continue working. This has an especially significant impact on women.

Numerous academic and government studies show that home equity has a paramount role in determining overall household wealth, especially among people over age 55, the group with the highest percentage of home ownership. A 2002 study found that 82% of participants, who were age 60 to 64, owned their own residence, with a typical home equity of $120,000.[31] A 2004 survey of consumer finances found that Social Security accounted for 42% of total wealth for a typical family approaching retirement (sample household headed by a person aged 55 to 64), followed by the principal residence (21% of total wealth).[32]

But more recent data shows a more dismal picture. Due to the decline in the housing market, home equity as a percent of home values fell from 59% in the first quarter of 2006 to 36% in the fourth quarter of 2009. "For the first time on record, the percent of home value that homeowners own outright dropped below 50%–meaning that banks now own more of the nation's housing stock than people do."[33] Nor did these wealth declines hit everyone equally. This same source found that the destruction of wealth that resulted from the start of the recession in 2007 to 2009 saw average annualized household declines in wealth of 16% for the richest fifth of Americans and 25% for the remaining four-fifths.[34]

In 2007, prior to the Great Recession, the median net worth of American households was $106,000, consisting primarily of home equity.[35] This increased by $17,000, or 2.9% annually, from 2001. In one simulation showing the effect of a decrease in housing prices for early Baby Boomers, a 13.5% drop in housing prices produced a 9% overall decrease in total net worth. For households in the median of the survey group, the median net worth loss would be 13%.[36]

Home price declines also affect retirement plans. A study released in October 2007 found that for every 10% increase in housing wealth (as measured by changes in house value), expected retirement dates were accelerated between 3.5 to 5 months.[37]

However, this study also found differences between men and women in planning their retirement dates as a result of increases in housing wealth. Women tend to revise their retirement dates without relying as much on the housing wealth effect.

Another complicating factor affecting housing wealth has been the significant assumption of greater mortgage debt among homeowners. While more people are carrying more mortgage debt, the increase among older households is significant.[38] In 1989, 54% of households headed by people aged 55 to 64 had paid-off mortgages, but in 2001 that figure had decreased to 41%.

In this same study group, 25% of households headed by people 65 or older were still paying off their mortgages. For people aged 55 to 64 holding mortgages, the median mortgage debt was $55,000 in 2001, an increase of $27,300 from 1989. For older mortgage holders over age 65, the median debt was $44,000, an increase of $31,500 from 1989.

As a result of the increase in mortgage debt and falling housing prices, many retirees and pre-retirees fall into the camp of being "cash poor, house rich." This group also faces the challenge of converting house equity into disposable income, often through a reverse mortgage, while also treading through a declining or slowly recovering housing market.

As the 78 million Americans born between 1946 and 1964 approach retirement age, more attention is being focused on the sources, importance and stability of retirement wealth. This wealth is commonly comprised of a combination of Social Security, Medicare, pension plans, 401(k) plans, and, increasingly, home equity. Retirement experts and academics also factor other financial and non-financial wealth components into this calculation, including human capital (expected labor earnings), personal savings, life insurance, annuities, gifts and inheritances.

While these wealth sources differ by race, sex, household status, and income, the reality is that this group of individuals (Baby Boomers) "has saved virtually nothing for retirement."[39] This problem arose for a variety of reasons as evidenced by an overall low savings rate and small 401(k) account balances.

This problem will only be aggravated by any increase in the Social Security retirement age, the continued demise of employer-sponsored pension plans, a changing tax structure, and longer life spans. The most disruptive force will be stem from attempts to privatize Social Security, which will only benefit insurance companies and the mutual fund industry.

The two relative bright spots in this otherwise grim picture are wealth sources derived from any future appreciation in home prices (and the slow recovery in home equity) and Social Security.

For most American households, these are the two greatest sources of total wealth. But this is a precarious situation. For the first time in 63 years, owners' equity in household real estate fell below 50%, according to data from 1945 to 2008.[40]

As a result, any shock to home prices and Social Security presents a major disruption to retirement plans of millions of Americans.[41] Of these two components, Social Security benefits range from approximately 45% for the least wealthy individuals to approximately 10% for the wealthiest individuals. Home equity (defined as purchase price less the mortgage balance) accounted for 9% to 14% of total wealth.[42] The shock to home equity wealth has serious ramifications in terms of wealth destruction. At the national level, the estimated loss in housing equity is between $460 billion to $1 trillion, based on 2008 data.[43]

In terms of any housing recovery, declines in housing should persist since pre-retirees will not be able to absorb the supply of housing stock offered by retirees as they sell their homes. One study found that while housing market corrections have historic cycles lasting three to seven years, any post-2008 recession housing recovery would be shaped by very different demographic changes.

As a result of the current housing market bubble, any new housing cycle correction could take over 20 years to reach an equilibrium state where buyers and sellers are proportional. The reason: When Baby Boomers aged 65 to 75 begin to sell their houses, there will be three sellers for every buyer.[44] This will create a "generational housing bubble" on top of the speculative housing bubble that developed from 2005 to 2007. This shift (more sellers than buyers) could last until 2030. In the past, without major changes like this in demographics, housing corrections historically lasted three to seven years.

What Happened to Housing When the Music Stopped

In February 2012, 49 attorney's generals reached an agreement with the major banks involved in committing mortgage fraud: Bank of America, Citibank, Wells Fargo & Co., J.P Morgan Chase and Ally Financial (formerly GMAC). While the settlement was billed as being in the range of $25 billion, it actually only cost the banks less than $5 billion, including $1.5 billion paid to borrowers who lost their homes in foreclosure from 2008 through 2011.[45]

It is also noteworthy that even though a mortgage lender loses an average $60,000 on every foreclosure, according to figures the federal government disclosed in connection with the February 2012 mortgage fraud settlement announcement, many lenders chose not to renegotiate mortgages held by troubled borrowers. The reason: many of these mortgages were re-sold to other investors, who could profit from these mortgages.

Since the housing market collapsed in 2008, over two million owners lost their homes to foreclosure during the four-year period ending in 2011. In addition, approximately 11 million homeowners had mortgages which are worth more than their homes. This amounts to an aggregate of about $700 billion combined, or an average of nearly $65,000 per homeowner. As part of the settlement, about 750,000 homeowners received a settlement of $2,000 each.

New Mutual Fund Company Business Models Needed

Fund companies, especially load-fund companies, can do this by changing some key components in their business models. Most load-fund companies are based on pre-ETF business models, developed before the housing implosion, the anti-Wall Street sentiment and deep 2007 recession. Any one of these would necessitate a change in the load-fund business model, but due to organizational inertia and structural buffers, fund management has avoided facing these problems.

One obvious area for change is in the load-fund wholesaler distribution model. This model is expensive and anti-investor. According to industry statistics, each wholesaler office visit to a financial professional costs about $500. These visits typically last 30 minutes. If you deduct the time for formalities, any substantive conversation can last about 20 minutes.

The expenses every wholesaler incurs on these visits is 100% reimbursable by the fund company, and every visit is supported by 12b-1 fees, which are ultimately borne by shareholders. When sales management hears complaints about the inefficiency of wholesalers, they respond that the wholesaler "owns the relationship" with the financial rep, yet when the redemptions occur, the wholesaler often claims they do not own the relationship. Even if the wholesaler did own the relationship, their link to the ultimate shareholder is non-existent. For most load-funds, their customer connection is restricted to a quarterly newsletter and Web site, both of which are passive responses to serious shareholder concerns. Given this reality, it's difficult to justify the financial benefits of the external wholesaler model.

The Dangers of Fund Commoditization

Classic brand theory names trust and awareness the sole determinants of brand value. The other key component of a brand's power is the powerful emotional connotation which a brand generates to supplement the consumer's ego. In today's market, consumers have begun focusing on brands which are exciting and have new features. These brands separate themselves from competitors and capture the public's attention by being different and linking to a purpose which is larger than themselves.

With only a few exceptions, the financial services sector does not have many fund company names which make it into the recurring lists of the nation's most admired brands. The financial services sector certainly does not rank high on the emotional quotient meter, either. These may all be inherent in the entire category. But one large problem is due to the rampant commoditization of the mutual fund industry.

CHAPTER 4

The Investment Company Institute lists over 8,000 mutual funds, including 4,800 equity funds at year-end 2008. Of these funds, 1,809 were large-cap growth funds. It takes full-time analysts to discern what separates one fund from another.

So it is no surprise that a mutual fund industry panel discussion noted that the mutual fund industry suffers from "too much capacity." That is analyst jargon for too many mutual funds. "We've competed away the alpha," according to Jeff Hopson of Stifel Nicolaus, a brokerage firm. "I clearly think that the golden age of the fund industry is behind us, unfortunately."[47]

Hopson is correct in that manager performance has become more average. It is more difficult for managers to beat the market, which is what he means by "competed away the alpha."

It's difficult to explain how funds differ from one another, so fund companies rely on revising quarterly data and touting their star ratings from the two major fund data companies, or creating carefully selected comparisons, or hypos, which compare funds against the competition on some esoteric data or over a select time frame. But these sales comparisons have been used so frequently that they too have become commoditized. As a result, selling rankings based on fund performance rotations has become too familiar to veteran investment professionals.

In consumer marketing, commoditization is countered by price reductions. While this provides more maneuvering room for consumer product marketers, load mutual funds have historically not reduced overall expense ratios, despite wide advances in computer processing productivity, reduced client communications costs, and increases in assets under management. One of the most controversial fees in today's negative return environment is manager fees. Simply put, there is no reason for shareholders to pay active manager fees when the active manager only produces index-like returns.

But fund marketers have an alternative if they change the business model. In turn, this could change people's minds, but given today's reality, change is not a real possibility for most funds companies.

Historically, relationships in the financial services industry are guided by inertia. When it comes to a fund's overall expense ratio,

|4|

the general rule is they stay the same or increase, even as assets under management increase.

When it comes to changing consumer's minds, research shows this is very difficult since belief systems and attitudes can be altered if you change the information on which the belief rests. This cannot be done in ads or commercials. Changing peoples' minds can be done by altering their perception of the competition. Successful brand campaigns outside of the financial services industry succeeded since they highlighted their competitors' weaknesses.[46] This changed customers' perceptions. Unfortunately, the current balance of power today finds that ETFs have the upper hand since they have capitalized on the fund industry's deficiencies.

CHAPTER 5

SHOW ME THE MONEY: WHY AVERAGE
PEOPLE DO NOT BECOME GREAT INVESTORS

Thirty years after the start of 401(k)s is enough time for retirement policy makers to see how well individual investors have done managing their own money for retirement.

So after years of formalized investment education, access to individual investment advice, repeated calls to maximize contributions, and first-hand experience managing various investment strategies, how well have America's 401(k) investors done?

Not too well. But that answer carries some qualifications.

The first problem is that discovering the "average balance" in a 401(k) plan is problematical. Estimates are difficult to make and are based on limited samples, such as those from a specific mutual fund company. Another main problem is that younger workers have lower balances compared to their older co-workers, who may have been participating for decades. This helps explain the disparity of account sizes for workers in their 60s, with 401(k) balances of $159,654, compared to the total average 401(k) of $67,438 (median balance $17,863), while the average IRA individual balance (all accounts from the same person combined) was $91,864, according to Employee Benefit Research Institute data released May 2012 and the Investment Company Institute. (The average IRA balance for men was $120,719 and $71,112 for women, according to the May 2012 EBRI study.)

To complicate matters, these average 401(k) balances do not necessarily provide a complete picture of total portfolio assets. For example, a person may have money in an IRA, SEP and 401(k), and they certainly could have more than one account in each.

But given available data, complete with these caveats, some experts assume the average 401(k) balance is between $69,000 and $60,329 (EBRI-ICI data at year-end 2010.)[1] Still, experts do not know the average age of 401(k) participants, which makes it difficult to calculate how many years they have until retirement, as well as their other sources of retirement income.[2] (Note: According to Fidelity, one reason why average balances did not increase was due to the increased number of individuals who recently joined 401(k) plans as a result of automatic enrollment.)

However, other data from a 2011 *USA Today* poll found that 54% of retirees have less than $25,000 in savings, while 25% of the population has nothing saved for retirement at all.[3] These numbers have increased "dramatically" from 2006, the survey found, when 42% said they had less than $25,000 saved. To generate an income of $50,000 annually in inflation-adjusted dollars, a 65-year-old retiree would need to have $1.1 million saved, assuming 3% inflation rate and a 5% annual return on investments.

This is certainly not enough money to last the first wave of Baby Boomers (persons born between 1946 and 1964), who turned 65 in 2011. Data shows that 57% of this group has less than $100,000 saved. This group also cannot expect much from inheritances; less than 2% of Baby Boomers will receive more than $100,000 from an inheritance. This moots the issue of inter-generational wealth transfers and excessive talk of the ill-effects of estate taxes impacting a large number of people. Worse, any inheritance possibilities have been hit even harder as a result of the 2008 recession and its lingering ill-effects.[4]

So with an expected lifespan of 75 for men and 81 for women, this money will provide some support for a few years. After all, 401(k)s were originally only designed to supplement pensions, savings, Social Security and real estate equity. But today's harsh economic reality has significantly changed this formula and severely reduced the power of other income sources. Given the uneven job market, wage growth and economic recovery, it is all but impossible for many people to replace lost or reduced income sources.

Of course, people planning for retirement have other assets–homes, savings, Social Security, pensions, 403(b)s–but 401(k)s have been touted by the fund industry and employers as being the main contributor to an individual's financial security, as well as an important employee benefit. But since the serious recession that lasted from December 2007 to June 2009, according to the National Bureau of Economic Research, every wealth generator commonly available to individuals has been severely disrupted.[5] Worse, the tremendous wealth destruction that ravaged housing equity, savings and portfolio returns, will take years to recover.

While the impact of portfolio losses in stocks and bonds has been extensively covered in the financial media, the impact of the decimated residential real estate market is murkier. The declines in real estate equity and home prices had a disproportionate impact on moderate-income households because real estate is this segment's largest asset, representing about 23% of consumer wealth. For households with assets between $100,000 and $1 million, the principal residence represents about 37% of household assets.

Housing plays such an important part in wealth creation that the housing wealth lost since late-2007 has reduced the home ownership percentage from 69% in 1985 to just 39% in 2010. This lost wealth is reflected in median home prices, which are now back to around year 2000 levels ($160,000) compared to $156,000 in the first quarter 2011. Home prices peaked in 2006, when the median was $230,000, according to Tiburon Strategic Advisors.[4]

This lost wealth impacts investor confidence, political positions, spending patterns, retirement plans and belief in the American

Dream. Since people felt less wealthy, they also justifiably questioned the merit of investing and, in some cases, the operations of the capitalist system. Worse, correcting these losses will take decades, despite the ever-optimistic pronouncements from the resident real estate industry that a housing recovery is imminent and just around the corner.

The other main contributor to re-building personal wealth is job creation. But even here, some economists suggest that it will not be until 2013, 2015 or 2018 that any recovery sparks enough employer confidence to reduce the unemployment rate. But even then, they caution that it will not be as low as pre-recession (mid-2007)levels.[6] None of this inspires confidence, but the economic shocks caused by the combined global credit, banking and housing failures still have not been properly addressed to prevent a future repetition of these events.

This is complicated because benefits paid by Social Security are too meager for most people to live on (it never was intended to do so), yet Social Security has become a greater percentage of monthly income for retirees. Given limited income sources, many people will be forced to lower their standard of living in retirement.

"America's real pension problem is not that Social Security is going bust, but that the retirement incomes it will provide are too small," according to columnist Clive Crook.[7]

"Too many people will rely exclusively on Social Security. Private pension saving, increasingly through 401(k)s and other defined-contribution vehicles rather than traditional defined-benefit plans, is inadequate, and fees eat up too much of the return for small savers. For many families, saving through home equity has turned out to be a catastrophic mistake. When they retire, many Baby Boomers will see a far bigger drop in their standard of living than they had expected. Many will have to work longer, whether they want to or not," Cook said.

Crook's summary shows the limitations of saving for retirement using the existing options. Given the incessant political attacks on Social Security and its stigmatization as an "entitlement system," future retirees face a dismal choice: If Social Security is privatized and handed over to insurance and mutual fund companies, the fee and expense abuses will affect millions more Americans on a wider scale. The net effect will be the same: more mediocre products, lower returns and high fees.

There is also another problem to consider: taxes. With so many imponderables, investors have to estimate the taxes that will be paid on their various retirement accounts, which include their 401(k)s, but also IRA and Roth-IRAs. In some 401(k) accounts, the highly-touted tax benefits in these accounts could be neutralized by the high fees.

While there are strong opinions about the benefits of Roth and traditional 401(k)s, a tax analysis comparing the two is inconclusive. One study found the tax advantages in a conventional 401(k) and Roth are equivalent, assuming no change in tax rates before and after retirement.[8]

But if tax rates do change and tax rates decline after retirement when retirees withdraw their funds, they will pay less tax and have more after-tax income with a conventional 401(k) than with a Roth.

Alternately, if rates increase, employees and retirees will pay more in taxes, but will have more after-tax income with a Roth 401(k) than a conventional one. The good news is that regardless of whether taxes increase or decrease, the difference will be insignificant for most retirees.[9]

Declines in Median Incomes

To complicate matters, employee-investors must also contend with an economic environment which is lowering their median incomes. Between June 2009, (the date some officially cite as being the end of the most recent recession) and June 2011, inflation-adjusted median household incomes fell 6.7% to $49,909, according to a study by two former U.S. Census Bureau officials.[10] During the most recent recession–from December 2007 to June 2009–household income fell 3.2%.

The full 9.8% drop in income (6.7% plus the 3.2% decline) from the start of the recession in late-2007 to June 2011–the most recent month in the study–appears to be the largest in several decades, according to Census Bureau data. The authors of the study, called the decline "a significant reduction in the American standard of living." In their study, the authors found that income dropped more, in percentage terms, for some groups who were already making less. This event contributed to rising income inequality between different racial groups.

From June 2007 to June 2011, median annual household income declined by 7.8% for non-Hispanic whites, to $56,320, and by 6.8% for Hispanics, to $39,901, according to a Sentier study. For blacks, household income declined 9.2%, to $31,784. For people who were already unemployed, the real median annual income fell by 18% (from $41,037 to $33,487) compared to a household headed by a full-time worker, whose income dropped 5% (from $72,104 to $68,454.)[11]

While shorter-term time frames paint a bleak picture, the decade from 2001 until 2011 has seen the smallest wage gains since the Great Depression, according to the Commerce Department.[12]

This may be a by-product of a structural shift in the U.S. labor market. Since the end of 2009, it has taken 20 months to reduce the unemployment rate by just 0.5%. Given that slow rate, it will take almost seven more years for the unemployment rate to fall 3.4% more to reach the historical average unemployment rate of 5.7%. To reach the unemployment rate of 5% that existed before the recession began, it will take 8.2 more years.[13]

This combination of real low real-wage growth and a job market riddled with unpaid internships, age discrimination, perma-temp positions, and hundreds of over-qualified persons applying for a single open position is the job market's new bleak reality.

It also has serious implications for the housing market's recovery. Any recovery implies that a new home owner will be able to sell their home at a significant profit in the next decade. But that may be an optimistic assumption given the huge inventory of fore-closed homes that are worth less than their mortgage balances. These are the reasons why the nation's economic policymakers are tepid about recovery projections and their time frames. Given the snail's pace of new job creation, accompanied by the high potential for lower wages and temporary hiring, should make home buyers very weary of entering the housing market.

Given this bleak background and the widening wealth gap between the nation's wealthiest and other working people, the elevated role of 401(k)s in the wealth creation process seems to be an insurmountable assignment. This becomes even more problematic when investors discover that the mutual fund industry is more preoccupied with the wealth creation of its own brokers and executives than with the wealth creation of its own shareholder-customers.

More Challenges From Recessions and Volatility

In the investing world, average investors have to cope with a stream of unpredictable economic and stock market events, including recessions and volatility. These are events which would derail any professionally-managed investment strategy, but can seriously harm any portfolio managed by an amateur investor.

While market volatility is good news to the small numbers of day traders, it is universally bad for long-term investors. Volatility is a by-product of global markets and it has been accelerated by operational factors (more computerized trading), more popular leveraged investments (hedge funds), as well as the belief that central banks and large national governments cannot dampen speculation or adequately manage their own fiscal and tax policies. For long-term investors, this means that planning any long-term account draw down strategy becomes more risky.

So why have markets become more risky? One commentator said "the reality is that in their crusade to manufacture extraordinary personal wealth, Wall Street insiders have engineered volatility into the capital markets. This change is permanent."[14]

According to Shah Gilani, "the same dangerous volatility that destabilizes markets creates innumerable trading opportunities for Wall Street's proprietary traders. These traders feed off each other and off their banking-industry clients."

Since the volatility provides more entry and exit points for strategies, it also shakes out traders with less capital and lower risk tolerances. All this was made easier because of decimalization (a rule change that allowed trading in pennies as opposed to trading in one-eighth increments), electronic trading and the elimination of the up-tick rule that facilitated short-selling. All of these changes benefited large professional traders at the expense of individuals. Or, as Gilani put it: "By increasing volatility in stock, bond, commodity and real estate markets, The Street has created a self-perpetuating moneymaking machine."

As the markets have become more complex and volatile, the offerings inside most 401(k) plans have remained limited and expensive. Most 401(k) plan mutual funds consist of actively managed, mediocre-rated mutual funds available from a limited number of fund families. One study found there are 18 to 20 investment plan options, including mutual funds, offered inside a typical 401(k) plan, but only a few plans offer ETFs.[15]

This is also complicated by offerings from some fund companies known for offering low-expense funds, such as Vanguard and Fidelity that provide look-alike, higher cost funds to their 401(k) plans.

For instance, when Vanguard offers an S&P 500 Index fund in a 401(k) account, it is not necessarily the same fund offered to retail investors in terms of its cost structure. To cover expenses inside a 401(k) structure, Vanguard may offer a collective investment trust (CIT) or a separately-managed account, both of which carry higher fees. For example, one advisor found a that a CIT based on the Vanguard S&P 500 Index fund had an expense ratio of 0.53%, which was almost 300% over the same fund offered to individuals that carried an expense ratio of 0.18%. In addition to the higher expense ratio, plan participants were also being charged a wrap fee of 0.50%.[16]

Similarly, unknowing 401(k) investors may discover they are investing in more expensive, sub-advised accounts, often found in group annuity 401(k) products. These specialized offerings are more expensive than what is found in the individual investor retail world because they contain separate "warp fees." These "wrap fees" are extra charges from a fund manager or investment advisor for managing or adding a special service to the investment. But in a fund which is already professionally managed, the wrap fee is often superfluous since the management service is already provided. It could be argued that a wrap fee charged on a professionally managed account is charging for the same service twice.

In another example, an advisor found that a plan contained a variation of the Vanguard 2030 target-date fund that carried an expense ratio of 0.94%, plus two separate wrap fees of 0.37% and 0.25%. This converted to a total expense of 1.52% to fund participants, which was 800% over the cost of the exact same fund offered to retail non-401(k) investors.[17] What accounted for the cost difference? From an investment perspective, it was the exact same product. But since the fund offered the opportunity to add more fees inside the 401(k) plan structure, the provider did so.

Investors and plan sponsors often assume that if a fund company is known for being a "low-cost provider" then all of their products offer the same low-cost benefits. This is not the case. The DOL fee disclosure regulations likely will shock many plan sponsors who assumed they were buying a low-cost alternative. If they made this mistake, their employees suffered and the employer failed to fulfill their fiduciary responsibilities.

List of Recessions in the 20th Century

20th Century Business Cycle Reference Dates		Duration in Months			
Peak	Trough	Contraction	Expansion	Cycle	
Quarterly dates are in parentheses		Peak to Trough	Previous Trough to this Peak	Trough from Previous	Peak from Peak
Sep 1902(IV)	Aug 1904 (III)	23	21	44	39
May 1907(II)	Jun 1908 (II)	13	33	46	56
Jan 1910(I)	Jan 1912 (IV)	24	19	43	32
Jan 1913(I)	Dec 1914 (IV)	23	12	35	36
Aug 1918(III)	Marc1919 (I)	7	44	51	67
Jan 1920(I)	Jul 1921 (III)	18	10	28	17
May 1923(II)	Jul 1924 (III)	14	22	36	40
Oct 1926(III)	Nov 1927 (IV)	13	27	40	41
Aug 1929(III)	Mar 1933 (I)	43	21	64	34
May 1937(II)	June1938 (II)	13	50	63	93
Feb 1945(I)	Oct 1945 (IV)	8	80	88	93
Nov 1948(IV)	Oct 1949 (IV)	11	37	48	45
Jul 1953(II)	May 1954 (II)	10	45	55	56
Aug 1957(III)	Apr 1958 (II)	8	39	47	49
Apr 1960(II)	Feb 1961 (I)	10	24	34	32
Dec 1969(IV)	Nov 1970 (IV)	11	106	117	116
Nov 1973(IV)	Mar 1975 (I)	16	36	52	47
Jan 1980(I)	Jul 1980 (III)	6	58	64	74
Jul 1981(III)	Nov 1982 (IV)	16	12	28	18
Jul 1990(III)	Mar 1991(I)	8	92	100	108
Mar 2001(I)	Nov 2001 (IV)	8	120	128	128
Dec 2007 (IV)	Jun 2009 (II)	18	73	91	81

Source: National Bureau of Economic Research
The NBER does not define a recession in terms of two consecutive quarters of decline in real GDP. Rather, a recession is a significant decline in economic activity spread across the economy, lasting more than a few months, normally visible in real GDP, real income, employment, industrial production, and wholesale-retail sales

The Role of the Financial Media

While the free flow of information is essential for public discussion in any democracy, the post-2000 investment and financial media, especially Web and TV, have a different agenda.

While it is very difficult to generalize about the financial media, certain Web sites and popular business TV networks emphasize the glories of trading, not investing, and certainly do not explain how fees and revenue sharing taint many financial relationships. TV financial media especially are guilty of trying to convey the energy of the trading floor into an individual investor's own home or office.

While this attracts advertisers, it is misleading to most investors, who have limited discretionary income, limited risk tolerances, and invariably pay high retail commissions compared to professionals. But the televised trading frenzy is well-suited to tout the next buying opportunity. Whether the S&P Index rises or falls, there are always buying opportunities, according to on-air announcers and their guests.

The contrast between the investing and trader personas is best illustrated by the completely different investment shows hosted by Louis Rukeyser and any CNBC announcer. Rukeyser's set was a comfortable living room, complete with couches, end tables and a formally-dressed assistant, who silently guided investment guest experts to a stuffed armchair across from Rukeyser. There was no background noise; only face-to-face discussions. Compare that to the free studio space offered by exchanges to contemporary financial networks, complete with background floor trading action, data-ridden banter, and ambient trading floor noise.

The differences between Rukeyser's and CNBC's on-air personas and stage sets also indicate the differences between investing and day-trading. Rukeyser's entire presentation and format was designed to appeal to investors. CNBC, and other fast-paced trading shows emphasizing volatile sectors, companies and strategies, intentionally appeal to short-term traders. Future retirees, who are long-term investors, get caught in the video frenzy. This only raises anxiety levels, distorts time horizons, compromises investment goals and, in general, only adds to the confusion of an already complicated global market.

Another problem is that financial journalism is a victim of its own self-imposed timetable. Since it has become a 24-hour global production, it has to often synthesize "news" when there is none or when U.S. markets are closed. This explains why monthly personal investor magazines, mutual fund and investing Web sites, and dedicated TV business shows find themselves continuously touting new mutual funds, industry sectors, and investment strategies, even when these same financial media outlets have noted the benefits of long-term investing.

Part of this is due to satisfying advertisers, while simultaneously adhering to a publishing calendar. But it should make veteran reporters and editors cynical to see this continuous stream of tactical and strategic portfolio changes coming out on a regular basis. It should also trigger a more cynical reaction among readers, who must wonder whether the advice they received a month ago was outdated or incomplete. This makes investors feel inadequate since they can never allocate enough money into these new strategies to receive their promised full benefits (if there are any.) This may also explain why people over-trade (more men than women are guilty of this), hold positions for too short a time, and buy at the top of a market.

But all this belies a simple fact: most Americans do not directly own stocks. Even at the 2007 economic peak, half of all U.S. households owned no stocks at all–either directly or indirectly through mutual or retirement funds. Less than half of households owned any stock, and only about a third had stock holdings–either direct or indirect–that were worth more than $6,000. To a large extent, low- to moderate-income households depend on labor income alone to meet their financial obligations, as they own very little stock that can be cashed in during times of economic hardship.[18]

As a result, "the news media devote much time and entire outlets to minute by-minute dissection of the stock market. But data on stock ownership show that the stock market, by and large, is of little or no direct financial importance to the majority of U.S. households."[19]

Some elements in the investment media have also failed the public by regularly recommending stocks without ever posting an audited record of their recommendations. These stock touts continue to make recommendations for years and are never held accountable, yet advertisers continue to support their shows, even when they know the uneven or dismal quality of the host's recommendations.

The Wild West aspect of investment journalism has increased on the Internet. Since most Web sites do not have fact checkers, researchers, copy editors, research budgets or libraries, many financial recommendations have questionable origins and may not meet any higher-level financial industry research standards.

Large mutual fund Web sites, such as Morningstar, combine their large databases with providing financial advice to individual investors, while also endorsing mutual funds on a continuous basis. This presents conflict-of-interest problems, especially when Morningstar produces daily advice or news stories on the funds it covers, while also making millions from licensing its fund ratings results to fund company clients. Given this balancing act, Morningstar has produced stories on the dangers of high-expense funds and revenue sharing, but it has not pressed the industry to curtail these practices or publicized them to individual investors. In essence, it has all its bases covered since it can proclaim itself a friend of consumers, while also sponsoring mutual fund industry trade events that demand licensing fees.

Forbes noted that Morningstar provides good quantitative fund data, but "Morningstar does have some conflicts-of-interest because the company provides services to the mutual fund industry." *Forbes* said Morningstar charges funds to use its star ratings in direct marketing campaigns and in investor letters. Morningstar charges a licensing fee, about $8,000 per year for one fund.[20]

Since Morningstar has a huge retail investor following, the predictive validity of its star-rating system should also be tempered. As Morningstar itself has said, "The star rating isn't a complete solution, but rather an aid that helps you to narrow the field and improve your chances for success." Others have qualified the star system more and say it has little predictive accuracy. Indeed, rotation among "top-rated" fund managers and asset classes is constant on a year-to-year basis.

The Relationship Between Financial Journalism and Investors

The markets rely on a steady source of new and repeat customers, who invest with the serious intent of making a profit. Since successful markets are comprised of a variety of traders, who meet in a centralized location with a range of purposes (hedgers, speculators, investors) and time frames (scalpers and long-term investors), the financial media plays a critical role in educating, informing and keeping market interest and confidence high.

At times, such as during the technology and millennium bubbles of late-1990s and 2000, the financial media played an important role in pushing investors into a buying frenzy. More recently, Web-based investment and business news sites offer the greatest range of investment information ever to all types of investors. The good news is that more of this information is free or readily available for a modest subscription fee. The challenge for investors is to sort through the clutter to find the most objective and professional news sources. Yet while investors today suffer from financial journalism overload, it is not clear whether investors have become more profitable traders or merely victims of the confusion.

Early Days of Financial Journalism

The strength of American financial markets cannot be separated from the crucial role that financial and business journalism played in developing and supporting the expansion of business and investing. As U.S. democracy and commerce developed, it fuelled vibrant public discussions in the early days of the American republic.

The first newspaper in the U.S., *Publick Occurrences, was* published in Boston in 1690. By 1801, when Thomas Jefferson became president, there were about 200 newspapers in the United States covering local and national news and political opinion.[21] Business news of this period and through the 1800s was commonly comprised of transportation events (shipping arrivals, departures, railroad developments) commodity and bond prices. Business news and prices were often printed in specialized publications.

Through the 1930s, business reporting developed significantly as the middle class expanded and major economic developments created more general interest in business and economic developments. Specialty publications, such as the *Wall Street Journal, Forbes, Fortune,* or the general circulation New York Times, and magazines such as the *Literary Digest,* covered business news, but it primarily consisted of favorable profiles on companies and businessmen, while economic stories were largely limited to presenting government-issued data on short-term economic events related to inflation, unemployment, housing.

It was also during the latter part of this period, as the recovery from the Depression continued that the emerging business press began to develop the editorial vision of a prosperous United States driven by ingenuity and modern business techniques. This editorial vision was championed by publisher Henry Luce through what eventually became his flagship, glossy periodical, *Fortune.*

Luce and other editors of specialized business publications promoted themes about American business acumen, modern management techniques and the nation's vast manufacturing ability. This theme of American abundance, rising living standards and the expansion of the middle class became common in business journalism from the late-1940 to the early 1960s. "This was a period during which a new 'ideology of abundance' was articulated by the media, political and business leaders, educators and other opinion-shapers that linked American greatness and 'identity' with quantitatively defined prosperity."[22]

As part of an abundant society, business journalism expanded its economic coverage, with some major publications hiring their economists and specialty reporters. For example, Sylvia Porter began writing financial columns, many of them aimed at family money management and tax issues. She eventually became one of the most successful financial columnists and writers in America. At the height of her career, Porter's personal investing syndicated columns were read by over 40 million people, until she retired in the late-1970s. The availability of growing reams of economic and market data were converted into business stories that presented a vision of a dynamic economy. All this mirrored the expansion of

CHAPTER 5

the middle class, accompanied by the desire for new luxuries and leisure time.

By the mid- to-late-1960s, as economic growth slowed, the influence of economists as featured columnists waned and was replaced by stories about the vast opportunities presented in the stock market, especially for individual investors. This change in editorial emphasis paralleled the expansion of national, full-service brokerage firms, which took the allure of the vast opportunities offered in the stock market into areas of the country that never before had direct access to investing.

As the bull market of the mid-1960's developed, it provided the backdrop for greater editorial coverage about investing, individual company news, product developments and management innovations.[23] The period from 1962 to 1968 sparked interest by retail investors in the "Nifty 50" stocks and marked the rise of individual investor journalism and its related coverage of personal finance, stock speculation and specialized industry coverage.

The 1970s marked a new era in financial journalism through the rise of television business and financial coverage in prototype shows covering Wall Street. More continuous market coverage, complete with the novel display of equity prices which crawled along the bottom third of the screen, hit the airwaves in 1966. The first West Coast TV station to offer daily market news, accompanied by a digital stock ticker, was KWHY in Los Angeles. KWHY-TV worked out a deal with Quotron, a stock price data vendor, which provided brokerage houses nationwide with real-time stock market information. As a result, this made KWHY the first business news service for television. Programs, such as one that aired on WBTB-TV, Channel 68, in New York City in the fall of 1975, advanced the concept of showing more recent stock trades on the consolidated ticker that along the bottom third of the screen. This occurred through negotiations with the SEC's Manhattan office that allowed this display, provided the prices were delayed for two hours to prevent any price destabilization. After a year of broadcasting, the price delay was cut to 20 minutes. These developments were noteworthy because they identified individual investors as being a viable audience and that TV could be used to inform and foster trading.

Later, shows, such as *Wall $treet Week,* brought a very different tone to investment coverage. This show debuted on a regional basis on the Eastern Educational TV Network on Nov. 20, 1970. The Public Broadcasting System later began distributing it nationwide on Jan. 7, 1972. The program aired from 1970 to 2005 and was officially titled *Wall $treet Week with Louis Rukeyser,* who served as its host for 32 years. The show was very formalized, structured and decidedly highbrow, complete with a formal, opening market commentary written by Rukeyser, a veteran financial journalist, followed by a panel discussion, answers to viewer's letters, and another, more focused, guest interview featuring an expert. *Wall $treet Week* represented the idealized, genteel, pre-day trading era of Wall Street and provided advice for buy-and-hold investors on stalwart companies of the Dow-Jones index. Guest experts and panelists were primarily chief investment officers and senior equity analysts, who commanded attention.

Since equity price feeds were expensive and required a sophisticated home computer set-up, broadcasters recognized that a continuous display of near real time equity and index prices proved highly popular with local speculators. In 1996, the first fully automated stock ticker appeared on the CNNfn network. The use of actual prices attracted viewers, but financial stations also benefit from the free content they received from market analysts, traders, commentators and economists, who all made themselves available to a national audience. Later, stock and futures exchanges offered free broadcast booth space to publicize their traded products and local experts, many of them exchange members. The few on-air people who received salaries were the anchors.

While the quality of financial journalism coverage was erratic, it attracted enough interested viewers to foster different types of hard-sell TV commercials pushing investment newsletters, precious metals, magazines, brokerage firms of all qualities, computer trading software and analytics, and trade-from-home data services. FNN accepted long-form commercials, later called infomercials, which exceeded the standard one-minute, and also accepted a compensation structure based on leads. The quality of these commercials added to the frenzied pace, and their hard-sell "call now" pitch appealed to both aggressive speculators and promoters.

If the Rukeyser show was aimed at people sipping tea after dinner in their living rooms, the Financial News Network (FNN) catered to hungry speculators eating fast food in a cluttered office. Launched in 1981, FNN offered more on-air hosts, including some holdovers from Los Angeles financial radio, expanded coverage of commodities market prices and company profiles. Market analysts of every quality provided a steady stream of opinions and recommendations. Due to budget or compliance restrictions, many national brokerage firms did not provide their own steady stream of market and financial news. Their main form of branch communications was restricted to a "squakbox," which was essentially a speaker phone or loudspeaker that carried a market summary delivered by the firm's analysts.

To fill this information void, FNN was often shown continuously inside brokerage office nationwide, without the volume, so brokers could track daily market prices and business news. It was free, accurate and specifically devoted to market and business news, complete with interviews of investment professionals spanning the spectrum in quality and credibility. As the network grew, the quality of its commentators and analysts improved, but the network retained its individual investor and trader programming orientation. FNN was later purchased by CNBC in 1991, but it maintained its individual investor focus.

That focus made it an ideal vehicle to help promote and guide the development of the most democratic access to retail investing ever: the rise of day trading. This was a phenomenon that capitalized on cheaper and faster trading. This was fueled by more accessible trading hardware and software, combined with new electronic access via discount brokers, and expanded systems to the NASDAQ and NYSE. The new systems made it possible for average, unsophisticated investors, with little or no trading experience, to open accounts for as little as a few thousand dollars, to scalp in and out of the market.

ECNs and Day Trading

Since its formation in 1792, originally as a forum to trade Revolutionary War bonds, the New York Stock Exchange has become the symbol of America's capitalist system. Over almost the next 200 years, the NYSE's traditional specialist trading system has reluctantly evolved to accommodate new technology, competing powers and regulatory forces. Since change does not come easily to Wall Street, anything the public does notice is often the result of decades of behind-the-curtain brawls, old-fashioned horse trading and bare-knuckle deals.

Take the case of the New York Stock Exchange's decision in 2000 to convert to a new price reporting system that would trade stocks in dollars and cents. To the public, this was positioned as a price reporting advancement. The real story was that the traditional system of trading stocks in one-eighth (or 12.5 cent) increments would disrupt a profit system that existed since the beginning of the 19th century.

Changing the minimum price increment, or spread, endangered profit-making of the NYSE most powerful members, floor specialists, and top-tier brokerage firms. Narrower spreads (from a minimum of 12.5 cents to one cent) meant that the potential profit per trade to the most preferred members could decrease by as much as 50%.

Academic studies at the time (around 2000) found that eliminating the minimum price increments, which dictate the prices of trillions of shares traded annually, could save individual investors about $14 billion annually. But since most of that money would come out of the profits of brokerage firms and exchange members, who benefited from the larger one-eight spreads, it created a serious industry problem. But this development did not happen in a vacuum. At about this same time, Congress had become interested in the NYSE's operations as a result of a then-recent Justice Department and SEC investigation into price collusion at the NASDAQ, the nation's second largest stock exchange. To settle the charges, the National Association of Securities Dealers (NASD) agreed to create a separate regulatory arm (the precursor to FINRA) and open its trading system to competitors.

To avoid any public discussion about its internal operations at the member-run exchange, the NYSE caved in to pressure from editorials and a push from SEC Chairman Arthur Levitt, who is considered the most pro-investor SEC chairman in modern times. Decimalization (trading in one cent increments) was the new protocol. This profit compression pushed large trading firms to find new ways to cut their large execution costs. So with this mandate, large traders began to expand their use of electronic trading, which had become more essential since the 1987 stock market crash.

Electronic trading was not new. In 1969, Institutional Networks Corp. launched Instinet, the original off-exchange electronic communications network (ECN) designed for private use by institutional traders and dealers. After the 1987 Crash, large traders needed faster, cheaper and more anonymous ways to execute their more sophisticated portfolio trading strategies.

Then, to complicate matters, the reform-minded SEC issued a 156-page "concept release" on the topic of the need to expand electronic trading. In its typical cryptic language, the SEC said it was soliciting comments which might "determine whether rule making is appropriate" on issues that could affect the definition of what constitutes an exchange. Given the serious limitations of the NYSE's specialist system, combined with reform-minded regulators and advanced technologists, the NYSE was forced to change. This is when the NYSE announced the adoption of its new decimal price reporting system.

But there were more changes ahead. In 2005, the SEC passed its "trade through rule," which required that all trades be executed at the best price, even if stock exchanges had to fill the order through a competitor exchange.

The idea of providing investors with the best price was new for the 212-year old NYSE. Up until that time, the NYSE's price was the best one from the perspective of its specialists. But now, the SEC was reversing this definition and defining best price from the investor's perspective.

This was the game changer the NYSE could not tolerate. Within two weeks of the SEC's best price announcement, the NYSE said it would go public.[24] Individual member profitability and seat prices could not be sustained if the NYSE had to provide the best price to its customers, large and small, if it meant being forced to use prices from other competing national exchanges. The heated debate concerning the issue of providing best prices should also have alarmed the NYSE's customers, who may have been wondering about the quality of the equity prices they had been paying for the last few centuries.

All these regulatory and technological developments, combined with pent-up customer frustrations, provided the foundation for the rise of new and larger electronic exchanges. These changes eventually injected more competition into the closed member-run exchange system and it helps explain why both stock and futures exchanges eventually went public. The process of going public allowed the exchange's member-owners to cash out at the high before their exchanges and seat prices became less valuable from the onslaught of electronic trading.

The Rise of Electronic Trading Competition

The first experiment in injecting competition into the NASDAQ occurred by accident. During the October 1987 market crash, the NASDAQ system was inundated with orders and ground to a halt.

But due to the skills of an astute trader, Harvey Houtkin, the NASDAQ's own Small Order Execution System (SOES) was used by Houkin to place trades directly and electronically with NASDAQ market-makers. Houtkin's use of the system was novel because the SOES system was originally designed as an emergency back-up system for top NASDAQ market makers and was not intended for general use. Houtkin changed that and after a period of litigation, was eventually opened to provide a major avenue for individual traders to access a national electronic trading system.

By the 1980s, interest in personal investment journalism exploded from the volatile combination of these disparate factors: day-trading access via SOES, discounted brokerage (which began May 1, 1976), the proliferation of affordable market analytic software, the Internet, the rise of global equity and derivatives markets, and the need to feed the growing demand from the 24-hour media with continuous, cheap journalism.

Another main driver was new advances in electronic trading systems that began to emerge in the early-1990s as a result of the spectacular failure of the NYSE order handling in the 1987 market crash. These privately-developed electronic systems reflected the pent-up demand for changes in the way traditional listed exchanges, such as the NASDAQ and NYSE operated. The first system to offer individual investors access to NASDAQ's SOES system was developed by All-Tech Trading, in Montvale, New Jersey.

By putting pressure on market-makers to honor their posted prices, SOES traders forced discussions on expanding the number of limit orders honored on the SOES system, as well as a number of key trading issues, including the management of NASDAQ itself. By the mid-1990s, there were a number of independent electronic systems in place for both individuals and institutions to change the way equity trading was done.

At about this same time, a group of academics conducting some mind-numbing data scans noticed an unusual pattern in prices at the NASDAQ, the nation's second largest equity exchange. The professors, Paul Schultz (Ohio State University) and William Christie (Vanderbilt University), discovered that there were no odd-eighth quotes in NASDAQ stocks on one particularly volatile trading day in November 1991. To make sure this was not a statistical anomaly, a second sample was tested and the same results appeared: No odd-eighth bids or offers. Their results found that the inside bid was 25 cents, instead of 12.5 cents, on 71 of 100 actively-traded NASD securities, according to the study. This situation "raise[d] the question of whether NASDAQ dealers implicitly collude to maintain wide spreads."

To help interpret the data, the academics worked with Harvey Houtkin, founder of All-Tech Trading in Montvale, New Jersey, who was considered the father of day trading, through his pioneering use of the SOES system. The academics and Houtkin played a large role in explaining how the NASDAQ market operates at different levels, to politicians and regulators. Due to the high public interest in Wall Street after the 1987 Crash, people were very interested in news of new investor abuses.

One of the more interested parties was the U.S. Justice Department. After their own investigation, they found enough trading irregularities at NASDAQ, which billed itself as the "exchange for the next 100 years," to slam the electronic exchange with an unprecedented charge of price collusion.[25] The professors and Houtkin, an OTC trading expert, proved a powerful team. Their conclusions mark one of the few times when an academic study produced findings which precipitated a Federal investigation into possible fraud at the nation's largest stock market.

The academic paper, "Why Did NASDAQ Market Makers Stop Avoiding Odd-Eighth Quotes,"[26] focused more attention on trading in very visible tech stocks in the OTC market. The paper's seemingly esoteric discovery came at an opportune time. Traders were discovering the high-tech revolution, spurred by IPOs and promises of even larger future gains. The paper's results found their way into the growing day-trading inspired financial media, and soon the U.S. Justice Department began an investigation of NASDAQ market makers on charges of price fixing and collusion. This is the most serious charge which can be filed against a public exchange. The Justice Department's announcement came at about the same time that 13 separate class action lawsuits filed against key NASDAQ market makers had been consolidated in New York.

The unprecedented Justice Department lawsuit understandably focused national attention on the entire OTC market structure, according to Junius Peake, a former chairman of the NASD.

While there were many interesting aspects to the suit, one aspect dealt with the different ways individual investors were treated versus institutions. An article at the time quoted one institutional money manager as saying charges of collusion are "plausible with respect to retail investors. But it is hard to imagine how we (institutional traders) could ever have been hurt."[27] The money manager said this was possible because large traders pay smaller transaction costs as a percentage of their large trade size.

But that did not ring true to many individual investors. On Prodigy's Money Talk bulletin board, one of the first on the

Internet, members posted numerous notes ("NASDAQ=Ripoff"), citing instances of wide spreads in more liquid NASDAQ issues, and specifics of limit orders not being filled. The board provided first-hand descriptions of delayed order handling and poor quality trades from the growing number of active off-floor retail traders. The reality was that any Federal investigation charging price collusion on NASDAQ produced millions of victims. Some were more victimized than others, but they were all victims. It probably was also no coincidence, but one of the people who witnessed this closely was Bernie Madoff, an active OTC market-maker and trader, who later held senior level executive positions at NASDAQ.

If news of the NASDAQ investigation shook public confidence, it had an even greater impact inside the executive offices of the nation's stock and futures exchanges. The exchanges had always policed themselves and dispensed their own frontier style of justice, often behind closed doors. But to meet basic open-meeting standards, summaries of penalties and hearings were released in an abbreviated format in the form of executive committee summaries.

In an interesting case at the Chicago Mercantile Exchange (CME), the clerk of a large broker left the trading floor with a stack of orders folded into her pocket. A fast market developed and the price limits on many orders were hit, but because the clerk had inadvertently taken the orders with her and off the trading floor, the orders could not be filled. Since the offending clerk worked for a large politically-connected broker, he petitioned the pit committee for relief. The committee came up with a novel solution: they erased the ticks from the record. It was as if the trading had never occurred. Hence, the orders could never have been filled. Since the exchange was member-owned, there was little outsiders could do. Subsequently, the exchange conducted an investigation of this unusual event, but it proved inconclusive.

Similarly, there were numerous cases of trading violations which occurred on the NYSE trading floor, even though the exchange's own internal surveillance department was located in the same building and had complete access to all computerized trading records.

But perhaps the largest festering complaint against NYSE specialists came from institutional investors (such as pension funds), who regularly complained that NYSE specialists were trading in front of their large orders. These complaints of "front running" were handled in a sporadic way, without making the significant changes the institutions wanted. Frustrated and locked out, institutional traders decided the best long-term solution was to use the increasing power of sophisticated, computerized electronic trading systems to centralize institutional orders off of the exchange floor. This provided huge benefits: cheaper trades done via anonymous institutional trading platforms.

What emerged was institutional crossing systems, such as the Investment Technology Group's POSIT system; Instinet, owned by Reuters; a single price auction, such as the Arizona Stock Exchange; and hybrid systems, like Bridge. Merrin, Island and Optimark. These systems were specifically-designed for large institutional orders, and could also accommodate specialized and sophisticated trading algorithms that analyzed trading in real time to find the best prices for a specific strategy without market impact.

But these were only first generation trading developments. Under pressure from the NASDAQ price collusion lawsuits to stimulate competition, the SEC granted expedited approval to a new category of trading facilitators called Electronic Communications Networks (ECNs). These systems displayed market-maker quotes under the SEC's new order handling rules and provided trading services.

ECN's were essentially alternative trade execution systems. After the SEC's order handling rules went into place in 2001, it approved five ECNs to provide quotes, analytics and electronic executions on the NASDAQ and other listed stock exchanges. But that number rapidly expanded as more systems developed new ways to link analysis and instant market access.

This was a huge breakthrough. It effectively created an entirely new type of institutional and retail trading away from the NYSE floor, yet still maintained the benefits of a centralized market system. As a result, prices from all the independent systems were publicly displayed on the consolidated ticker. This benefited the nation's largest and most active institutional traders, as well as active individual traders, but it did not bode well for NYSE specialists.

Within a few years, it became evident that these profound technological changes would force significant political changes at the nation's exchanges.

Traditional member-owned stock and futures exchanges, some of which had been in business almost 200 years (the NYSE was formed in 1792), were soon going to experience an increase in surveillance and competition, accompanied by commission pressures, declines in seat prices and incomes, and greater market volatility. These fundamental changes fostered mergers between large NYSE clearing firms. Over time, these were the main forces which caused member-owned exchanges to entirely change their ownership structures and go public.

And that is exactly what happened. In 2002, the CME went public followed by the NYSE in 2005. Both member-owned exchanges succumbed to the increased institutionalization of the markets, electronic global trading, increased volatility, the need for greater amounts of trading and risk capital, and the specter (dramatically over-estimated) of federal regulation.

These events were accompanied by a growing tide of new media outlets, often without any quality controls, experienced editors, reporters, or journalistic standards. Since the emphasis was on speed and hyping, sensationalism became a main attraction.

What emerged was an investment-tilted journalism that rivaled the Tower of Babble. Experts emerged overnight as self-proclaimed successful day traders and technology experts. Since the markets were now global (futures trading went 24-hour in 1992), so-called experts could develop unverifiable stories and theories linking foreign currencies, market moves, business developments and micro-economic events into a trading story. For most, it never mattered whether the story was true or ever resulted in real profits since no one ever tracked the results.

The Y2K frenzy further fueled the new media. Some equity analysts, who were previously considered objective professionals, were pulled into making overly-optimistic recommendations on companies represented by their firm's own investment bankers.

Conflict-of-interest concerns were jettisoned for wildly favorable and largely unsubstantiated buy recommendations. Analysts developed new terms to make their recommendations, such as "mission-critical business processes," "best-of breed solutions," "significant home-page experience" and "an end-to-end solution for e-commerce personalization in the business-to-business space."

The curious role of how some equity analysts touted their recommendations to the hungry media did not go unnoticed. In a presentation by the AIMR in May 2001, a few years after the Y2K-related analyst scandal and the evaporation of the bubble in technology stocks, an AIMR executive acknowledged that individual investors get most of their information from the media.[28]

He was then asked: In the past few years, has the financial media dis-served the public?

The executive, AIMR President and CEO Thomas A. Bowman, candidly answered:

"I think maybe unconsciously so. Investing and reporting news on investing is serious business, and sometimes it gets confused with entertainment.

"It's very, very dangerous for an individual investor, especially an unsophisticated investor that has no real formal training in this, to make decisions based on an eight second sound bite where an analyst is asked, 'Well, should we buy it or sell it? And you've got five seconds to tell me.'

"That, for the less sophisticated investor, is really doing him a disservice in the sense that there's a lot more behind these recommendations: Is it appropriate for this individual? Where is he in his life cycle? What is his tax situation? Is he risk-tolerant? None of those can be addressed in a five second sound bite.

"As AIMR representatives, we have talked with investors all over the world in recent months and we've been struck by the number of even very high-net-worth investors who say their primary source of investment information is not a broker or an investment advisor, or even a CPA or attorney, but the news media, especially local business columnists and business television. Clearly, you and we have a responsibility to educate investors.

"At a minimum, investors should never make buy or sell decisions based on a sound bite. Investors need to read the analysts' full research report. Investors need to understand their own investment objectives, risk tolerance and time horizon, and the costs and risks of short term trading before they even begin to consider the appropriateness of a particular security. They need to understand who they are listening to and what conflicts-of-interests they may be subject to, especially how the person may stand to benefit from their following his or her recommendation.

"Perhaps most important, they need to know what they don't know. One lesson that has clearly hit home in the past year (since 2000) is that investing is not as easy as it may have looked in much of the 1990's. Mutual funds are usually much more appropriate for investors, who don't have professional training and are unable or don't want to hire their own professional investment advisor. Investing in individual stocks is a sophisticated and higher-risk investment strategy, and do-it-yourself investing only compounds the risk for most people."[29]

Impossible Questions: Impossible Answers

Due to advances in medicine and the financial service industry's role of finding new ways to sell their services, financial planners are now routinely asking people how long they expect to live? This is not a trick question. It is a way of determining if an individual will outlive the ability of their assets to pay living expenses past age 85 and beyond. (The fastest growing age demographic in the U.S. is people aged 80 and above.[30]) But the answer to this longevity question is simultaneously frustrating, highly personal, and impossible to answer, let alone quantify.

Still, that has not prevented some financial planners from proposing "longevity insurance" as a new product to answer this serious, but unanswerable, question. This question has more rhetorical value in financial planning than producing a hard answer, but it can stimulate discussion about the future. One firm calls the longevity question "money death" and proposes that retirees adopt a more aggressive investment strategy past age 60 or 65.[31]

That strategy would include a more aggressive portfolio comprised of 80% dividend-paying stocks and 20% bonds carrying higher-yields. In one scenario, a hypothetical portfolio was well-diversified globally and by asset classes. Since this was a high-performance portfolio, it also had to be regularly rebalanced.

The Federal Reserve has also proposed longevity annuities as being very appropriate for healthy people, who can somehow calculate that they will live 25 or 35 more years past their retirement age of 65. (The odds of living to 85 are only about 50-50 for people turning 65.) If they can do that and have $100,000 or more to invest in the policy, they will be able to collect up to %75,000 annually for every year they live past age 85. That's quite a bet. If the retiree loses and dies before age 85, or whatever age is specified in their policy, their premiums revert to the insurance company.

But this is only the more straightforward parts of the presentation. In order to make an intelligent buying decision about whether to buy longevity insurance, financial advisors also suggest that clients answer these questions: How long will you live? Can you make big financial adjustments to your spending and retirement dates? Can you calculate your "money-life ratio," which consists of determining your total financial assets and then dividing them by the difference between your planned spending and other income (from work, pensions, and Social Security) during the first year of retirement? Can an investor withstand the volatility of a higher-risk portfolio? Does the investor have at least $100,000 to buy the policy? How does the policy purchase impact the investor's other estate planning needs?

While these questions are imposing, the U.S. Treasury made it easier to buy longevity policies, regardless of their usefulness. On Feb. 2, 2012, the day the final DOL regulations on the fee disclosure rule were announced, the U.S. Treasury said "the use of annuities and other lifetime income in retirement plans has been diminishing. Unfortunately, defined benefit pension plans, a traditional source of low-cost lifetime income, have declined; and defined benefit plans have increasingly offered and made single-sum (or 'lump sum') cash payments, either by adding a lump-sum option to the plan's payout choices or by converting the plan to a 'hybrid,' lump-sum-oriented format."

Treasury noted that from a base of $11.2 trillion in private pension assets in 2011, only 21% were maintained in defined benefit plans, with 36% in defined contribution (401k) plans and 43% in IRAs. "In short, although the term 'pension' traditionally has referred to a regular stream of income guaranteed for life, the nation's private pension system has been steadily shifting away from lifetime retirement income payments to single-sum cash payments," the Treasury report said.

To replace the steady erosion of pensions, combined with the danger that retirees would outlive their assets, the IRS and Treasury announced that annuities, which provide a stream of income over time after a large payment is made, would replicate some of the lost benefits of pensions. To do this, Treasury made some allowances for employers and individuals to buy privately-issued "longevity annuities" in their IRAs. This would allow employees to use some 401(k) assets to provide lifelong retirement income beginning at age 80 or 85.[79]

While this was done to address the issue of retirees outliving their retirement incomes as they aged, some retirement experts considered this an acknowledgment that a more formal, predictable type of retirement income plan is needed to replace the shortcomings of the 401(k) system. While they did not specify a replacement, the obvious one would be pensions.

Benefits of Exchange Traded Funds (ETFs)

Exchange traded funds (ETFs) are more popular than mutual funds (as measured by their trading volume.) With $1.2 trillion in U.S. assets, (as of February 2012) ETFs have captured investor's attention because they are created as indexes, which can be sold short, offer exposure to a wide variety of asset classes, markets, leverage and strategies, and incur minimal trading costs.

Yet despite their popularity, ETFs have not become widely available in 401(k) plans as participant investment options. There are two main reasons for this: One is due to the unique trading and operational characteristics of ETFs. The other is due to the innate conservatism of the mutual fund and insurance industries to implement changes that benefit customers at the expense of their existing systems.

ETFs are structured as investment pools which trade in listed securities. ETFs trade like stocks, throughout the day at market prices, and can only be purchased and sold in whole shares. In contrast, mutual funds trade at a net asset value (NAV) closing price and can be purchased or sold in whole and fractional shares. This gives ETFs certain features which contribute to their low costs.

In contrast, mutual funds suffer buying and selling pressures due to changing investor sentiment, which forces them to trade shares of stocks. In an ETF, the pool does not have to buy or sell a large amount of stock since only certain approved financial institutions have the power to create or redeem an ETFs' shares through "creation units." While the ETF creation process is beyond the scope of this book, the net effect to investors is a lower cost structure, intra-day pricing, and the ability to go short during the trading day.

Fees Associated With ETFs

It is important to note that ETFs have a distinctively lower set of expenses, including a history of not paying revenue sharing to financial professionals.

While the DOL disclosure regulations do not mention ETFs, they are included here because they are a low-cost, index-like investment, which offer distinct benefits to investors. In many cases, the investment exposures offered by ETFs are more specific and focused than what a mutual fund delivers. They also have dramatically lower costs because they are based on indexing (passive investing) and often do not have the manager fees and high transactions costs associated with mutual funds. Importantly, they do not allow revenue sharing.

This practice, combined with the inability of recordkeepers to handle ETF accounting, has effectively kept ETFs out of the mainstream 401(k) investment product offerings provided by fund distributors. As a result, 401(k) participants have been denied the opportunity invest in lower-cost, passively managed investments, which offer the potential for high returns (based on their lower expense profile) and can help them meet their financial objectives. It also helps explain why the mutual fund industry is at an impasse. Its day-to-day operations and sales practices cannot accommodate pro-investor products, while it cannot change its sales-centric business model. This situation has not gone unnoticed. Financial advisor Ric Edelman says "the retail mutual fund industry is a dinosaur and won't exist in 10 to 15 more years, as investors are realizing the incredible opportunity to lower their cost, lower their risks and improve their disclosure by virtue of ETFs compared to mutual funds."[32]

Two main reasons why ETFs have low expenses are due to their structure. Since ETFs are traded through intermediary financial firms, who manage the trading in the component stocks that comprise a specific index, they are paid for supplying order flow to their trading partners. This source of revenue is passed on to investors in the form of reduced trading costs. When an ETF is traded inside a 401(k) plan, investors not only get the benefit of reduced trading costs, but they also do not have to pay for the trading costs of more frequent traders outside the plan.[33]

One academic paper estimated that 401(k) participants could save 0.7% % or asset or more" in the average 401(k) plan by using ETFs as opposed to actively traded mutual funds. The same paper found that compared to equity mutual funds that had a median trading cost of 0.66% of assets in a sample of equity mutual funds, ETFs reduced yearly expenses by up to 0.5% of assets.[34]

Another study between ETFs and low-cost index funds, conducted by BrightScope and Invest N' Retire, found that index mutual funds only become truly competitive in the retirement large-plan market comprised of funds with assets over $200 million. Using data from PlanSponsor, the data found that "the overwhelming number of plans (88%) in the United States have less than $200 million in assets and therefore would be better served by using ETFs, rather than mutual funds for their index investments."[35]

However, while ETFs have distinct benefits, they become more expensive in TDFs. When ETFs are used in TDFs in 401(k) plans, some plan participants can be exposed to two levels of fees which can accrue over time to make them more expensive. These two fees are comprised of the cost of the ETF itself, plus a second management fee used to administer the target dates fund. Plan participants should check with their plan sponsor to determine the specific fees charged by their plan's ETF target date fund manager.

Political Realities: Why ETFs are Absent in 401(k)s

Since the popularity, low expense and unique asset exposure benefits of ETFs are no secret to those in the 401(k) industry, it's logical to ask why they are not included in more 401(k) plans.

One possible explanation is that ETFs do not carry 12b-1 fees and engage in revenue sharing. Those two factors are the magic elixirs of the mutual fund and 401(k) industries and are the cash payments which lubricate the entire system. But there is also a critical factor related to the technology changes needed to accommodate ETFs in 401(k) plans that have been only designed to accommodate mutual funds.

While the vast majority of individual investors never consider the computer systems which support their investment company and its various service providers, the power of the "back office" determines the scope of services offered to investors. According to Neil Plein of Invest n' Retire, "The success of a 401(k) plan is based on the primacy of the record keeper's technology. ... But the record keeper sits at the absolute core of a retirement plan. The record keeper's capabilities are the building blocks of the 401(k) system, the elemental components that define *what* can be offered within a plan and *how* it can be offered to plan participants. These aspects together define the 'experience' of a plan."[36]

The technology also determines what is offered to plan participants. Importantly, 401(k) recordkeeper systems today do not have the ability to accommodate trading practices unique to ETFs or track residual cash.[37]

As it stands today, both unbundled and bundled providers cannot use ETFs in 401(k) s, unless the ETFs are packaged in a mutual fund or are using some creative application that makes them look like a mutual fund. But these machinations are designed to strip away the benefits of ETFs to end-investors, so they can continue to make it easier for plan sponsors and recordkeepers to maintain their systems unchanged. Adhering to the mutual fund only status quo is a disservice to investors which is especially egregious since the lower-cost ETF alternative has demonstrated benefits. In terms of costs alone, studies have found that actively managed mutual funds have very poor track records, under-performing their benchmark indexes 99.4% of the time over the past 30 years.[38]

The decision to delay the introduction of ETFs into 401(k) plans is transparently self-serving to the fund and insurance industries, and is jeopardizing the financial security of millions of future retirees.

Doing What's Good for Fund Companies

While 80% of all participants withdraw 100% of their money from company retirement accounts when it's time to leave the company, the portfolio managers of target-date funds prefer that you leave the money in their funds, so it can continue to be managed and generate fees. This is good for the fund company, but bad for investors. The reason: the investment needs of people close to retirement vary greatly. As people age, their health, marriage, job, risk tolerances and family situations change, some dramatically, so putting more assets into bonds or equities becomes more difficult to justify unless it is on an individual basis.

The situation becomes more complicated because older people may be better off using annuities or paying down their home mortgage using target-date assets. Fund companies know about these situations, but when people approaching retirement call to transfer target-date fund assets, they are frequently told to keep their assets invested in the fund, even after the retirement date has been reached. This policy boosts company profits by retaining assets under management, but it is often a disservice to investors.

This was noted in another form in a 2010 academic paper as part of an "agency problem," or mismatch of incentives between an investor (called a principal) and the fund company (called the agent.)[40] When there is a mismatch of incentives of information, the agent is able to profit at the principal's expense. This happens because fund companies are selling a fund's objectives, which are actually hopes that can be served by any glide path or strategy the portfolio manager chooses because there is no actual objective, i.e., a return 15% above the benchmark.

In contrast, a fund has an objective if, for example, it clearly states that it intends to increase an investor's total net return by 5% (net of expenses and fees) over the course of 10 years. That is a specific goal, something employees are frequently measured against if they are to earn a bonus or retain their jobs. But in the world of investment portfolio management, this is never done. Investment managers are infrequently fired, and if they are, it usually occurs many months after the deficit investment performance has been documented. In cases where a fund company hires an outside manager, even after a manager is dismissed, their contract states how their dismissal should be worded and publicly communicated to make it as innocuous as possible. It's no wonder that TDFs, the preferred investment default in millions of 401(k) accounts, can meander along for decades and never be expected to produce an above-index return to investors. While the passage of time takes the target-date fund to its conclusion, generating returns for investors are never an essential part of the equation.

What Investors Can Do To Protect Themselves

No one cares about your money more than you. Accept the fact that investment professionals make their living by generating commissions and fees based on your investments. Investors should understand what they are being charged and whether they are receiving those services. So with that in mind, here are some suggestions to protect your assets.

Work With RIAs

By definition, RIAs adhere to a fiduciary standard, and clearly state the origins of all revenues they receive. But like most other sales practices in the financial services world, things may not seem as they are. There have been numerous instances of sales people saying they are "fiduciaries," but who are not.

One investment professional relates that when managing a 403(b) plan (a retirement plan for educators), the committee managing the plan encountered numerous conflicts-of-interest from agents selling insurance products. The educators on the committee did not realize there were other investment options available. Worse, the professional said "the thought of requiring a competitive bid for TPA (third-party administrative services) brought on threats of lawsuits because the insurance lobby hides behind an obscene and archaic insurance code." The professional said his firm tried twice to change the law, but it was defeated by the insurance lobby. The professional went on to say that while many financial sales people say they are fiduciaries, their actions indicate they accept promotional payments from investment companies.

Unfortunately, given the history of the financial services industry over the past decade, investment professionals must bear the burden of proof to prove their integrity to customers. If you are not comfortable with an investment professional, or there is a breach of trust, end the relationship. When working with an investment advisor, make it clear that making a mistake which involves your money is cause for immediate dismissal. The new rule is: One strike and you are out.

Know Your Limitations and Be Disciplined

Investors are often their own worst enemies. While it has become a cliché, investors succumb to fear and greed, buy when stocks are expensive, switch funds too often, miss market moves and incur unneeded expenses and commissions, which consistently erode any hope of profits.

A 2011 Dalbar study over a 20-year period found that the average equity mutual fund investor posted an annualized 3.83%

return and asset allocation investors earned 2.56%, while the S&P 500 index returned 9.14%.[41] The main reasons for this gap are that investors over-traded and switched funds at the wrong times. They churned their own accounts by following general sentiment or over-thinking their own strategy.

These factors undoubtedly help explain why the average equity mutual fund holding period was only 3.27 years in 2010, according to Dalbar. Given this short time frame, it is no wonder investors miss the larger market moves, which play out over a decade and only if the investor holds a position. Instead, by making frequent mid-course investment strategy corrections, many investors lose their way or entirely miss the large tide that carries the market forward.

Participate in Your 401(k) Plan

401(k) plans are not as good as pension plans, but they are the best alternative currently available to fund retirement. The problem is that too many employees fail to take full advantage of these plans or even participate in them. Unfortunately, studies show that 25%-34% of eligible participants do not enroll in their plans. One reason may be that employees are intimidated by the paperwork required for participants to manually enroll in the plan.[42]

According to Vanguard data, two-thirds of employees participate in their company's defined benefit plan and make a 6% contribution from their paychecks. Of those who participate, one in five take out loans against their 401(k) accounts, a dangerous and fee-ridden practice, and about 2% of 401(k) participants are active traders inside of their accounts. While the 401(k) participation numbers should be higher, the surprising fact is that the median 401(k) balance is only $24,000, according to Vanguard.

Another, more understandable, reason may be that employees need all their take-home pay and cannot afford to defer any portion of their salary for future retirement needs. This dilemma gets to the heart of the nation's current financial problems–the erosion of financial security for the middle class. However, individuals must still confront and manage their own retirements. This means

401(k) participation becomes a matter of personal and family sacrifice as current take-home pay is sacrificed in favor of a (hopefully) larger future retirement savings account.

While this may be a difficult decision, make the effort to participate in your plan to the fullest extent possible. This will allow you to benefit from the tax deferral and matched contribution benefits. However, do not be fooled by the slogan that your 401(k) is offering "free money." Matching contributions from employers are an employee benefit; it is money you have earned, just as Social Security is money you have contributed to the Social Security trust fund through payroll taxes.

With this in mind, remember that the professionals who provide the services to every 401(k) plan in the U.S. are making a good, risk-free profit for providing the services. In many cases, providers have made more money administering 401(k) plans than many participants themselves, especially over the past decade when large-cap market returns were flat. The bottom line: participate in your 401(k) plan because experts predict you will need approximately 65% to 85% of your current income to maintain your present lifestyle in retirement.[43] Assume the burden of a smaller current take-home pay with the goal of having more money in retirement. Given the alternative (less money in retirement), this is the better choice.

Get Involved in Planning Your Retirement

Once you make the choice to participate in your employer's 401(k) plan, get involved in its management and in making the decisions related to your investments. This is a daunting task, but no one else will protect your money as diligently as its owner. While a study has found that only 41% of participants actually get involved in the management of their own plans, this number decreases significantly to only 19% of participants, who become actively engaged in making plans affecting their own retirement.[44]

Do not allow these crucial decisions to be made by default. Deciding not to act is a decision in itself, so make the effort to understand the variables involved in this admittedly complex investment planning process. This will make you a more knowledgeable investor, but you still may want professional advice from a fee-only financial planner. The reason: Professional investment management has been shown to outperform participant directed investment selection 84.6% of the time[45] which leads to higher portfolio balances.[46]

Be Realistic About Your Ability To Get Rich

The typical U.S. household's net worth was $120,300 and family income was $50,000 in 2007, according to the U.S. Census Bureau data, although that number certainly has decreased since the 2008 recession.[47]

Given the existing wealth-building engines available to Americans, a reality check would show that home equity, Social Security, personal savings and salaries have the ability to make people wealthy. But as we have seen, the power of these wealth-building engines has been compromised. To build wealth faster, many investors begin to trade in their 401(k)s. This is a mistake and investors should resist the temptation. The 401(k) is a savings vehicle and was not designed for trading. Active trading requires a low-commission, fast-access trading platform, specialized training, and the ability to sustain losses. That is the exact opposite of what a 401(k) is designed to do.

Studies also have shown that when non-professionals invest in actively-traded, higher-fee mutual funds, they do not do as well as professionals. Worse, some 401(k) plans are designed to benefit employers, by allowing them to borrow money from the plans or transfer assets.

The reality is that if a fund is not managed for the specific benefit of its employees, offers a poor choice of expensive funds, or the stock market suffers another steep decline (another highly-probable statistical event), investors will suffer from that disadvantage for years.

Another problem is complexity. "Thanks to the incredible complexity of the U.S. fiscal system, it is impossible for anyone to understand her incentive to work, save, or contribute to retirement accounts absent highly advanced computer technology and software."[48] Unfortunately, the ability to access and use such software is outside the ability of most people.

Monitor Fund Fees and Expenses

Read your Plan's Summary Plan Description, 5500 Statement, DOL fee disclosure information and all communications sent to you as a 401(k) or pension plan participant. The devil is in the details, so plan providers will meet their disclosure obligations simply by sending materials to employees. Even when employees do not open these materials or fail to understand them (this is often intentional), this information still constitutes "disclosure" from the points of view of securities regulators' and the courts.

If you have these materials and cannot understand them, contact your company benefits administrator. Keep notes about the date, time, name of the person you met with, and their responses to your questions. Be specific. This information could become valuable later. The goal of these meetings is is to bring more employee-plan participant accountability to the company's benefits administration department. Another concern is whether the fees investors pay for actively-managed mutual funds actually deliver any value. Most active fund managers fail to beat their own benchmarks, so why pay for something you are not getting?

Consider ETFs and Low-Cost Mutual Funds

Participants in 401(k) plans could achieve similar reductions in fees and trading costs by shifting their assets from actively managed mutual funds to low-cost index mutual funds, index ETFs, and index commingled trusts.

The benefits of ETFs are widely acknowledged. Numerous studies have noted the potential savings which accrue to participants when ETFs are used. One study conducted by the Center for Retirement Research found that participants in 401(k) plans "could earn significantly higher surplus returns" if their plans dropped actively-traded equity mutual funds and replaced them with ETFs and commingled trusts.

Remember the Ravages of Inflation

Inflation erodes the value of money and an investor's buying power. Unfortunately, data from the U.S. Bureau of Labor Statistics and Reuters shows that over the last 20 years (from December 1989 to December 2009), inflation has exceeded the Consumer Price Index in the following categories: college tuition, hospital services, medical care, drugs, energy, doctor services and housing. Of these, retirees require six of the seven, and all seven if they are paying for someone's tuition.

While inflation (measured by the Consumer Price Index) has remained at 3% for the past 20 years, its future direction is unpredictable. But still, the impact of that 3% inflation rate becomes significant over time. To maintain your buying power of $25,000 per year in today's dollars, you will need $33,600 a year in 10 years, $45,000 in 20 years, and $60,000 in 30 years. In just 20 years, your buying power will be reduced by 42% with a 3% inflation rate.[80] The risks of inflation are high due to post-2008 recession monetary policy. This poses a significant potential threat to retirees.

Avoid Annuities

Fixed, variable or hybrid, annuities are insurance contracts written by insurance companies for the benefit of insurance companies and the agents and brokers who sell them. Your role in the annuity sales process is to write the check, pay the commissions and wait for sub-standard returns. Yet despite the extensive warnings, people buy annuities since they fail to understand the product. This happens when the insurance industry cleverly weaves a story between the features involving life insurance and investments. Then, the annuity is selectively sold to present its "best" features, while skirting details about the key clauses that activate early surrender charges, limit upside potential and reduce net returns.

These "wrapped" products contain a minefield of fees and are designed for investor abuse.

Due to this product's bad publicity, insurance companies pay very large commissions to annuity salespeople. In some cases, variable annuity commissions typically range from 6% to 8% and can go as high as 14%. In practice, a salesperson who sells a $1 million annuity can earn $100,000 or more on a single sale. In the words of Ken Fisher, a well-known investment manager, "He or she is getting that huge commission to sell you something that is bad for you, that you wouldn't otherwise naturally buy, and that if you truly understood the product you would never, ever buy."[49] Then, if an investor changes his mind and wants to exit the contract there is a "surrender" charge which can start at 7% and decline 1% per year over the surrender holding period. And for a variable annuity that is in addition to fees for fund expenses, mortality and expense risk charges, administrative fees, and distribution.

Despite their well-acknowledged deficiencies (high fees, low returns), variable annuities are more prevalent in 403(b) plans due to the selling arrangement between teacher's union officials and insurance companies. According to people involved in the annuity business, about 80% of teachers own annuities in their 403(b) accounts largely due to the selling efforts of annuity sales-people working closely with teacher's union approval.

At this point, it is important to compare annuity to mutual fund fees. The average variable annuity fee charges 2.4% per year compared to the average mutual fund expense of 1.2% per years, according to Morningstar. This fee is paid regardless of the variable annuity's market return and effectively reduces any fund return the investor earns.

Just as in mutual funds, the long-term effect of fees is critical to return. If a person invests $1 million over a 20-year period in a variable annuity that delivers a 10% market return and carries annual expenses of 2.4% per year, they will end with $4.138 million. The same amount invested in a mutual fund with an expense of 1.2% over 20 years will produce $5.284 million. The difference of $1.146 million is strictly due to expenses.[50]

Understand the New Workplace and the Global Economy

Employers are shifting the costs of managing health care plans and all forms of retirement plans to their employees. Not only are employees paying a larger share of these costs than they were a decade ago, they also are assuming more risk in the form of rising health care costs and investment market uncertainty.

This means employees have to spend more time managing these large potential expenses. The largest source of personal bankruptcy in the U.S. is due to the burden of large hospital and medical expenses. This makes it essential that families have a basic form of health insurance to defray any fraction of these large potential expenses that can easily devastate any savings.

In the new workplace, employers are shifting more financial risk to their employees. In the past, employees had to be concerned with workplace safety issues (functioning machinery, good ventilation, uncluttered work spaces), but as manufacturing has been replaced by the service sector, and employees themselves are being considered expenses rather than assets, new financial engineering practices have encouraged employers to shift more financial risk to their own employees.

This is occurring even as employers know their workers are not qualified or have the resources to manage financial planning, interest rate, inflation and tax scenarios going out 50 years, while also attempting to quantify imponderables, such as how long they will live, or evaluating complex medical and pharmaceutical plans. This is further complicated when the employer only provides limited choices, which have been previously screened by full-time professionals who made plan choices that clearly favor employers. In essence, employees are now fully responsible for managing all aspects of their own careers, including the choice, and payment of medical and retirement benefits.

Avoid Front-End Load Mutual Funds

The insurance and mutual fund industries have been perfecting ways of compensating their brokers for selling products for years.

One of the proven methods is front-end load funds. In these funds, investors essentially pay their full commissions and additional expenses before any services have been rendered.

In the case of the Growth Fund of America front-end load fund offered by American Funds, investor pay 575 basis points (5.75%) up front and 68 basis points per year to have the honor of investing in the fund. To get any benefit over no-load funds, the investor would have to hold the fund eight years just to break even and this does not include volatility and performance-related issues faced by the investor.[51] The basic problem is that in front-end load funds, investors pre-pay all commissions and fees. This makes it more expensive to sell an under-performing front-end load. It also rewards the fund company before they have produced any results.

Investing in a Low-Return Environment

Warren Buffett has predicted that the next 20 to 30 years will be a low-yield investment environment, with fixed income yielding an average of 3% and equities 5%. These low returns will make their greatest impact on younger workers, who begin investing early in their careers, and will fail to build large principals that will generate higher returns over time due to the magic of compound interest. Still, the best alternative is to save more. This may be dull advice, but the new reality of saving more is important since medical advances should translate into longer lifespans, accompanied by smaller retirement savings accounts.[52]

Pity Generation X

People born between 1965 and 1974 will face an exceptionally difficult time building their assets for retirement for a number of reasons:

- They are part of a workplace transition where employers consider them liabilities rather than assets.

- Their employment gaps will be longer and more frequent. This will disrupt any savings and 401(k) accumulations, plus they may need to borrow from their 401(k) assets, which should be avoided at all costs.

- Political pressures to cut entitlements will continue to loom as conservatives seek to denigrate the middle-class.

- The home equity wealth engine will take years to rebuild, thus denying this generation a key source of savings.

- Global economic conditions will continue to disrupt markets and personal savings plans.

- An EBRI study released May 24, 2012 found that 44% of Generation X is expected to not have enough money in retirement. A more detailed breakdown found that 87% of low-income households and 13% of the top income households will suffer a retirement shortfall.

Pity Generation Y Even More

Gen Y (persons born in the early-1980s through the 1990s) will essentially be on their own in terms of retirement financing, especially if there are any significant changes to Social Security or a decline in the quality of 401(k) fee and expense disclosure. Pensions will be a rarity in this group.

This generation will also suffer from a more unstable wage situation and longer lapses in unemployment. This slow start in wage traction is especially detrimental to building long-term wealth since 70% of lifetime wage growth happens in the first 10 years of a career.[53] Any delays due to unemployment or underemployment in this early career period can derail wealth creation.

Students in this generation will carry an average of $23,300 in student debt. This initial debt burden will hamper their ability to buy a home. This debt can't be discharged through bankruptcy and almost two million Americans with student debt are over 60, according to the New York Federal Reserve. In March 2012, the Consumer Financial Protection Bureau said U.S. student-loan debt reached $1 trillion.

Don't Tolerate Mistakes From Your Advisor

The new rule of thumb governing relationships between investors and their professional financial advisors in the post-2008 recessionary world is: one strike and the financial professional is out.

Given the new era of market volatility, low investment returns and limited real-wage growth, any lost investment money will be extremely difficult to recoup before retirement. This makes it imperative to watch current investment balances, returns, risk levels, and expenses. Since so much is out of the control of investors (Eurodollar volatility, political instability, monetary and fiscal policy, corporate misbehaviors), the new rule is to control what you can control. The short list of what is within your domain of control starts with who you choose as a financial advisor. Whenever possible, work with RIAs and FINRA-registered advisers.

Absent a formally adopted fiduciary standard, the investment advisory industry has to assume the burden of responsibility to prove they are acting in the best and exclusive interests of their clients. In turn, if clients do not receive evidence that their financial advisor is acting exclusively in their best interests, get professional advice elsewhere.

Re-Consider "Long-Term Investing"

Average investors often think of stock market returns in terms of percentages. That is a mistake, at least according to some experts, who think in terms of probabilities. The probability argument is better suited to investment professionals and the industry since it effectively evades comparisons between returns in different time frames.

For example, while returns during the 1990s were above average, returns for the decade beginning in 2000 were essentially flat. For the 10-year period from Sept. 30, 2001 to March 31, 2012, the S&P 500 delivered a 2.07% annualized return, accompanied by significant volatility. While long-term historical market returns are in the range of 8% to 10% annually, that number only applies to the long term (10 to 20 years into the future.)

That is not much consolation to the investor approaching retirement, including younger investors. Consider that from

October 2007 until March 2009, the market declined by 58%. In order to recover to this previous level, the market had to post a gain of 138% (not the commonly assumed 58%) just to break even.[54] No one will venture a guess on how many years this could take, so it is no wonder that Gus Sauter, chief investment officer of Vanguard, said "so if you're saving to spend on something a year from now, you shouldn't be in the stock market." [55] This gives an entirely new meaning to "long-term" investing, but it should not instill confidence in the average investor.

More Global Meltdowns Are Inevitable

Despite public hand wringing from regulators and some elected officials, fundamental financial reform has not happened. There will be another global financial crisis because the powers driving global trading will not surrender their powers to any nation. This is due to the sheer power and size of this market, and the characteristics of its protagonists.

The size of the global over-the-counter derivatives market, which provides the leverage and links key global financial institutions, is estimated at over $1 quadrillion, according to 2008 estimates from the Bank of International Settlements. As of June 2008, there was $683 trillion in outstanding OTC swaps for the G-10 nations and Switzerland alone.[56] This dwarfs the size of the largest U.S. market, the New York Stock Exchange. Similarly, the popularity of hedge funds is due to their use of sophisticated strategies and leverage, but these funds are not suitable for the vast majority of individual investors due to their income, net worth and risk tolerance requirements. Still, despite their limited mass retail appeal, these strategies and the amount of money they control affect market activity worldwide.[59]

Even when regulators try, they will not be able to curb abuses in this market since it is truly global, complex and governed by private contracts between global parties. Regulators and courts are unable to untangle these webs of contracts and their actual owners. For example, Porsche held such a large derivative position in Volkswagen that it effectively controlled the company.[57]

While it may have been true only a decade ago that activities in prime brokerage and hedge funds did not significantly affect average investors, which has now changed. Since the bailout of Long Term Capital Management in 1998, the OTC derivatives market and prime brokerages have become larger and more integrated. This is propelling the expansion of global finance and the financial engineering of huge individual profits, often through leverage.

But the now-accepted policy of "too big to fail" and the socialization of risk subsidized by individual taxpayers means average Americans are now financing this wealth transfer as their own personal financial futures are degraded. Yet despite all the rhetoric, nothing is being done to insulate U.S. taxpayers from another inevitable global financial failure. Seemingly unrelated events, such as the TARP program, bailouts of Bear Stearns, regulations affecting swaps dealers and international accounting standards, the $7.8 million Maiden Lane CDO mortgage swap, and the questionable stability of the Eurodollar, will all hurt investors, accompanied by the looming threat of another recession, lost jobs and higher taxes.

Then, there is the critical issue of conflicts-of-interest at all levels of the investment business. Lloyd Blankfein, CEO of Goldman Sachs, said "no one who is going to be effective can avoid conflicts-of-interest coming up," he explained, simply because investment banks act as lenders to their clients. As a result, the firm has a vested interest in their continued solvency and profitability at all costs in order to preserve their investment and the ongoing relationship.[58]

This is one of the clearest statements about why conflicts-of-interest will continue at the institutional investment level. But it does not explain why a local broker, working in an office at a suburban shopping mall, would sell an inappropriate or very expensive investment, such as an annuity, to an unsophisticated investor in exchange for a revenue sharing percentage and additional fees. That conflict-of-interest can be best explained by pure greed. The better explanation from Blankfein is predicated on a mutually-beneficial interest. For too many retail brokers, however, the majority of benefits only flow one way.

Another reason why future financial crises are very probable is that lobbyists have captured the Congress and regulatory agencies.

An example: On March 12, 2012, President Obama signed the Stop Trading on Congressional Knowledge Act into law, which was intended to ban insider trading by members of Congress and other appointed federal officials. While the bill was hailed as a major piece of ethics legislation, its final version contained a loop-hole which neglected to ban the little-know practice of "political intelligence." As a result, the bill failed to correct the problem.

While not well known, political intelligence is a $100 million industry employing over 2,000 people. In practice, people ply-ing this work (often lobbyists and former legislative aides), who use their access to Congressional staffers and elected officials to obtain unpublicized news about pending legislation. This news then becomes a valuable commodity to hedge and private equity funds, which make trades based on the involved parties and the affected industries. Basically, this amounts to political insiders sell-ing the information they gather to Wall Street traders and hedge funds, which then use it to make investment decisions.[78]

In another example, speaking before the U.S. House of Representatives Committee on Banking and Financial Services, legendary hedge fund manager George Soros said:

"This hearing is very timely because the global capitalist sys-tem which has been responsible for the remarkable prosperity of this country in the last decade is coming apart at the seams. The current decline in the U.S. stock market is only a symptom, and a belated symptom at that, of the more profound problems that are affecting the world economy."

He then went on to say: "banks are frantically trying to limit their exposure and de-leverage and reduce risk. Bank stocks have plummeted. A global credit crunch is in the making. It is already restricting the flow of funds to the periphery, but it has also begun to affect the availability of credit in the domestic economy." He then explained the complicated world of OTC derivatives and intertwined counter-parties.

While many would think Soros was describing the 2008 hous-ing and financial crises, he was speaking in 1998 and describing the global market fallout from the collapse of Long-Term Capital Management, a hedge fund which leveraged itself 300 to 400 times and amassed debts of $1 trillion. This fund then became the first "too big to fail" entity, mainly because it included well-connected investors and top-shelf counter-parties worldwide. This helped explain why the fund was bailed out by the Federal Reserve and some major investment banks.

While both cases occurred at different times, they both address the same system of selective legislation designed to allow insider trading and preferential treatment for connected firms and executives to continue uninterrupted. Despite the TARP and other bailouts, the multi-trillion hedge fund, investment banking and prime finance industries require special regulatory and legislative exemptions to continue. They need special treatment, so they can provide leveraged income-producing opportunities to large speculators. Even after the 2008 Wall Street bailout, the system remains unchanged. It is only a question of time before the next crisis develops.

Beware the Health Care Sword

While the Obama administration has made an attempt to contain health care costs long-term, the program is under attack. If parts of the program are reversed, employees will find themselves paying higher costs for medical costs. Employers will choose plans with higher deductibles. Out-of-pocket expenses will increase, reducing employee take-home pay. New health insurance plans will be accompanied by tax-free accounts for routine expenses, paid for (to some degree) by employers' contributions. Health care, accompanied by long-term care will continue to consume larger portions of disposable incomes, continuing the trend of individuals paying more to insurance companies for many of their 401(k) and health care needs.

Beware of Buy-and-Hold Investing

For the 10-year period from Sept. 30, 2001 to March 31, 2012, the S&P 500 delivered a 2.07% annualized return. This so-called "Lost

Decade" of investment returns presents an unpleasant truth for the industry that although investors continued to pay significant fees, while assuming all the investment risk, volatility and opportunity costs of buying-and-holding, they received nothing in return. Alternately, fund companies are paid for their assets under management, so they clearly benefited.

In an investment world impacted by events totally outside the realm of average investors, the mainstream investment industry insists that over the long-term investors will be rewarded as markets deliver their historical averages. The "long term" (often defined in an investment context as 10 to 20 years) is an unacceptable time frame for people approaching retirement, who have to absorb investment losses, accompanied by the time needed to recover that loss. This commonly offered advice ("Hold on and the market will recover.") should be considered pure speculation since it is devoid of strategy.

The alternative is to use diversified investment strategies and asset classes. Alternative strategy funds, including long-short, arbitrage, opportunistic and event-driven, are tested in the hedge fund world and increasingly becoming available to qualified, more risk-tolerant investors. Alternative strategy funds make sense and have a role in large, diversified portfolios.

The goal is to find active tactical strategies designed to capture positive returns, regardless of market direction. The irony is that investors of all types and account sizes will have to become more risk tolerant, but existing, long-only mutual funds do not meet this new need.

Fewer Wealth-Building Engines Available

The other new reality is that the number of wealth-building engines has been seriously reduced or is seriously under-performing.

Consider the following:

When Home Equity Evaporates

For Baby Boomers planning to retire, housing wealth accounts for a majority of their total net worth. While this figure is skewed according to demographics (education, race, age within the Baby Boomer segment, marital status, sex), home equity accounts for one-third of net worth at the mean and 50% at the median. This makes Baby Boomers especially susceptible to housing price shocks, both positive and negative, which can significantly affect retirement planning and consumption patterns.

Recent declines in home prices have slashed household wealth by as much as $7 trillion, according to Federal Reserve Board Chairman Ben Bernanke.[60]

From this staggering amount, approximately $400 billion alone was lost between 2007 to mid-2008. These combined losses have significantly altered the retirement plans of millions of Americans. At the end of the first quarter 2011, data showed that 22.7% of all residential homes with mortgages had negative equity, down from the fourth quarter 2010 when 23.1% of U.S. homes were under-water.[61] The decrease in housing equities and values are especially important since home ownership increases with age. As a result, older people rely more on their home equity as a source of wealth and as insurance against unforeseen negative life events, such as a serious illness or the death of a spouse. Decreased home values also have resulted in reduced confidence in future retirement planning for people of all ages.[62]

As of February 2012, eight million U.S. homes, representing about 25% of all homeowners, are worth less than their mortgage balances.

When Real Wages Become Stagnant

Since the mid-1970s, real wages have not increased. According to the Economic Policy Institute, the average hourly wage for workers in the U.S. in 2007 dollars (adjusted for inflation) was $18.90 in 1973 and $21.34 in 2006. This converts to a 13% wage increase in 33 years, or a growth rate of 0.04% per year. This increase applies only to wages, but when wages and benefits (aka "overall compensation") are tallied together, the numbers are even smaller: the median worker compensation from 1983-1989 grew at a rate of 0.01% annually and between 2002–2007 there was no growth rate at all.[63]

Alternately, the cost of family medical premiums from 2003 to 2010 increased by 50%, and by 64% for individuals from 2003 to 2010, according to a study by the Commonwealth Fund. This is part of a trend which has seen employers shifting the cost of premiums from businesses to employees.[64]

Stagnant real wage growth is one of the largest contributors to a stagnant standard of living. Yet while this is a critical economic metric, it begs the need for a political explanation that most economists and elected officials are reluctant to make. It is also a difficult concept to communicate and politically radioactive, so some opportunistic political activists have noted that the decline in buying power should be linked to raising taxes. This re-focuses the argument away from a discussion on the causes of wage stagnation and into a whole new fable about the dangers of raising taxes and "big, inefficient government," rather than one correctly centered on the reasons for wage stagnation and the nation's high level of income disparity.

When Pensions Become Less Available

Since the 1980s, an increasingly smaller number of American workers are being covered by pension plans. Today, three workers in 10 had a defined benefit plan, including 15% of public workers. While many employees today are nostalgic about pensions, the reality is that people crave the predictability of a specific monthly payment, not necessarily the payment amount itself.

Also, most pensions were not as generous as many people believe. The median pension payment benefit payment in 2004 was $6,700 a year. This amount was higher for retirees from public plans and the military, often because larger pensions were used as a hiring incentive to offset lower salaries. In order to receive a pension, employees often had to remain with the same firm for 20 to 25 years.

Today, long-term employment is a near-impossibility due to volatile global markets, frequent company operational changes and the uncertainty of long-term planning. The first victims of these changes are line employees, who are expensive in terms of benefits and expendable as business evaporates. Pensions also have been looted by top management either to fund their own retirements and severance packages, to fund corporate expansions or boost earnings. As a result, pension plans are being frozen or closed. Experts do not foresee them becoming popular again in the corporate world.

Beware of Rising Market Volatility

The new reality facing modern workers is that they have assumed more risk over their own financial futures. Corporate paternalism is dead and corporate management is rewarded for transferring financial risk and benefit expenses to employees. This includes investment and health care risks, which take the form of uncertain portfolio returns and rising premiums for health care. Job security and clear paths to promotion also have been derailed.

During the 2008 bear market, an estimated $1 trillion was lost in employee 401(k)s.[65] These losses were assumed by average people acting as amateur, employee-investment managers, the majority of whom were managing their entire portfolios without any outside professional assistance.

Another caveat is that investors have to be concerned about market volatility. Market gyrations affect retirement planning and withdrawals. Investors should realize that even in a bull market, a 15% correction is the norm. This is complicated because some professional traders thrive on volatility, and trading techniques designed to benefit from it.

For instance, a study on "flash trading" (a sub-set strategy of high-frequency trading) found that professionals are using this special type of order to arbitrage trades between exchanges in New York and Chicago to take advantage of the 11 millisecond transmission delay between the two markets. To capitalize on price disparities, flash traders are devoting millions of dollars to the strategy, which is not illegal, although it may cause temporary price imbalances. One example happened on May 6, 2010, when just 16 traders accounted for 29% of the trades in S&P 500 index futures and E-Mini S&P 500 futures. These futures contracts affect other equity trading prices.[66] In August 2009, SEC Chairwoman Mary Schapiro said her agency would begin an investigation into the practice. But by May 2012, the SEC had not taken any action on this issue.[67]

Disposable Incomes and Savings Rates

According to the Economic Policy Institute, disposable personal incomes for Americans in 2012 rose at only a 0.8% rate after adjusting for inflation. This small growth rate occurred was partially financed by a reduction in the personal savings rate.[68]

Since the 1980s when it became easier for homeowners to obtain a home equity loan, Americans have begun to cash out their home equities and spend it on consumption. While this practice became popular, it only fostered more credit abuse. Subsequent studies found that for every $1 since 1980 that people withdrew in home equity, they added $2 more in debt, primarily from the unrestrained use of credit cards.[69]

The Two-Salary Family Is A Necessity

As a result of stagnant real wages, American families began working more hours, accompanied by the addition of women to the workforce in increasing numbers beginning in the 1970s. At about that time, 40% of adult women had entered the labor force. Today, the number of women in the workforce is about 80%.[70] The entry of full-time working mothers into the workforce transformed American families, who have now become dependent on two salaries. While this may have raised family's incomes and standards of living, it has also created a host of other family and societal stresses and expenses.

Most Will Not Get Rich by Inheriting Assets

Inheritances are becoming smaller and for many people, non-existent. According to John Gist, who has analyzed extensive

Federal Reserve survey data for AARP's Public Policy Institute, as of 2004, only 20% of Baby Boomers (people born between 1946 and 1964) said they received an inheritance. That number has been consistent since 1989, with a median value for an inheritance of $49,000.

The bad news is that due to the prolonged 2008 recession and its severe impact on personal savings among older Americans, the percentage of Baby Boomers expecting inheritances has diminished from 27% to 15%. Accompanying these diminished hopes, Gist said that only one-quarter of those expecting any largess will receive anything.[71]

Limit Exposure to Company Stock

Companies occasionally offer employees a small discount to invest in their own company's stock. This can be done for a variety of reasons (as an incentive, to make employees feel more "involved" etc.), but while a small number of shares (3% to 5%) of the total portfolio should accomplish this task, employees should not assume larger positions in company stock. Nationally, more than 10% of the total assets in 401(k) plans are invested in company stock.[72]

When an employee's company stock exposure exceeds 10% of their entire portfolio, they have become too closely aligned with their company's fate. As numerous examples in this book have shown, a company's direction and long-term goals are not the same as its own employees. In too many cases, they are the exact opposite. Nor are employees well informed about the company's full range of operational, investment, executive compensation, management and strategic activities.

There have been a number of high profile ERISA cases where employers, such as Lucent and Enron, misled their own employees about the value of company stock. Other well-known corporate failures, such as Washington Mutual, Pan American Airlines, AIG, and Lehman Brothers, wiped out many employee accounts from workers, who believed in the infallibility of their executive management. That proved to be an irrecoverable mistake.

Study YOUR 401(k) Fee DisclosureS

When a 401(k) plan presents its investment performance and fee information to participants, it must be displayed in a comparative format. Experts recommend that participants look at the fees for each of their investment options. Second, participants should find the rates of return for each investment option because fees for each investment directly impact their rate of return. The last step is to compare investment options with other available plan options to determine whether there is a better choice (in terms of cost and performance) that will still fit the investor's goals.

When examining fees, the most important factor is the dollar amount charged per thousand dollars invested. For instance, if you have $100,000 invested in a fund, and the cost-per-thousand is $10, the total cost for the fund is $1,000. In addition to showing a dollar amount, the new reports must disclose the total cost, as an annual percentage of each fund the employee is invested in, as well as any other fees charged against the individual account, such as those for loans or distributions. By adding these two amounts, you can determine the total cost of investing in your company's 401(k) plan.[73]

Paying someone to manage your 401(k) is expected. But the more important question is whether the fees you are paying are commensurate with the services you are receiving. What is reasonable can vary depending on the plan's size. For example, plans with over $100 million in assets usually carry fees of less than 1%, while plans in the $50 million to $100 million range may cost 1.5 %; smaller plans often incur higher fees.

The other key variable is whether you are getting your money's worth in terms of dollars paid for services rendered. Experts recommend that a fee of 75 to 100 basis points (0.75% to 1%) is justified if the advisor is holding regular quarterly client meetings. But if that is not the case, the investor is paying too much, especially since no-load fund families commonly offer globally-diversified portfolios for less than 15 basis points (0.15%.)

As a general rule, if a plan is charging 0.5% or less, and quality services are being provided, it pays to maintain the relationship. However, if a plan is charging 2% to 4%, the fees should be considered excessive and investors should consider making a change quickly. The reason: Over the course of 25 to 30 years, these fee differentials can cost an investor with a significant portfolio about $1 million.

Use the DOL's Charts to Compare Fund Fees

If you believe the investment fees you are paying in your 401(k) are unreasonable, make sure it's not because of your own choices. For instance, if you've elected a variable annuity with layers of funds, that could be the source of your increased costs.

Once you've checked your investment choices, talk with your employer about improving the quality of your plan by offering lower-cost choices or access to new strategies or asset classes. If the plan itself is too expensive, you may need to ask your employer to charge less or limit your plan participation after you have reached the maximum match limit from your employer. To determine how a company's plan compares to others, investors can use the fund rating comparison program available on BrightScope. This data can then be presented to plan sponsors to see why plan fee rates differ. A similar comparison chart is available from the DOL.[74]

The new DOL charts will offer investors the following:

- For each available investment option, participants can see total operating expenses expressed as a percentage and as a dollar amount for an assumed investment of $1000;

- The ability to see plan expenses, such as those related to administration, using third-party investment options, and legal and accounting fees;

- The ability to see historical performance data for investment options. This includes one-, five- and 10-year returns compared to key benchmarks, such as the S&P 500, or other broad-based benchmarks for bonds and non-U.S. equities.[75]

The issue is not whether any of the commission rates are improper, but instead whether the commission structure is appropriate based on the size of the plan and the services provided to participants. Such comparisons will allow employee-investors to make intelligent buying decisions for the first time in the history of the 401(k) industry.

How Fees Can Be Reduced

Plan participants can work with their employers to reduce plan expenses, but with certain caveats. A main concern is to recognize that 401(k) plans achieve a certain economy of scale based on their size, so participants should recognize that the services provided by larger plans may not be cost effective for smaller ones.

Another approach is to ask employers or plan sponsors to assume more of the plan's costs or to unbundle services so participants can take advantage of only those services they use. This would include paying for impartial fiduciary-conscious advice from outside professionals on an a la carte basis.

Investors seeking above-market returns assume greater risk and will also pay more for the effort. It must also be noted that the decision to buy an index versus an actively-managed fund is not always justified. When actively-managed funds are bought directly from a fund company, and the fund expenses are fully disclosed, they can provide many of the same benefits as index funds in terms of fees.

Remember: Powerful Forces are Working Against Investors' Interests

Most businesses value their customers, but the inherent conflicts-of-interest in the financial services industry erode this assumption. In addition to the daily business practices described in this book, designed to separate investors from their money, there are organized forces working full time to shape regulations and laws that favor the financial services industry over their own customers.

While there are a number of individual mutual funds and financial services industry trade and lobbying groups that conduct their own lobbying campaigns, the largest for the fund industry is the Investment Company Institute (ICI.) In 2011, the ICI had about $50 million in lobbying funds and employed five full-time, 30 part-time, and 75 outside lobbyists to get their pro-industry positions across to regulators and elected officials. The ICI gets their money from mutual fund companies, which, in turn get it from their own customer-shareholders. In essence, shareholders' fees are converted into contributions by fund companies for lobbying activities which are then used to erode their own customers' interests.

But this is only one of many financial services lobbying groups working against investors. From 1998 to 2008, the financial services industry spent $1.7 billion on campaign contributions and $5 billion on lobbying expenses. During this period, the securities industry alone spent $1.7 billion on campaign contributions and $3.4 billion on lobbying. The insurance industry led the lobbying effort by spending $1 billion, largely to repeal any reforms passed since the New Deal. To put this into perspective, when these campaign contributions are compared to other industries during the period starting in 1989, contributions from the financial services industry alone are greater than the contributions from the energy, health care, defense and telecommunications industries combined.[77]

This is an extraordinary amount. Accordingly, anyone with common political sense would ask why the financial services industry would go to such great and expensive lengths to lobby elected officials and delay all types of financial reform and regulation, if the expected profits from the status quo were not worth defending. Of course, the rewards far outweigh these tremendous cash outlays. This better explains the essentially confrontational relationship that exists between financial services companies, including mutual funds, and their own customers.

When Possible, Buy Directly from Fund Companies, Not Brokers

Numerous academic studies have found that funds sold directly by fund companies outperform those sold by brokers by about 1% per year.[79] This is partially due to the extra expenses needed to compensate brokers, but also to other factors, such as the drag on performance from advisor-focused marketing expenses. These results also trigger a fiduciary responsibility for plan sponsors, who should recognize the difference between the suitability and the fiduciary standards.

Deal With RIAs for Investment Advice

Since conflicts-of-interest are an inherent part of many financial relationships, investors can protect themselves by dealing with the only category of investment advisors that explicitly acknowledges their fiduciary duty. This is the SEC-registered category known as Registered Investment Advisors (RIAs).

RIAs often are members of the Investment Advisor Association, a professional group, which has codified standards of practice for its members. Since the advisory industry is so fragmented, advisors can have different definitions and standards. For example, broker-dealers are also included under the Investment Advisors Act of 1940, but their business practices may not align with either the Standard of Care or the fiduciary standard. The confusion that exists between the various professional titles (such as, brokers, advisors, consultants) does not benefit investors. It may even be intentional, so the industry can evade responsibility for being accused of providing investment "recommendations" versus "advice," which may carry a more limited legal obligation.

Investors should use RIAs because of this straightforward definition: "An investment advisor is a fiduciary whose duty is to serve the best interests of its clients, including an obligation not to subordinate clients' interests to its own. Included in the fiduciary standard are the duties of loyalty and care. An advisor that has a material conflict-of-interest must either eliminate that conflict or fully disclose to its clients all material facts relating to the conflict."[78] In addition, when an RIA is acting as principal for an account, they have to disclose in writing if they have a conflict-of-interest in the transaction.

While this industry-regulatory debate continues as a result of the Dodd-Frank Wall Street Reform and Consumer Protection Act of 2010, investors can bypass the excessive recommendations, studies and legal challenges produced by the various industry and special interest groups. To act in their best interests, investors should find, interview and work directly with RIAs, who put their clients' interests ahead of a commissioned broker. Putting in a few hours of research to find the right RIA can save investors thousands of dollars over time and reduce the aggravation of time-consuming and emotionally draining arbitration or lawsuits.

CHAPTER 6

WHAT INVESTORS AND PLAN SPONSORS GAINED—AND LOST—FROM POOR DISCLOSURE

While the DOL's fee and expense disclosure regulations may trigger a reactive response from plan sponsors, they can turn this new 401(k) plan transparency into a new pro-employee and corporate branding effort. To do this, plan sponsors can borrow from the playbook used by companies adopting environmentally-sustainable practices.

In the world of environmentally sustainable products, research from Proctor and Gamble found that consumers will only buy environmentally-friendly products if they do not have any disadvantage in terms of price and performance with a comparable product. In terms of a 401(k) plan, cost can be a decision-critical factor, but it can also be offset by the quality and frequency of investor communications and product offerings, especially low-cost ETFs or index funds. In short, higher expenses can be justified if plan participants get the services and investment results they are paying for.

Companies can adopt three different approaches when it comes to communicating expense information to plan participants.

The first is to list the broad and detailed plan expenses from an unbundled 401(k) compared to a benchmark. A basic employee education-communications program can be built around this release without any impact on the company's reputation and brand.

A second approach would introduce a new "sub-brand" of a low-cost 401(k) plan offering. This could involve a new platform of ETFs, such as one offered by Invest 'n Retire, comprised of ETFs selected for 401(k)s, accompanied by a new dedicated recordkeeping platform and professionally-managed, fiduciary-compliant advisory services. This not only offers the opportunity to complement an existing 401(k) plan, but to supplement it with a new sub-brand that offers distinct, low-cost alternatives from different types of investment vehicles. This approach also acknowledges that the average investor needs professional help to manage modern markets. Long-term financial planning is a challenge for professionals, so it is immensely more foreboding to the average 401(k) participant.

A third approach applies to companies whose 401(k) plans rank high in terms of expenses. Offering a high-cost plan may force plan sponsors to revamp their entire offering. If the plan sponsor wants to rebuild their reputation, they can re-launch their plan as one which has low-cost investments that are automated, compliant and responsive to employee needs.

Companies that fail to note the change in public opinion, which is decidedly against corporate and Wall Street abuses, will continue to forge ahead with total disregard for their employees, only to find no one is following them. But for employers who want to develop high-quality 401(k) plans in this new DOL-inspired fee disclosure environment, companies will be forced to push their recordkeepers and fund companies to develop more transparent, cheaper, unbundled services. If this occurs, many corporate 401(k) plan administrators will be creating new branding and marketing strategies that meet their employee's needs.

CHAPTER 6

What Investors Lost From Poor Disclosure

For those plans which have inadvertently or intentionally overpaid their service providers for decades, the sad reality is that decades of management inaction have cost 401(k) participants an incalculable amount in lost investment returns.

If a plan sponsor failed to contain plan costs and offered a poor choice of investments, employees should ask: Why weren't costs contained? Who benefited from any systematic over-payments? What will be done about it?

While many plans which failed to monitor costs had no ulterior motive, there have been cases where some executives responsible for administering their 401(k) plans consciously decided to elevate the interests of their vendors over the interests of their own employees. This fundamental shift is a violation of ERISA and the traditional employee-employer relationship, where an employee could assume (incorrectly) that their employer would protect their interests.

As the new DOL regulations begin to gather enough data to make cost comparisons between plan sponsors, it will be possible to determine who allowed overpayments to service providers and how much these cost participants.

Once these comparisons can be made, it is highly likely that a pattern will emerge among corporations which allowed significant overpayments to occur to plan providers at the same time companies were reducing pension and health care benefits, froze pension plans, or cut contributions to their 401(k)s.

Unfortunately, there have been instances when major companies, such as include Ford, Unisys, GE, IBM, Verizon, Lucent, and DuPont[1] diverted pension plan assets to enrich their top executives.

In the 1980s and 1990s, corporations began to consider pension plan assets, many of which were over-funded, as underutilized pools of capital that could be freely used for acquisitions and market speculation. According to reporter Ellen Schultz, "With perfectly legal loopholes that enable companies to tap pension plans like piggy banks, and accounting rules that rewarded employers for cutting benefits, retiree benefits plans soon morphed into profit centers, and populations of retirees eventually became portfolios of assets and debts, which passed from company to company in swirls of mergers, spin-offs, and acquisitions. And with each of these restructuring deals, the subsequent owner aimed to squeeze a profit from the portfolio, always at the expense of the retirees."[2]

The other beneficiaries of pension plan abuses were executive compensation and retirement plans. This represents one of the greatest and under-reported transfers of wealth in U.S. history.

But it would be a mistake to assume these new disclosures only affect plan participants. If anything, they will have a greater effect on all employers. One by-product of the new DOL fee disclosure regulations is that companies must make extra efforts to demonstrate their commitments to employees. Companies should expect that employees should take nothing for granted, especially when they hear statements from their employers about being "part of the team," "their work is valued," or there is "need for shared sacrifice."

If a company overpaid 401(k) service providers for years, no explanation will be sufficient to employees. When these 401(k) over-payments are presented alongside the looting of the pension system over the past few decades, a dangerous pattern emerges. Along with the shift of health care benefits to employees, this trifecta of abuse–diminished benefits for pensions, 401(k)s and health care–marks a sea change in the employer-employee relationship. These abuses, combined with changes in tax burdens, help account

Can the Mutual Fund Industry Change?

Greater disclosure also will shift the burden of change to the mutual fund industry. No longer should the industry be able to get along by largely offering and managing expensive funds that deliver mediocre returns.

Instead, the industry should be expected to realistically assess whether 401(k) plans can deliver on their implied promise of "providing excellent financial security for people," in the words of Vanguard CEO Jack Brennan, who boldly proclaimed that 401(k) investors "will be better off in 25 years than we are today." If this fails to materialize, financial industry executives and public policy makers must acknowledge they have lost their huge retirement gamble and reduced the quality of life for a few generations of Americans.

This will become more devastating if calls for privatizing Social Security gain political traction. This will not only increase the level of financial insecurity for millions, but will be part of the greatest wealth transfer in the nation's history. Privatizing Social Security will result in higher fees for investments, while evading the fact that it remains very difficult to deliver consistent, above-index level returns that will improve the lives of investors.

But as long as the fund industry deals with uninformed customers, it will survive unchanged. It is betting on uninformed investors to continue its business-as-usual offering of expensive actively-managed funds, even as it acknowledges that ETFs have superior features.

The problem is that the entire mutual fund industry's business operations are built around the old mutual fund product structure, pay-to-play, revenue sharing deals. Shifting to a new business model, where advisors buy products without revenue sharing, requires changes in management, operations, marketing and philosophy. Selling without confronting the conflict-of-interest dilemma requires new sales techniques and messages. These are events that will re-shape the fund industry that has essentially hit an intellectual brick wall from the marketing and portfolio management perspectives.

This also helps explain why there have been so few new product introductions in the fund industry since target-date funds. Even with the push from the DOL to make target-date funds the default options for 401(k) participants, the jury remains undecided on whether these products will meet investors' investment objectives in the next few decades.

So where does this leave individual investors?

If you have read this far, you have seen how powerful financial industry forces have structured retirement plans to work better for employers and investment professionals than employees. This is an age-old story. If history is correct, it takes an extraordinary effort to introduce a new business model which will introduce new, less expensive investments designed for retirees.

Today, technology has isolated workers, so they cannot hold the needed face-to-face discussions to address common problems. But most importantly, investors must recognize that the interests of regulators, the financial services industry and employers are not aligned for the common benefit of improving retirement financial security for 401(k) plan participants.

Finally, as this is being written (June 2012), Jamie Dimon, CEO of JP Morgan Chase, testified before a Senate Banking Committee to explain the $2 billion trading loss his sophisticated traders made in a bungled hedging strategy. JP Morgan has a $1 billion technology budget, 230,000 employees worldwide and operates one of the most sophisticated global trading networks in history.

However, in today's global trading market structure, JPMorgan traders and others as sophisticated, ply the same waters daily as novice individual investors trying to generate consistent small profits for their retirement funds. For many investors, this will prove to be a fool's errand. This is the new retirement reality. So, if you are concerned about your retirement, control what you can: risk levels, asset allocation, costs, and choosing qualified, ethical advisors. Only then can you take the required actions that can help you secure your financial future.

APPENDIX

A variation of this article was published in Barron's, "Where Are the Customers' Advocates?" in the Other Voices section, Aug. 28, 2011.

How Fund Companies Can Accommodate the New Fee Disclosure Rules

By Chuck Epstein

As former SEC Chairman Manuel Cohen taught, "Wall Street rarely moves toward reform unless it is pushed."

While the mutual fund industry wrestles with regulators, consumer groups, independent advisors and Congress about the need for reducing fund fees, disclosure and increased transparency, no one seems to be asking how all this is affecting the industry's customers.

After all, it's their money. While everyone is affected by volatile markets, new regulations, contentious elections, depressed home prices, and sunken portfolios, the fund industry's very visible public intransigence against any type of industry reform should be considered a remarkable political blunder. Not only has this position alienated key professionals involved in the debate–independent financial advisors, pro-shareholder groups, independent trustees–but it's also affecting individual shareholders and even fund company employees.

For this reason, load fund companies should become active and innovative. They should create a new executive-level position of shareholder advocate. The advocate would examine fund activities involving products, sales materials, sales practices, shareholder communications, key account relationships and lobbying to determine how fund company's activities are benefiting shareholders–if at all.

A shareholder advocate could offer a new perspective to counter the build-in slant of selling funds using 12b-1 fees, revenue sharing and selective transparency. Since these practices are being challenged at the national level, it's only fitting that a load-fund company would want to anticipate future changes and be prepared for new rules which would affect its daily operations. Even if any reform is beaten back, the effort will be so contentious and visible that it will further alienate reform-minded investors. The advocate would work to bridge the misalignment of interests that exists between load-fund companies and their customers.

Shareholder advocates would work at the management level and would not be independent board members. While many fund-company boards have independent directors, they are more advisory, rarely implement daily business actions and have limited contact with company staff.

"Independent fund directors have failed as fiduciaries in their legal roles as shareholder watchdogs," says J.A. Haslem, professor emeritus of business at the University of Maryland, in College Park. Alan R. Palmiter, professor of law at Wake Forest University, declares that the 1940 Investment Act, which handed regulatory oversight of mutual-fund advisors to the independent directors rather than to the SEC, "has not provided essential fiduciary protections to fund shareholders."

Independent directors also have not been successful when placed in other roles at major financial institutions. For instance, when independent directors were allowed to sit on the board of the NYSE in the late-1930s, the move was done to restore public confidence in America's capitalist centerpiece, the NYSE, during its most bleak period. This was the time when former NYSE chairman Richard Whitney (who served as NYSE president from 1930-1935), was considered one of the most arrogant foes of federal securities regulation.

Writing in *The House of Morgan*, author Ron Chernow recounts how Whitney "personified the smug arrogance of the ancien regime on Wall Street. When he (Whitney) testified about securities reform before the Senate Banking and Currency Committee in 1932, he lectured the senators on the need for a senatorial pay cut. Opposing creation of the SEC, he (Whitney) told Pecora's investigators, 'You gentlemen are making a great mistake, The (NYSE) Exchange is a perfect institution.'"

Whitney continued to oppose any reform, until eventually SEC Chairman William O. Douglas, who succeeded Joseph P. Kennedy as the first SEC chairman, reached his breaking point. In the fall of 1937, Douglas told NYSE leaders: "The job of regulation's got to be done. It isn't being done now, and, damn it, you're going to do it or we are." With the New Deal steamroller bearing down, NYSE Chairman Charles R. Gay became convinced that this SEC chairman was serious. Gay did what any exchange executive did: He appointed a committee to study reform. In January 1938, the committee recommended "a complete revamping" of the NYSE, including having a full-time paid president, professional staff and non-member governors. (For a complete description of Richard Whitney's subsequent difficulties, including his embezzlement of NYSE funds, see *The House of Morgan: An American Banking Dynasty*, Ron Chernow, pp. 421-429.)

It was in that atmosphere that public governors were installed at the NYSE. The role of public governors was reinforced in 1975 when regulators again mandated a public orientation towards protecting the investing community. Given the authority and shareholder support, an empowered, non-independent director, full-time advocate would be able to change this.

While the advocate idea may be new in the securities industry, they exist in other industries and professions, where they are entrusted with assisting over people who are unable or less sophisticated to make complicated decisions. This situation exists where there is a "standard and care" guideline in the real estate and health care industries, for example, where less sophisticated buyers rely on the professional judgment of trained professionals to provide the best possible advice needed to deliver the best possible long-term result.

In the financial industry, fund companies and advisors polish a professional reputation to attract more business. But the entire industry suffers when a fund company or advisor is cited for breaking regulations because the average shareholder or advisor's customers cannot distinguish among high-quality, medium-quality and unethical or incompetent providers.

This "information asymmetry," according to Yale Law School Professor Jonathan R. Macey, "reduces the market's demand and willingness to pay for financial planners because consumers have less information than producers."

Shareholder advocates would voice employee concerns about their employer's business practices. In my experience at two large fund companies, I heard these concerns voiced privately, but people remained silent in discussions about fees, revenue sharing, the role of wholesalers and other sensitive business practices. They were afraid of losing their jobs.

Silence should not be construed as approval of sales practices. Fear about job loss is commonly translated into poor morale and reduced productivity. Indeed, there is extensive management literature indicating that employees' goals often are not well aligned with those of their employers. Advocates could help bridge this gap.

Advocates would not be popular people inside a fund company. They would have to openly question the viability of the existing load-fund company business model, including sales expenses and the role of wholesalers.

But the public debates over the need for fund reform have become an openly adversarial situation. This has eroded confidence in the investment markets, fund companies, and the quality of professional investment advice.

Fund companies that dare to create shareholder advocates would publicly acknowledge that they are working to bridge this gap and address issues which work against their own customers. Is there even one fund company willing to work for them?

GLOSSARY

Actuary–A specialist in the mathematics of risk, especially as it relates to insurance calculations, such as premiums, reserves, dividends, and insurance and annuity rates. Actuaries work for insurance companies to evaluate applications based on risk. Actuaries have also been the target of many jokes. One involves the question: How do you identify an actuary who is extroverted? The answer: In a crowd, he is the one who talks, while looking at another person's shoes.

Agency–The fiduciary relationship which results from the manifestation of consent by one person to another, so that the other person acts on his behalf and is subject to his control, and consent.

Annuity–A series of periodic payments, usually level in amount or adjusted according to some index, e.g., cost-of-living, that typically continue for the lifetime of the recipient. In contrast, an installment payment is one of a specific number of payments that will be paid whether or not the recipient lives to receive them.

Collective Investment Trusts (CITs)–A commingled or collective fund that is more commonly being found in pension and 401(k) plans. CITs are tax-exempt, pooled investment vehicles maintained by a bank or trust company exclusively for qualified plans, and are subject to banking regulations, not to the Investment Company Act of 1940. As a result, they are less regulated and not registered with the SEC.

Covered Plan–To be ERISA-qualified, the terms "employee welfare benefit plan" and "welfare plan" mean any plan, fund, or program which was established or maintained by an employer, an employee organization, or both, to the extent that the plan, fund or program was established or maintained for the purpose of providing for its participants or their beneficiaries some pension or other benefit.

Defined Benefit (DB)–Commonly known as pension plans, a DB plan is designed to provide participants with a definite benefit at retirement, e.g., a monthly benefit of 20% of compensation upon reaching age 65. Contributions under the plan are determined by reference to the benefits provided, not on the basis of a percentage of compensation.

Defined Contribution (DC)–A defined contribution plan, on the other hand, does not promise a specific amount of benefits at retirement. In these plans, the participant or the employer (or both) contribute to the participant's individual account under the plan, sometimes at a set rate, such as 5 % of their earnings annually. These contributions generally are invested on the participant's behalf. The participant will ultimately receive the balance in their account, which is based on contributions plus or minus investment gains or losses. The value of the account will fluctuate due to changes in the value of investments. Examples of defined contribution plans include 401(k) plans, 403(b) plans, employee stock ownership plans, and profit-sharing plans. The general rules of ERISA apply to each of these types of plans.

Designated Investment Alternative–A designated investment alternative is any investment alternative the plan designates into which participants may direct the investment of their individual account assets. For example, if the plan designates 10 identified mutual funds into which participants may direct their investments, each of the 10 funds is a designated investment alternative. The term does not include a brokerage window, a self-directed brokerage account or similar arrangements permitting participants to select investments beyond the designated investment alternatives. This definition is identical to the definition of the same term used in the July 2010 service provider fee disclosure regulations.

Dodd-Frank Wall Street Reform and Consumer Protection Act–Passed in 2010, the Act seeks to improve accountability and transparency in the financial system, end the "too big to fail" bailouts and protect consumers from abusive financial services practices.

Duty of Care–A fiduciary must discharge their duty with the "care, skill, prudence and diligence under the circumstances then prevailing that a prudent man acting in a like capacity and familiar with such matters would use in the conduct of an enterprise of a like character and wit like aims." This is also known as the Prudent Man Standard.

Duty of Loyalty–A fiduciary must discharge their duties solely in the interest of plan participants. A fiduciary must also avoid conflicts-of-interests when managing plan assets.

Duty to Diversify–A fiduciary must diversify its plan's investments so as to minimize the risk of large losses unless under the circumstances it is clearly not prudent to do so.

Duty of Obedience–A fiduciary must discharge their duties in accordance with the documents and instruments governing the plan as they are consistent with ERISA.

Eligible Indirect Compensation—includes broadly defined, indirect compensation that directly reduces the value of the plan's investments.

ERISA–The Employee Retirement Income Security Act of 1974 is a federal law that sets minimum standards for most voluntarily established pension and health plans in private industry to provide protection for individuals in these plans.

ERISA Section 404(c)—This section of the law states that fiduciaries are not held responsible for investment decisions made by the participants, as long as certain requirements are met. However, this relief does not apply to participants who fail to direct the investment of their assets and are subsequently placed in a default option.

Exclusive Benefit Rule–The fiduciary "must discharge his duties with respect to a plan solely in the interest of the participants and beneficiaries and for the exclusive purpose of: (i) providing benefits...and (ii) defraying reasonable expenses of administering the plan." (Source: 29 U.S.C. §1104 (a)(1)(A).

Exclusive Purpose Rule–A fiduciary must discharge his or her duties for the exclusive purpose of providing benefits of defraying reasonable expenses only. The plan must not pay excessive compensation to its investment and service providers.

FASB (Financial Accounting Standards Board)–Formed in 1973, the FASB has been the designated organization in the private sector for establishing standards of financial accounting that governs the preparation of financial reports by non-governmental entities. Those standards are officially recognized as authoritative by the Securities and Exchange Commission (SEC) and the American Institute of Certified Public Accountants. Such standards are important to the efficient functioning of the economy because decisions about the allocation of resources rely heavily on credible, concise, and understandable financial information.

Fiduciary–ERISA defines a person or entity as a plan fiduciary if that person: (1) exercises any discretionary authority or discretionary control respecting management of the benefits plan, or disposition of its assets; or (2) has any discretionary authority or discretionary responsibility in the administration of the benefits plan.

Financial Advisors (FAs)–FAs work for broker-dealers and are regulated under provisions of the Securities Exchange Act of 1934. FAs receive commissions from securities trading. FAs also recommend suitable investments, which may, or may not be, the best possible investments for their clients.

FINRA–The Financial Industry Regulatory Authority is the largest independent regulator for all securities firms doing business in the United States. FINRA's mission is to protect America's investors by making sure the securities industry operates fairly and honestly. As of 2012, FINRA oversees nearly 4,435 brokerage firms, about 161,450 branch offices and approximately 630,155 registered securities representatives.

Form 5500–Pension plans file a Form 5500, a publicly available document, which is a joint form of the DOL, the IRS, and the Pension Benefit Guaranty Corporation (PBGC). This form reports the status and activity of retirement plans to the Internal Revenue Service (lRS). The IRS uses this form to determine whether a retirement plan is in compliance with all requirements. Form 5500 must be filed with the IRS by the last day of the seventh month following the plan's year-end.

403(b) Plan–A retirement plan similar to a 401(k), but one offered by non-profit organizations, such as universities, schools and charitable organizations, rather than corporations.

Indirect Compensation–This includes revenue sharing, 12b-1 fees, sub-transfer agency fees, administrative services fees, subsidies to TPAs, and so on. It is "indirect" because the expense was not paid from the plan.

Investment Advisor–Any person who, for compensation, engages in the business of advising others either directly or through publications or writings, as to the value of securities or to the advisability of investing in, purchasing, or selling securities.

Law of Large Numbers–The theorem in probability theory that the number of successes increases as the number of experiments increases and approximates the probability times the number of experiments for a large number of experiments.

Mutual Fund Wholesalers–Commission salespeople who sell a family of mutual funds to financial professionals and advisors. Wholesalers are compensated from revenue sharing and 12b-1 fees, which are often cited as being the origins of the conflicts-of-interest that exist between investors and their financial advisors and brokers.

Plan Asset–An asset in a retirement plan that serves as an investment vehicle for participating employees. Plan assets are managed by an investment manager and chosen for their ability to generate appropriate revenue to maintain the plan, as well as their ability to manage risk.

Plan Sponsor–An entity that establishes and maintains a pension or insurance plan. This may be a corporation, labor union, government agency, or nonprofit organization. Plan sponsors must follow government guidelines in the establishment and administration of these plans, including informing plan participants about the financial health of the plan and the benefits available.

Prohibited Transaction–Specified transactions may not be entered into (directly or indirectly) by a party in interest with the plan. Those include, for example, sales or exchanges, leases, and loans between the parties. The DOL may exempt a specific transaction from the prohibited transactions restrictions.

Prudent Man Rule–The standard under which the fiduciary must act. The fiduciary is required to act "with the care, skill, prudence, and diligence under the circumstances then prevailing that a prudent man acting in a like capacity and familiar with such matters would use in the conduct of an enterprise of a like character and with like aims."

Real Wages–A measure of an individual's or nation's purchasing power minus the impact of inflation.

Recordkeeper–Recordkeepers receive the contributions made by employees from the plan sponsor. The recordkeeper also tracks the participants' contribution rates, investment selections and balance. This includes tracking the amount of employer matching contributions, providing account statements, and maintaining the information about any outstanding 401k loan(s) participants might have, such as balance due, monthly payment and interest due.

Registered Investment Advisors (RIAs)–Regulated by the Investment Advisors Act of 1940, RIAs receive fees based on assets managed. They owe a fiduciary standard of care to clients, which requires that they place clients' interests ahead of their own.

Revenue Sharing–Revenue sharing, as defined by the Securities and Exchange Commission, occurs when the investment advisor to a fund, or another affiliate of a fund, makes payments to a broker-dealer. In some cases, the investment advisor may describe those payments as reimbursing the broker-dealer for expenses it incurs in selling the shares. Those payments, regardless of whether they are labeled as reimbursements, may give the broker-dealer a greater incentive to sell the shares of that fund or affiliated funds. Revenue sharing can take many forms. A common means of revenue sharing in the mutual fund industry is the use of 12(b)1 fees. Another common method of revenue sharing between investment management firms and other service providers to retirement or savings plans is an agreement known as a sub-transfer agency agreement.

Roth 401(k)–Since 2006, employers have had the options of offering a Roth 401(k). Under this arrangement, initial contributions are not deductible. But investment earnings accrue tax free and no tax is paid when the money is withdrawn. This arrangement is considered by some to be superior to savings outside a plan because no taxes are ever paid on the investment returns.

Safe Harbor–A legal provision to reduce or eliminate liability as long as good faith is demonstrated.

Securities and Exchange Commission (SEC)–The SEC is the primary federal regulatory agency for the securities industry. Its main responsibility is to promote full disclosure and protect investors from fraudulent and manipulative practices in the securities markets. The SEC enforces, among other acts, the Securities Act of 1933, the Securities Exchange Act of 1934, the Investment Company Act of 1940, the Trust Indentures Act of 1939 and the Investment Advisors Act.

Standard of Care–The degree of prudence that a reasonable man (or person) may be expected to exercise when caring for something

SEC Rule 12b-1—This rule, enacted in 1980, created two types of 12(b)-1 fees: (1) sales commission 12(b)-1 fees, paid to a registered representative for selling mutual funds for an individual or within a plan; and (2) servicing 12(b)-1 fees, paid to a person or entity who services an account after the sale. This rule is partially responsible for the proliferation of mutual funds in individual account plans. 12b-1 charges (which are named for the rule that authorized them) are used to pay the companies and individuals through which investors buy fund shares. As a result, investors are paying those agents indirectly, through charges that reduce their funds' returns.

Third-Party Administrators (TPAs)–An organization, often an insurance company, that processes insurance or benefits claims for employee benefit plans, including pension and 401(k)s. This is considered a form of outsourcing for the plan sponsor.

2006 Pension Protection Act–The Pension Protection Act is the most comprehensive reform of the nation's pension laws since the enactment of the Employee Retirement Income Security Act of 1974 (ERISA, P.L. 93-406.) It establishes new funding requirements for defined benefit pensions and includes reforms that will affect cash balance pension plans, defined contribution plans, and deferred compensation plans for executives and highly compensated employees.

BIBLIOGRAPHY

Abrahamson, Darwin, "Avoiding Fees in 401(k) Plans," Invest n' Retire, June 2005.

Aikman, J.S., *When Prime Brokers Fail*, Bloomberg Press, 2010.

AIMR Annual Conference, Comments of AIMR President and CEO Thomas A. Bowman, CFA, July 2001.

Ackley, Dennis, "401(k) Fee Disclosure for the 'You Never Told Me' Employees," *Society of Human Resource Management*, Feb. 25, 2011.

Alexander, Steve, "Ameriprise workers seek class-action suit on 401(k)," *Minneapolis Star-Tribune*, Sept. 29, 2011.

Alfred, Ryan, "Reviewing the DOL's Final Rule on Participant Fee Disclosure," Brightscope, Oct. 18, 2010.

Loeper, David, *Stop the Retirement Rip-off*, John Wiley, 2009.

Aon Hewitt/Financial Engines, "401(k) Participants Using Professional Investment Help Continue to Do Better Than Those Who Go It Alone," September, 2011.

Beshears, John (Stanford University and National Bureau of Economic Research), James J. Choi (Yale University and NBER), David Laibson (Harvard University and NBER), Brigitte C. Madrian (Harvard University and NBER), "The Availability and Utilization of 401(k) Loans," National Bureau of Economic Research, May 31, 2011.

Bogle, John C., *The Battle for the Soul of Capitalism*, Harper Collins, 2005.

Braverman, Beth, "79% of fund managers didn't beat the S&P," CNNMoney, Feb. 23, 2012.

Brinson, G.P., L.R. Hood and G.I. Beebower, "Determinants of Portfolio Performance," *Financial Analysts Journal*, January/February 1995.

Brown, James Douglas. *An American Philosophy of Social Security: Evolution and Issues.* Princeton University Press, 1972.

Buckman, Carol, "Get Ready for Investment Comparison Charts: U.S. Department of Labor Beefs Up Required Participant Fee Disclosure," Mondaq Labour and Employment, Oct. 26, 2010.

Carlton, Diana, "Justify high rates, health secretary tells execs," *San Francisco Chronicle,* Hearst Washington Bureau, March 5, 2010.

Carosa, Christopher, "Exclusive Interview with Ron Rhoades: Revenue Sharing – Two Hats are Worse than One," Fiduciary News, Jan. 31, 2012.

——"Does New Study Seal the Deal for Fiduciary Standard – or Just Warn Plan Sponsors?" Fiduciary News, Jan. 19, 2011.

CBS News, "Trapped in Unemployment," 60 Minutes broadcast, Feb. 26, 2012.

Cendrowski, Scott, "Is your 401(k) ripping you off?" CNN Money, June 25, 2012.

CFA Centre for Financial Market Integrity/Business Roundtable Institute for Corporate Ethics, "Breaking the Short-Term Cycle," 2006.

Chernow, Ron, *The House of Morgan: An American Banking Dynasty,* Grove Press, 1990.

Christie, William G., Jeffrey H. Harris, Paul H. Schultz, "Why Did NASDAQ Market Makers Stop Avoiding Odd-Eighth Quotes?" *Journal of Finance,* vol. 49, no. 5, December 1994.

Constable, Simon, "It's Not Your Fault Your Fund Can't Keep Up," *Wall Street Journal,* April 8, 2012, p.D3

Court, Jamie, "Will Patients Beat Blue Shield Again... This Time With the First Online Ballot Petition for Rate Regulation?" *Huffington Post,* Feb. 8, 2012.

Coile, Courtney, Kevin Milligan, What Happens to Household Portfolios After Retirement?, Center for Retirement Research at Boston College, November 2006.

Cowdrick, Edward. 1928. Pensions: A Problem of Management. New York: American Management Association, Annual Convention Series, No. 75.

Crook, Clive, "Crook: U.S. Retirees Face a Private-Savings Crisis," Bloomberg, March 13, 2012.

BIBLIOGRAPHY

Dalbar, "ERISA 404(a)(5): A Game Changer? – 401(k) Participant Disclosure Requirements Could Reconstruct the Industry, October 2010.

Davidson, Joe, "Federal workers to pay more for health care," *Washington Post*, Oct. 1, 2010.

Deloitte Consulting, "Inside the Structure of Defined Contribution/401(k) Plan Fees: A Study Assessing the Mechanics of the 'All-In' Fee," Conducted by Deloitte Consulting LLP for the Investment Company Institute, November 2011.

——"Annual 401(k) Benchmarking Survey, 2011: Plan sponsors and providers work at closing the retirement readiness gap while getting ready for new fee disclosure regulations," 2011.

Domhoff, William G., "Who Rules America: The Unexpected Origins of the Social Security Act of 1935," Sociology Department, University of California at Santa Cruz, 2009.

Drinker Biddle, "How You Are Paying What You Don't Know: A Primer on Indirect Mutual Fund Payments," Feb. 1, 2008.

——"Excessive 401(k) Plan Fees and Costs: The Coming Storm in ERISA litigation," Feb. 1, 2010.

Ellis, Charles, Financial Analysts Journal, "Investment Management Fees Are (Much) Higher Than You Think," May/June 2012.

——Winning the Loser's Game, McGraw Hill, 2008.

Epstein, Chuck, "Wall Street's Double Standard," Investing Online, January 1995.

——"Are Target-Date Funds the Ideal Default Investment Choice?," Mutualfundreform.com, Feb. 11 2012.

——"How Housing Wealth Affects Retirement Planning," Principal Financial, June 2008.

—— "Financial Industry Lobbyists Move to Delay Investor Protections," Mutualfundreform.com, May 1, 2012.

—— *Managed Futures in the Institutional Portfolio*, John Wiley & Sons, 1992.

——"New 401(k) Fee Disclosure and Revenue Sharing Disclosures Could Re-Shape DC Plans,"

Mutualfundreform.com, Dec. 23, 2011.

———"Revenue Sharing Taints 401(k) Plans," Mutualfundreform.com, Oct. 29, 2012.

———"The DOL: An Individual Investor's Best Friend," Mutualfundreform.com, April 26, 2012.

———"Thinking the Unthinkable: Selling Mutual Funds Without Revenue Sharing, Mutualfundreform.com, March 2012.

———"Why Fee Disclosures Will Be Traumatic for Many 401(k) Plans," Mutualfundreform.com, Nov. 30, 2011.

Fabio, Michelle, "Can Your Employer Make Money on Your Death? Corporate-Owned Life Insurance Policies," LegalZoom, September 2010.

Faucher, Joe, Reish Luftman Reicher & Cohen, "Spate of Class Action Lawsuits Targets 401(k) Fees and Expenses," *ERISA Litigation Bulletin*, Oct. 6, 2006.

Federal Reserve Flow of Funds Accounts of the United States, cited in Investment News, June 2, 2008, p. 26.

Fletcher, Winston, *Powers of Persuasion: The Inside Story of British Advertising*, Oxford University Press, 2008,

Franham, Martin, Purvi Sevak, "Housing Wealth and Retirement Timing," University of Michigan Retirement Research Center, October 2007.

Frazier, Ian, "Out of the Bronx: Private equity and the cookie factory," *The New Yorker*, Feb. 6, 2012.

Friedman, Hershey H., "Placing a Stumbling Block Before the Blind Person: An In-Depth Analysis," *Jewish Law Articles*, 2002.

Georgia State University, "The Replacement Ratio Study," 1997.

Gilani, Shah, "The New Abnormal: Permanently Engineered Market Volatility," Money Morning, Aug. 19, 2011.

Glazer, David A., "The effect of commission versus non-commission benefits on customer value: the case of life insurance policy performance," Financial Services Review 16 (2007), p. 135–153.

Grant, H., Insurance Reform: Consumer Action in the Progressive Era, (1979) as cited in "Statutory Prohibitions on the Negotiation of Insurance Agent Commissions: Substantive Due Process Review Under State Constitutions," Robert H. Jerry II and Reginald Robinson, *Ohio State Law Journal*, Vol. 51, No. 4, 1990.

Greenhouse, Steve and Reed Abelson "Wal-Mart Cuts Some Health Care Benefits," *New York Times*, Oct. 20, 2011.

Hanson, Joyce, "401(k)s to Overtake Pensions as Primary Retirement Vehicle in 2012: State Street 'Leakage' from DC plans threatens employee savings during job switches," AdvisorOne, Jan. 26, 2012.

Hartmann, Thom, *Screwed*, Berrett-Koehler Publishers, Inc., 2006.

Henry Kaiser Family Foundation, "Average Annual Premiums for Family Health Benefits Top $15,000 in 2011, Up 9 %, Substantially More than the Growth in Worker's Wages, Benchmark Employer Survey Finds," Sept. 27, 2011.

Hiltzik, Michael, "Mortgage settlement is great–for politicians and banks, *Los Angeles Times*, Feb. 11, 2012.

Hutcheson, Matthew D., "Uncovering and Understanding Hidden Fees In Qualified Retirement Plans," The *University of Illinois Elder Law Journal*, Third Edition, Fall 2007. An insightful, historic paper which deserves attention for presenting an early discussion of the hidden costs and expenses in 401(k) plans.

Israelsen, Craig, and Joseph Nagengast, "Popping the Hood IV, 2011: An Analysis of Target Date Families," BrightScope, Inc. and Target Date Analytics, Oct. 18, 2011.

Jackson, Nancy Mann, "What To Look For in Your New 401(k) Report," Nancy Mann Jackson, Second Act, You. Part Two, Jan. 18, 2012.

Jaffe, Charles, "Fund Fees Don't Always Mean Better Business Practices," *Reading Eagle*, Jan. 16, 2005.

John Hancock, "John Hancock Study of 401(K) Participants Investment Outcomes Reveals Common Investing Behaviors," PR Newswire, October, 2007.

Kasina, "Trends in Wholesaler Compensation," January 2006.

Koenig, David, "Feds pressure American Airlines to save pensions," Associated Press, Feb. 1, 2012.

Kopcke, Richard W., Francis M. Vitagliano, and Zhenya S. Karamcheva, "Reducing Costs of 401(k) Plans with ETFs and Commingled Trusts," Center for Retirement Research, July 2010.

——"Fees and Trading Costs of Equity Mutual Funds in 401(k) Plans and Potential Savings from ETFs and Commingled Trusts,"

Boston College, Center for Retirement Research, November 2009, WP#2009-27.

Krantz, Matt, "Many have little to no savings as retirement looms," *USA Today*, Dec. 4, 2011.

Kristof, Kathy, "Coming Up: The True Cost of Your 401(k)," *Kiplinger's Personal Finance*, p. 12, April 2012.

Lauricell, Tom, "Spitzer Aims At Another Mark: Fee Disclosure," *Wall Street Journal*, Fund Track, Oct. 10, 2006.

Lessig, Lawrence, *Republic, Lost: How Money Corrupts Congress–and a Plan to Stop It*, Twelve, 2011.

Leuchtenburg, William E. *The Supreme Court Reborn: The Constitutional Revolution in the Age of Roosevelt.* Oxford University Press, 1995.

Liu, John, "Are New Yorkers Ready for Retirement?" New York City Comptroller, January 2012.

Lusardi Annamarie, Olivia S. Mitchell, Baby Boomer Retirement Security: The Roles of Planning, Financial Literacy, and Housing Wealth, Michigan Retirement Research Center, University of Michigan, April 2006.

Maiello, Michael, "Ignore Morningstar's Stars," Forbes.com, Jan. 30, 2009.

Main, Carla, "Mutual Fund Fees, Watchdog List, Helaba Stress Test, CDS Probe: Compliance," Bloomberg, May 2, 2011.

Mensack, Mark D., "Caveat Emptor for 401(k) Plan Sponsors," InvestorOne, May 18, 2011.

Mishel, Lawrence and Heidi Shierholz, "The sad but true story of wages in America," Economic Policy Institute, March 15, 2011.

Miller, Mark, "Target date funds get better and bigger," Reuters Money, Oct. 18, 2011.

Montopoli, Brian, "Will 'political intelligence' stay in the dark?' CBS News, Feb. 9, 2012.

Morrissey, Janet, Still Searching for a bottom in the housing crisis, *Investment News*, p. 50, June 9, 2008.

Morningstar, "What Is Your 401(k) Really Costing You?' The Short Answer, March 13, 2012.

Mui, Ylan Q., "Higher prices, stagnant wages chip at savings rate," Washington Post, Nov. 23, 2011.

Munnell, Alicia H., Laura Quinby, and Anthony Webb, "What's the tax advantages of 401(k)s?" Center for Retirement Research, Boston College, February 2012, No. 12-4.

Munnell Alice H., Mauricio Soto, Jean-Pierre Aubry, Do People Plan to Tap Their Home Equity in Retirement? Center for Retirement Research at Boston College, May 2007.

My Money Blog, "More Statistics on 401(k) Target Date Retirement Funds," March 15, 2012.

Nunberg, H. and D. P. Lackey, "Ethical reflections on company-owned life insurance," *Journal of Business Ethics*, 2008, Volume: 80, Issue: 4, Pages: 845-854.

O'Connor, Sandra Day, Stanley Prusiner, Ken Dychwald, "The Age of Alzheimer's," *New York Times*, Oct. 27, 2010.

O'Neil Institute for Global and National Health, "The McCarran-Ferguson Act of 1945: Time to be Repealed," Oct. 22, 2009.

Olshan, Jeremy, "Nobel Prize-Winning 401(k) Advice," Smart Money, Feb. 11, 2012.

———— "Secrets of the 401(k) Millionaires: They don't necessarily have higher salaries, or the investing IQs of Warren Buffett, advisors say," *Smart Money*, Feb. 8, 2012.

Phipps, Jennie L., "Union retirees take a hit," Bankrate.com, Oct. 4, 2011.

Pisani, Bob, "When Will ETFs Break Into 401(k) Business?" CNBC, Jan. 24, 2011.

Plansponsor.com, "Plan Sponsors Should Not Delay Preparing 404(a)(5)," April 6, 2012.

————"Employer to Pay for Failing to Monitor RK Costs," April 3, 2012.

————"Delayed Retirement, Early Withdrawals Results from Economic Downturn," May 14, 2008.

Plein, Neil, "401(k) Manifesto–Attributes of the Ideal Plan," Invest n' Retire, Dec. 15, 2011.

————"2012 Study of Indexing in DC Plans," Invest n' Retire, March 7, 2012.

————"Asset Allocation Models Are The Only Way Forward For 401(k)'s," Invest n' Retire, July, 2011.

Polek, Gregory, "Transport Workers Union, Objecting to AMR's Hiring of Bain, Picket Romney Campaign," <u>AIN Air Transport Perspective</u>, Jan. 30, 2012.

Pozen, Robert and Theresa Hamacher, The Fund Industry: How Your Money Is Managed, Wiley Finance, 2011.

Rand Corporation, InvestmentInsights, BGI.

Randstad Workmonitor Global Press Report: Employee Outlook for 2012: A Mixed Picture," Q4 2011, November 2011.

Reish, Fred, Bruce Ashton and Debra Davis, "The DOL's Proposed 408(b)(2) Regulation: Impact of the Mandated Disclosures on Registered Investment Advisors (RIAs)," Reish, Luftman, Reicher and Cohen, Feb. 4, 2008.

Reuters, "Bernanke urges action to heal U.S. housing markets," Feb. 10, 2012.

Riese, Tom, "Why your employees may balk at their 401(k) fees," *Washington Post*, March 13, 2012.

Riley, Charles, Household wealth down 23% in 2 years–Fed," CNNMoney, March 28, 2011.

Roland Criss, "A Different Perspective on the New DOL Regulations: What "Fee Disclosure" Rules Really Mean for Plan Sponsors," 2011 Roland|Criss Fiduciary Services.

Senior Network, "A Brief History of the Pensioners Movement," Pensions 100, http://www.pension100.co.uk/index.html.

Sentier Research, "Household Income Trends During Recession and Economic Recovery," Oct. 10, 2011.

Shilling, Gary A., "Will U.S. Avoid Recession in 2012? (Part 1)." Bloomberg News, April 9, 2012.

Smith, Ann Kates, "What's Lurking in Your Fund," *Kiplinger's Personal Finance*, September 2011.

Spectrem's Millionaire Corner, "401(K) Plan Participants Using Almost Double the Investment Funds Significant Growth in Past 15 years," May 18, 2001.

Staley, Oliver, "England Student Debt Unprecedented as Government Shifts Funding," Bloomberg, April 23, 2012.

Starkman, Dean, "What Is Financial Journalism For?" *Columbia Journalism Review*, January 13, 2009.

Stephens, Mitchell, History of Newspapers, 1994.

Toth, Robert, "Annuity Investment Accounts and 408(b)(2)," *Business of Benefits*, Feb. 19, 2011.

Taub, Stephen, "NYSE Goes Public, Goes Electronic," CFO.com, April 21, 2005.

Triche, Ronald J., Trucker Huss and Brian A. Montanez, "A Guide to Retirement Plan Fees & Expenses," Multnomah Group, February 2010. A good summary of all the fees associated with the menu of possible investments in a 401(k) plans, including insurance products, wrap accounts and annuities.

U.S. Department of Labor, "Final Rule to Improve Transparency of Fees and Expenses to Workers in 401(k)-Type Retirement Plans," U.S. Department of Labor, Employee Benefits Security Administration, Oct. 14, 2010.

———"A Look At 401(k) Plan Fees, http://www.dol.gov/ebsa/publications/401k_employee.html

U.S. Government Accountability Office, "401(K) Plans" Improved Regulation Could Better Protect Participants from Conflicts of Interest." Report to the Ranking Member, Committee on Education and the Workforce, House of Representatives, January 2011.

Venneberg, Donald L., and Barbara Welss Eversole, "The Boomer Retirement Time Bomb," ABC-CLIO, 2010.

Vicci, Gino, "Critics Weigh in on High Frequency Trading on Flash Crash Anniversary," *Huffington Post*, May 9, 2012.

Weller, Christian, "The Consequences of Conservatism," Center for American Progress, March 25, 2011.

Winerman, Lea, "Workers Paying More for Health Insurance as Cash-Strapped Companies Shift Costs," PBS, Sept. 2, 2011.

Yarrow, Andrew L., "The Big Postwar Story: Abundance and the Rise of Economic Journalism." *Journalism History*, Summer 2006.

FOOTNOTES

1. Public Broadcasting Service: Frontline with John C. Bogle, the Vanguard Group, Feb. 7, 2006.

Introduction
1. Federal Reserve study cited in "Household wealth down 23% in 2 years–Fed," CNNMoney, Charles Riley, March 28, 2011.
2. "The U.S. Retirement Market, Second Quarter 2011," Investment Company Institute, September 2011.
3. "401(k)s to Overtake Pensions as Primary Retirement Vehicle in 2012: State Street 'Leakage' from DC plans threatens employee savings during job switches," Joyce Hanson, *AdvisorOne*, Jan. 26, 2012.
4. "The sad but true story of wages in America," Economic Policy Institute, Lawrence Mishel and Heidi Shierholz, March 15, 2011.
5. "Higher prices, stagnant wages chip at savings rate," *Washington Post*, Ylan Q. Mui, Nov. 23, 2011.
6. *Screwed*, Thom Hartmann, Berrett-Koehler Publishers, Inc., 2006.

Chapter 1: A Brief History of Retirement and the Fiduciary Standard
1. Academics frame the pension question in terms of an economic model based on wealth accumulation. To make it more complicated, this model consists of making savings and consumption decisions "in a forward looking context." This requires that any young worker optimize their savings during their working years to get a discounted lifetime expected utility" which factors in essential unknowns, such as expected

salary, future pensions, social security benefits, inflation rates, retirement ages of the wage earner and their partner, and family needs, including health conditions, lifestyle and marital status over time. Cited in Annamaria Lusardi, Olivia S. Mitchell, *Baby Boomer Retirement Security: the Roles of Planning, Financial Literacy, and Housing Wealth*, Michigan Retirement Research Center, University of Michigan, April 2006.

2. Senior Network, "A Brief History of the Pensioners Movement," Pensions 100. http://www.pension100.co.uk/index.html.

3. "Who Rules America: The Unexpected Origins of the Social Security Act of 1935," G. William Domhoff, Sociology Department, University of California at Santa Cruz, 2009.

4. William E. Leuchtenburg, *The Supreme Court Reborn: The Constitutional Revolution in the Age of Roosevelt*. New York, NY: Oxford University Press, 1995.

5. Domhoff, "*Who Rules America.*"

6. Sass 1997, p. 65. Klein 2003.

7. Ibid.

8. "The Risk Pool," Malcolm Gladwell, *The New Yorker*, Aug. 28, 2006.

9. Private conversation with author.

10. U.S. Bureau of Labor Statistics, Union Membership Data from the National Directory Series/1 Table A. 1930-1980.

11. Miller, M. and F. Modigliani, 1961. "Dividend policy, growth, and the valuation of shares." *Journal of Business*, 34, (4), 411-433.

12. Corporate Pension Funds Suffer Worst Year Ever in 2002; Wilshire Associates Study Finds 89 Percent of Plans Underfunded," May 14, 2003, PR Newswire. www.PBGC.gov

13. Ellen E. Schultz, *Retirement Heist: How Companies Plunder and Profit from the Nest Eggs of American Workers*, Portfolio/Penguin, New York, 2011, p. 23.

14. Shultz, p. 25

15. "401 (k)s to Overtake Pensions as Primary Retirement Vehicle in 2012: State Street 'Leakage' from DC plans threatens employee savings during job switches," Joyce Hanson, *AdvisorOne*, Jan. 26, 2012.

16. Hanson, *AdvisorOne*

FOOTNOTES

Chapter 2: Why Fund Expenses Matter

1. "The Tyranny of Compounding Fees: Are Mutual Funds Bleeding Retirement Accounts Dry?" *Stewart Neufeld, Journal of Financial Planning*, December 2011.
2. *Powers of Persuasion: The Inside Story of British Advertising.* Winston Fletcher, Oxford University Press, 2008, p. 176.
3. "How 401(k)s are failing millions of Americans," *The Week*, April 12, 2012. This same article notes that the average balance in the nation's 50 million 401(k) accounts is just over $60,000, according to the Employee Benefit Research Institute. People who are within 10 years of retirement have saved an average of only $78,000; more than a third of them have less than $25,000; and over half of U.S. workers have no retirement plan at all.
4. Hutcheson, p. 333
5. "What Is Your 401(k) Really Costing You? The Short Answer," Morningstar. March 13, 2012.
6. "How 401(k)s are failing millions of Americans," *The Week*, April 12, 2012.
7. "What Is Your 401(k) Really Costing You?" Morningstar, p. 146.
8. "A Look at 401(k) Plan Fees," U.S. Department of Labor, revised October 2010.
9. "Reducing Costs of 401(k) Plans with ETFs and Commingled Trusts," Richard W. Kopcke, Francis M. Vitagliano, and Zhenya S. Karamcheva, Center for Retirement Research, July 2010.
10. "401(k)s to Overtake Pensions as Primary Retirement Vehicle in 2012: State Street 'Leakage' from DC plans threatens employee savings during job switches," Joyce Hanson, *AdvisorOne*, Jan. 26, 2012.
11. Fisher, p. 32
12. "Get Ready to Reduce Retirement Expenses," Emily Brandon, U.S. News Money, March 16, 2010.
13. "How to Take Advantage of New 401(k) Fee Disclosures–Workers can use this fee information to build a bigger nest egg and maybe even retire sooner," Emily Brandon, *U.S. News and World Report,* Jan. 30, 2012. "How Target-Date Fund Fees Impact Retirement Income, Emily Brandon, U.S. News Money, April 6, 2010.

14. "Mutual Fund Fees, Watchdog List, Helaba Stress Test, CDS Probe: Compliance," Bloomberg, Carla Main, May 2, 2011.
15. "Plan Sponsors Lack Knowledge of Revenue-Sharing Fees," *Society of Human Resource Management*, Stephen Miller, Jan. 16, 2012.
16. "2012 Defined Contribution Trends Survey: Where Have We Come from and What Lies Ahead, Callan Associates.
17. "Plan Sponsors Lack Knowledge of Revenue-Sharing Fees," Society of Human Resource Management, Stephen Miller, Jan. 16, 2012.
18. Hutcheson, p. 364
19. "Mutual Fund Fees, Watchdog List, Helaba Stress Test, CDS Probe: Compliance," Bloomberg, Carla Main, May 2, 2011.
20. Financial Industry Regulatory Authority (FINRA) Web site, www.finra.org.
21. "BrightScope's Transaction Cost Algorithm: Helping Fiduciaries Understand and Discharge Their Fiduciary Duties," Brightscope, June 24, 2009.
22. Ibid.
23. "False Discoveries in Mutual Fund Performance: Measuring Luck in Estimated Alphas," Barras, Laurent, Scaillet, O., Wermers, Russ, March, 2008, as cited in 401(k) Manifesto, Plein.
24. Karceski, Livingston, and O'Neal 2004; Edelen, Evans, and Kadlec 2007.
25. Deloitte 2009a
26. "Fees and Trading Costs of Equity Mutual Funds in 401(k) Plans and Potential Savings from ETFs and Commingled Trusts," Richard W. Kopcke, Francis M. Vitagliano, and Zhenya S. Karamcheva.
27. "79% of fund managers didn't beat the S&P," CNNMoney, Beth Braverman, Feb. 23, 2012.
28. "It's Not Your Fault Your Fund Can't Keep Up," Simon Constable, *Wall Street Journal*, April 8, 2012, p.D3.
29. "How To Take Advantage of New 401(k) Fee Disclosures—Workers can use this fee information to build a bigger nest egg and maybe even retire sooner." Emily Brandon, U.S. News and World Report, Jan. 30, 2012.

30. "Mutual Fund Fees," Watchdog List, Helaba Stress Test, CDS Probe: Compliance," Bloomberg, Carla Main, May 2, 2011.
31. "Plan Sponsors Lack Knowledge of Revenue Sharing Fees," Society of Human Resources Management, Stephen Miller, Jan. 16, 2012.
32. Retirement Heist, Schultz

Chapter 3: The Power of Disclosure: Introduction to the DOL's 2012 Fee Regulations
1. Deloitte Touche Tohmatsu Limited, 2001.
2. "Are New Yorkers Ready for Retirement?" New York City Comptroller John Liu, January 2012.
3. Ibid.
4. *Paychecks for Life*, Charles D. Epstein, 2012, p. 20
5. Education Portal, http://education-portal.com/academy/lesson/opportunity-cost-definition-real-world-examples.html.
6. "ERISA 404(a)(5): A Game Changer?–401(k) Participant Disclosure Requirements Could Reconstruct the Industry," Dalbar, October 2010.
7. "Report of a possible delay in DOL's fee disclosure rule sparks apprehension among advisors and industry observers," *RIA Biz*, Lisa Shidler, Jan. 5, 2012.
8. "$2.7 trillion 401(k) market source," *RIA Biz*, Sara Hansard, March 3, 2010.
9. "Why the DOL's massive new 401(k) disclosure requirements are a 'very, very big deal'" Elizabeth MacBride, *RIA Biz*, Oct. 15, 2010.
10. "401(k) Plan Participants Using Almost Double the Investment Funds, Significant Growth in Past 15 years," Spectrem's Millionaire Corner, May 18, 2001.
11. "401(k) Plan Participants: Characteristics, Contributions and Account Activity," ICI Research Series, Spring 2010.
12. "How 401(k)s are failing millions of Americans," *The Week*, April 12, 2012.
13. "401(k) Fee Disclosure for the 'You Never Told Me' Employees," *Society of Human Resource Management*, Dennis Ackley, Feb. 25, 2011.

14. "Reviewing the DOL's Final Rule on Participant Fee Disclosure," Ryan Alfred, Brightscope, Oct. 18, 2010.
15. Hutcheson, p. 328. Taken from "Mutual Funds: Trading Practices and Abuses That Harm Investors," Hearing Before the Subcommittee on Financial Management, The Budget, and International Security of the Sub-Committee on Governmental Affairs, 108th Cong. 3 (2003) Statement of Sen. Peter Fitzgerald, Chairman, Subcommittee on Financial Management, The Budget, and International Security.
16. "A Look at 401(k) Plan Fees," U.S. Department of Labor, revised October 2010.
17. "Why Active Investing is a Negative Sum Game," Eugene F. Fama and Kenneth R. French, Fama-French Forum, June 3, 2009.
18. "State of Financial Services Industry," Tiburon CEO Summit XXI, Oct. 12, 2011.
19. "How 401(k)s are failing millions of Americans," *The Week*, April 12, 2012.
20. "The Consequences of Conservatism," Christian E. Weller, Center for American Progress, March 25, 2011.
21. The housing bubble evaporated huge swaths of the nation's wealth, but it did not impact all income levels equally. A study by Sylvia Allegretto found that "on average, the top 20% lost 16.0% and the bottom 80% lost 25.1% of their total wealth in 2008 and 2009. Average wealth of the bottom 80% was just $62,900 in 2009—a drop-off of $40,900 from 2007 and slightly less, in inflation-adjusted terms, than it was more than a quarter-century ago in 1983." The State of Working America's Wealth 2011, EPI Briefing Paper #292, p. 7.
22. *Republic, Lost: How Money Corrupts Congress—and a Plan to Stop It*, Lawrence Lessig, Twelve, 2011, p 83.
23. Dalbar
24. Private conversation on LinkedIn
25. "Annuity Investment Accounts and 408(b)(2)" by Robert Toth, *Business of Benefits*, Feb. 19, 2011.
26. "United States: U.S. Department Of Labor Releases FAQs On Implementation of Participant-Level Fee Disclosures," May 29, 2012.

FOOTNOTES

27. "Placing a Stumbling Block Before the Blind Person: An In-Depth Analysis," Hershey H. Friedman, PhD., Jewish Law Articles, 2002.
28. U.S. Department of Labor, Employee Benefits Security Administration, February 2012.
29. "Plan Sponsors Should Not Delay Preparing for 404(a)(5)," Plansponsor.com, April 6, 2012.
30. "Employer to Pay for Failing to Monitor RK Costs," Plansponsor.com, April 3, 2012.
31. "Changes to Final Disclosure Rule," U.S. Department of Labor, Employee Benefits Security Administration, February 2012
32. Employee Benefit Research Institute, "History of 401(k) Plans: An Update," February 2005, as quoted in 401(k) Manifesto–Attributes of the Ideal Plan, Neil Plein, Invest n' Retire, Dec. 15, 2011.
33. "Study of 401(k) Plan Fees and Expenses," Pension and Welfare Benefits Administration, April, 1998, as cited in 401(k) Manifesto, Neil Plein.
34. "Excessive 401(k) Plan Fees and Costs: The Coming Storm in ERISA Litigation?" published in the *ERISA Controversy Newsletter*, Joe Faucher (of the law firm Reish Luftman Reicher & Cohen.)
35. "The Age of Alzheimer's," Sandra Day O'Connor, Stanley Prusiner, Ken Dychwald, *New York Times*, Oct. 27, 2010
36. "401(k) Participants' Awareness and Understanding of Fees," AARP, February 2011.
37. "Determining Whether 401(k) Fees are Reasonable: Are Disclosure Requirements Adequate?" AARP Policy Institute, September 2008, as cited in "401(k) Participants' Awareness and Understanding of Fees," February 2011, AARP.
38. "Will U.S. Avoid Recession in 2012? (Part 1)" A. Gary Shilling, Bloomberg News, April 9, 2012.
39. "My 9 Rules for Picking Mutual Funds," Steven Goldberg, *Kiplinger*, May 4, 2011.
40. "What's Lurking in Your Fund," Kiplinger's Personal Finance, September 2011, Anne Kates Smith, p. 32. "Rising Rates: A Case for Active Bond Investing?" Vanguard Research, August 2011.
41. Ibid, p. 32.

42. "Determining the True Cost of Retirement Service Industry" FEI Institute, December 2001

43. "More Statistics on 401(k) Target Date Retirement Funds," My Money Blog, March 15, 2012.

44. G.P. Brinson, L.R. Hood and G.I. Beebower, "Determinants of Portfolio Performance," *Financial Analysts Journal*, January/February 1995.

45. "Defined Contribution/401(k) Fee Study: A Study Assessing the Mechanics of What Drives the All-In Fee," Deloitte-Investment Company Institute, updated June 2009.

46. "Ric Edelman: Mutual Fund Era End in Sight," Oliver Ludwig, *Index Universe*, May 15, 2012.

47. This book contains references to numerous studies on the ill-effects of fees on net investor returns. One of the most cited comes from the U.S. Department of Labor, "A Look At 401(k) Plan Fees," October, 2010. Separately, Burton Malkiel noted that costs alone mark the prime difference between active and passive management returns, so "after costs, passive managers will outperform most active managers." Cited in "Passive Investment Strategies and Efficient Markets," *European Financial Management*, vol. 9, no. 1, 2003, 1-10, p. 3.

48. "Target date funds get better and bigger," Mark Miller, Reuters Money, October 18, 2011.

49. "Popping the Hood IV, 2011: An Analysis of Target Date Families," Craig Israelsen and Joseph Nagengast, BrightScope, Inc. and Target Date Analytics, Oct. 18, 2011.

50. Popping the Hood III, page v.

51. "Recovery in Target Date Funds", Joe C. Nagengast, *Target Data Analytics*, February 2010.

52. Winning the Loser's Game, Charles Ellis, McGraw Hill, 2010, p. 2.

53. "Investment Management Fees Are (Much) Higher Than You Think," Charles Ellis, Financial Analysts Journal, May/June 2012.

54. Ibid.

55. "Is your 401(k) ripping you off?" CNN Money, Scott Cendrowski, June 25, 2012.

56. "Determining the True Cost of Retirement Service Industry, Insights from McHenry Consulting Group," FEI Research Foundation, December 2001, p. 4.

57. Hutcheson, p. 326

58. "401(k) Plans Improved Regulation Could Better Protect Participants from Conflicts of Interest." Report to the Ranking Member, Committee on Education and the Workforce, House of Representatives, U.S. Government Accountablity Office, January 2011.33 "SEC Proposes Measures to Improve Regulation of Fund Distribution Fees and Provide Better Disclosure for Investors," SEC, press release, July 21, 2010.

59. "Mutual Funds Hike Short-Term Redemption Fees," Jonas Max Ferris, Feb. 16, 2004, as quoted in "Avoiding Redemption Fees in 401(k) Plans, Darwin Abrahamson, June 2005, Invest n' Retire.

60. Fred Reish, *The Starting Point: A Shift in Focus for the 401(k), Plan Sponsor*, June 2006, as quoted in Hutcheson, p. 341.

61. T. Harrison, "Understanding the behavior of financial services consumers: a research agenda," **Journal of Financial Services Marketing**, 8, 6-9-2003, as cited in "The effect of commission versus non-commission benefits on customer value: the case of life insurance performance," David A. Glazer, Financial Services Review 16, (2007) p. 135-153.

62. As quoted in "Investment Professionals: Are You Earning Your Keep?" Kurt Schacht, CFA Institute, Oct. 26, 2011.

63. Ibid.

64. Personal e-mail from manager.

65. "Breaking the Short-Term Cycle," CFA Centre for Financial Market Integrity/ Business Roundtable Institute for Corporate Ethics, 2006.

66. "$135 Billion Redeemed From U.S. Equity Mutual Funds In 2011, 34 Of 35 Consecutive Weekly Outflows," Tyler Durdenon, *Zerohedge*, Dec. 29, 2011.

67. "2011 ETF Inflows Twice That of Mutual Funds," Index Universe, Matt Hougan and Olly Ludwig, Jan. 13, 2012.

68. "Why Fees Matter for 401(k) Plan Fiduciaries, But Not Defined Benefit Pension Plans," *Smart Investor*, June 20, 2011.

69. Cited in Hutchinson and sourced as *Cf.* Mark R. Paul & Charles A.A. Whitefoord, *All Buyouts Are Not the Same: It Can Be Different in England, Business Law Today*, March.–April. 2000.
70. "A Different Perspective in the New DOL Regulations: What 'Fee Disclosure' Rules Really Mean to Plan Sponsors," Roland-Criss, 2010.
71. *Federal Register*, July 16, 2010.
72. Roland Criss
73. Ibid.
74. Ibid.
75. Stephen Winks interview, Jan. 31, 2012.
76. "Exclusive Interview with Ron Rhoades: Revenue Sharing–Two Hats are Worse than One," *Fiduciary News*, Christopher Carosa, Jan. 31, 2012.
77. "Is Your 401(k) Ripping You Off?" CNN Money, Scott Cendrowski, June 25, 2012.
78. Kasina, Research, 2006.
79. Hutcheson. p. 351.
80. Ibid.
81. Chris Burand, "Provide Good Service to Set Your Agency Apart," *American Agent & Broker*, Oct.10, 2002, p. 74; (quoting Scott Adams) as quoted in Hutcheson. p. 351.
82. McHenry Consulting Group, "Revenue Sharing in the 401(k) Marketplace: Whose Money Is It?" (2001).
83. Hutcheson, p. 328.
84. "New Rules Will Clarify 401(k) Fees," Kathy Kristof, *Kiplinger's Personal Finance*, April 2012, p. 12.
85. "Exclusive Interview with Ron Rhoades: Revenue Sharing–Two Hats are Worse than One," *Fiduciary News*, Christopher Carosa, Jan. 31, 2012.
86. "Determining the True Cost of Retirement Service Industry," Insights from McHenry Consulting Group, FEI Research Foundation, December 2001, p. 4.
87. **The Fund Industry: How Your Money Is Managed**, Robert Pozen and Theresa Hamacher, Wiley Finance, 2011, p. 392.
88. Pozen and Hamacher, p. 510.

Chapter 4: The Great Wealth Transfer and Wealth Destruction
1. *Retirement Heist,* Ellen Schultz, Portfolio-Penguin, 2011, p. 204.
2. Ibid
3. Ibid., p. 4.
4. "Executive Pensions Eclipse Years on the Job," David Cay Johnson, *New York Times,* Dec. 17, 2002.
5. Schultz, p. 202.
6. "Out of the Bronx: Private equity and the cookie factory," Ian Frazier, *The New Yorker,* Feb. 6, 2012, p. 57.
7. Schultz, p. 57.
8. Schultz, p. 131.
9. Nunberg and Lackey, p. 1.
10. "Can Your Employer Make Money on Your Death? Corporate-Owned Life Insurance Policies," Michelle Fabio, LegalZoom, September 2010.
11. NYLEX Benefits Web site.
12. "Ethical reflections on company-owned life insurance," H. Nurnberg, D. P. Lackey, *Journal of Business Ethics,* 2008, Volume: 80, Issue: 4, pages: 845-854.
13. Martin, 2004, as quoted in Nunberg and Lackey, p. 1.
14. "State workers to pay more for health benefits," *Stateline,* Melissa Maynard, May 25, 2011.
15. "Justify high rates, health secretary tells execs," *San Francisco Chronicle,* Diana Carlton, March 5, 2010.
16. "Will Patients Beat Blue Shield Again... This Time With the First Online Ballot Petition for Rate Regulation?" Jamie Court, *Huffington Post,* Feb. 8, 2012.
17. "Average Annual Premiums for Family Health Benefits Top $15,000 in 2011, Up 9 Percent, Substantially More than the Growth in Worker's Wages, Benchmark Employer Survey Finds" Henry Kaiser Family Foundation, Sept. 27, 2011.
18. "Workers Paying More for Health Insurance as Cash-Strapped Companies Shift Costs," Lea Winerman, PBS Newshour, Sept. 2, 2011.
19. "Federal workers to pay more for health care," Joe Davidson, *Washington Post,* Oct. 1, 2010.

20. "Wal-Mart Cuts Some Health Care Benefits," Steven Greenhouse and reed Abelson, *New York Times*, Oct. 20, 2011.
21. "Feds pressure American Airlines to save pensions," David Koenig, Associated Press, Feb. 1, 2012.
22. "Transport Workers Union, Objecting to AMR's Hiring of Bain, Picket Romney Campaign," Gregory Polek, *AIN Air Transport Perspective,* Jan. 30, 2012,
23. Annamaria Lusardi, Olivia S. Mitchell, "Baby Boomer Retirement Security: The Roles of Planning, Financial Literacy, and Housing Wealth," Michigan Retirement Research Center, University of Michigan, April 2006.
24. Sylvia A. Allegretto, EPI Briefing Paper, "The State of Working America's Wealth, 2011," #292, March 23, 2011.
25. Ibid., p. 2.
26. Lusardi and Mitchell.
27. "Bernanke urges action to heal U.S. housing markets," Reuters, Feb. 10, 2012,
28. Allegretto, p. 2
29. Courtney Coile, Kevin Milligan, "What Happens to Household Portfolios After Retirement?" Center for Retirement Research at Boston College, November 2006.
30. Munnell et al,, "Do People Plan to Tap Their Home Equity in Retirement?"
31. Allegretto, p. 2
32. Ibid.
33. Ibid., p. 6
34. Lusardi and Mitchell
35. Martin Franham, Purvi Sevak, "Housing Wealth and Retirement Timing," University of Michigan Retirement Research Center, October 2007.
36. Morrissey, p. 50.
37. Alice H. Munnell et al, "Do People Plan to Tap Their Home Equity in Retirement?"
38. "Federal Reserve Flow of Funds Accounts of the United States," cited in *Investment News,* June 2, 2008, p. 26.
39. The bear market in the summer of 2008 caused workers aged 45 to 64 to delay their retirement dates and borrow from their

401(k) accounts. "Delayed Retirement, Early Withdrawals Results from Economic Downturn," May 14, 2008, PlanSponsor.com.

40. InvestmentInsights, RAND Corporation, BGI. p. 12.
41. "Boomer Retirement Portfolios after the Housing Bubble," Advisor Perspectives, May 20, 2008.
42. "Still searching for a bottom in the housing crisis," Janet Morrissey, *Investment News,* June 9, 2008, p. 50.
43. Dowell Myers, SungHo Ryu, "Aging Baby Boomers and the Generational Housing Bubble," *Journal of American Planning Association*, Winter 2008.
44. "Mortgage settlement is great–for politicians and banks," Michael Hiltzik, *Los Angeles Times,* Feb. 11, 2012.
45. *The Brand Bubble,* John Gerzema and Ed Lebar, Josey-Bass, 2008.
46. "Analysts See 'Too Much Capacity' in Asset Management," Neil Anderson, MutualFundWire.com, Oct. 4, 2011.
47. Simon Constable.

Chapter 5: Show Me the Money: Why Average People Do Not Become Great Investors
1. "Above Average," EBRI.org Blog, Feb. 6, 2012.
2. "Many have little to no savings as retirement looms," Matt Krantz, *USA Today,* Dec. 4, 2011.
3. "State of Financial Services Industry," Tiburon CEO Summit, XXI, Oct. 12, 2011.
4. "Mid-Incomers Suffer in Polarized U.S. Job Market: Economy," Bloomberg, Alex Kowalski , April 11, 2012.
5. "Adjusting to the 'New Normal': The Consequences of Long-Term High Unemployment," Knowledge@Wharton, Dec. 8, 2010.
6. "Crook: U.S. Retirees Face a Private-Savings Crisis," Clive Crook, March 13, 2012, Bloomberg.
7. "What's the tax advantages of 401(k)s?" Alicia H. Munnell, Laura Quinby, and Anthony Webb, Center for Retirement Research, Boston College, February 2012, No. 12-4.
8. Ibid.
9. "Household Income Trends During Recession and Economic Recovery," Sentier Research, Oct. 10, 2011.

10. "Recession Officially Over, U.S. Incomes Keep Falling," Robert Pear, *New York Times*, Oct. 9, 2011.
11. "10-Year Real Wage Gains Worse Than During Depression," Jed Graham, *Investor's Business Daily*, June 2, 2011.
12. "State of the Financial Services Industry," Tiburon CEO Summit XXI, Tiburon Strategic Advisors, Oct. 12, 2011.
13. "The New Abnormal: Permanently Engineered Market Volatility," Shah Gilani, *Money Morning*, Aug. 19, 2011.
14. "Fundamentals," Vol. 10, No. 5, Investment Company Institute, September 2010. This ICI report found that Hewitt Associates 2007 indicated 90% of the 292 plans surveyed in the spring of 2007 considered themselves compliant with ERISA Section 404(c). Profit Sharing/401k Council of America 2009 indicated that in 2008, the average number of investment fund options available for participant contributions was 18; Hewitt Associates 2009 indicated an average number of investment options of 18 in 2008.Deloite Consulting LLP, International Foundation, and the International Society of Certified Employee Benefit Specialists 2009 reported that the average number of funds offered by the 606 401(k) plan sponsors in their survey was 20 in early 2009.
15. "Caveat Emptor for 401(k) Plan Sponsors," Mark D. Mensack, *InvestorOne*, May 18, 2011,
16. Ibid.
17. Allegretto, p. 17.
18. Ibid., p. 12.
19. "Ignore Morningstar's Stars," Michael Maiello, *Forbes*, Jan. 30, 2009.
20. *History of Newspapers*, Mitchell Stephens, 1994.
21. "The Big Postwar Story: Abundance and the Rise of Economic Journalism." A. L Yarrow, *Journalism History*, Summer 2006.
22. "NYSE Goes Public, Goes Electronic," Stephen Taub, CFO. com, April 21, 2005.
23. From 1962 through 1968, the market increase was greater than the famous bull market of the 1920s.
24. At the time this book was being written (July 2012), regulators in Europe were pursuing investigations against some major

European banks about efforts to influence the London Inter-Bank Offering Rate, or LIBOR, which sets the rate for trillions of dollars in interest-sensitive loans. In July, 2012, Barclays Plc. was fined $455 million for rigging LIBOR after U.S. and UK regulators found the bank "systematically" attempted to manipulate the rate for profit.

25. "Why Did NASDAQ Market Makers Stop Avoiding Odd-Eighth Quotes?" by William G. Christie, Jeffrey H. Harris, Paul H. Schultz, *Journal of Finance*, vol. 49, no. 5, December 1994.

26. *Pensions & Investments*, Oct. 31, 1994.

27. The Association for Investment Management and Research (AIMR) merged with the CFA Institute in 1999 and in 2004, AIMR voted to change its name to the CFA Institute.

28. Comments of AIMR president and CEO Thomas A. Bowman, CFA, July 2001 AIMR Annual Conference.

29. "Transgenerational Design Matters," www://transgeneratinal. org, states: "The fastest-growing segment of the total population is the oldest old—those 80 and over. Their growth rate is twice that of those 65 and over and almost 4-times that for the total population. In the United States, this group now represents 10% of the older population and will *more than triple* from 5.7 million in 2010 to over 19 million by 2050."

30. "Do You Face "Money Death' in Old Age?," Philip Moeller, *U.S. News & World Report*, Feb. 10, 2012.

31. "Ric Edelman: Mutual Fund Era End in Sight," Oliver Ludwig, *Index Universe*, May 15, 2012.

32. "Reducing Costs of 401(k) Plans with ETFs and Commingled Trusts," Richard W. Kopcke, Francis M. Vitagliano, and Zhenya S. Karamcheva, Center for Retirement Research, July 2010.

33. Ibid.

34. "2012 Study of Indexing in DC Plans," Neil Plein, Invest N' Retire, March 7, 2012.

35. 401(k) Manifesto, Plein.

36. Ibid.

37. "False Discoveries in Mutual Fund Performance: Measuring Luck in Estimated Alphas," Barras, Laurent, Scaillet, O.,

Wermers, Russ, March, 2008, as cited in 401(k) Manifesto, Plein.

38. The agency problem is discussed in numerous papers. See "Financial Duties of Brokers-Advisors-Financial Planners-Money Managers," Tamar Frankel, Boston University School of Law, Working Paper No. 09-36, Aug. 10, 2009; "The New Reality of Financial Advisors and Investors," John A. Haslem, http://ssrn.com/abstract=1536029; "A Simple Code of Ethics: A History of the Moral Purpose Inspiring Federal Regulation of the Securities Industry," John H. Walsh, *Hofstra Law Review*, vol. 29: November 2001.

39. "Investors Can Manage Psyche to Capture Alpha," Dalbar, April 1, 2011.

40. "Auto Enrollment Grabs Reluctant Retirement Savers," Global Action on Aging, Associated Press, February, 201

41. The Replacement Ratio Study, Georgia State University. 1997.

42. "Asset Allocation Models Are The Only Way Forward For 401(k)'s," Neil Plein, Invest n' Retire, July, 2011.

43. "John Hancock Study of 401(k) Participants Investment Outcomes Reveals Common Investing Behaviors," PR Newswire, October, 2007.

44. "401(k) Participants Using Professional Investment Help Continue to Do Better Than Those Who Go It Alone," Aon Hewitt–Financial Engines, September 2011.

45. "Romney would rank among richest presidents ever," *USA Today*, Jan. 29, 2012.

46. Lawrence J. Kotlikoff and David Ransom, 2007, "Does It Pay at the Margin to Work, and Save? Measuring Effective Marginal Tax Rates on Americans' Labor Supply and Savings," *Tax Policy and the Economy*, ed. James M. Poterba, Boston, MIT Press, p. 1

47. *Debunkery*, Ken Fisher, John Wiley, 2012, p. 62.

48. Ibid., p. 64.

49. "Bloomberg Attacks Front-End Loads," Mutualfundwire.com, May 1, 2012.

50. "401(k)s to Overtake Pensions as Primary Retirement Vehicle in 2012: State Street 'Leakage' from DC plans threatens employee savings during job switches," Joyce Hanson, *AdvisorOne*, Jan. 26, 2012.

51. *The Defining Decade: Why Your Twenties Matter–And How to Make the Most of Them Now,* Dr. Meg Jay, Twelve Books, 2012.

52. *Debunkery,* Ken Fisher, John Wiley, p. 31.

53. "Vanguard's long-term outlook for stocks and the economy," Vanguard.com, April 30, 2012.

54. *When Prime Brokers Fail,* J.S. Aikman, Bloomberg Press, 2010.

55. Ibid., p. 122.

56. Bloomberg News, April 25, 2012.

57. *Managed Futures in the Institutional Portfolio,* Chuck Epstein, John Wiley, 1993.

58. "Bernanke urges action to heal U.S. housing markets," Reuters, Feb. 10, 2012.

59. First Quarter Sees Slight Decrease in Negative Home Equity," Alyssa Gerace, *Reverse Mortgage Daily,* June 8, 2011.

60. The Impact of Diminishing Wealth on Future Consumption: How Housing Wealth Affects Retirement Planning," Chuck Epstein, Principal Financial, September 2008.

61. *23 Things They Don't Tell You About Capitalism,* Ha-Joon Chang, Bloomsbury Press, 2010. p 150.

62. Richard D. Wolff, WBAI Radio, Jan. 28, 2012.

63. Schultz, p. 210.

64. "Critics Weigh in on High-Frequency Trading on Flash Crash Anniversary," Gino Vicci, *Huffington Post,* May 9, 2012.

65. CNBC, Half-Time Market Report, May 15, 2012.

66. Economic Policy Institute, Jan. 27, 2012.

67. David Cay Johnson, Bill Moyers interview, PBS, Jan. 18, 2008.

68. "What Wealth Transfer?: Baby-Boomers and their children shouldn't expect large inheritances. Their elders are spending it fast," Anne Kates Smith, *Kiplingers,* September 2006.

69. Schultz. p. 209.

70. "What To Look For in Your New 401(k) Report," Nancy Mann Jackson, Second Act, You. Part Two. Jan. 18, 2012.

71. Ibid.

72. "Get Ready for Investment Comparison Charts: U.S. Department of Labor Beefs Up Required Participant Fee Disclosure," Carol Buckmann, Oct. 26, 2010.

73. "Fund Fees Don't Always Mean Better Business Practices," Charles Jaffe, *Reading Eagle*, Jan. 16, 2005.
74. "Study on Investment Advisors and Broker-Dealers: As Required by Section 913 of the Dodd-Frank Wall Street Reform and Consumer Protection Act," SEC, January 2011, p. iii.
75. "Financial sector spent $5 billion lobbying DC last decade," Greg Morcroft, MarketWatch, March 4, 2009.
76. "Does New Study Seal the Deal for Fiduciary Standard – or Just Warn Plan Sponsors?" Christopher Carosa, Fiduciary News, Jan. 19, 2011.
77. Fisher, p. 125.

Chapter 6: Conclusion: What Investors Gained—and Lost—From Poor Disclosure

1. Schultz, *Retirement Heist*
2. Ibid., p. 4.

INDEX

Quotron, 157

Ragatz, Julie Anne, 117
Railways Employees National Pension
  Association, 3
Railroad Retirement and Carrier
  Taxing Acts of 1937, 20
Railroad Retirement Board v. Alton
  Railroad Co., 3
Randstad, 19
Real wage growth, 148, 187, 193, 194,
  196; defined, 220
Recessions, 149; list of, 151
Record-keepers, 39, 51, 56, 58, 72, 75,
  78, 79, 81, 84, 85, 206; defined,
  220, 74; compensation of, 103;
  and ETFs, 172, 175
Recovery times needed to recoup
  housing price loss chart, 135
Redemption fees, 30, 31
Registered Investment Advisers
  (RIAs), 94, 104, 107, 111, 112,
  114, 118, 150, 177, 202; defined,
  219, 220
Regulation, historic impact of, 115,
  117, 151; and plan sponsors, 205-
  208, 211; and individual investors,
  207
Reish, Fred, 83, 96
Retirement, 59, 209, 210, 216; impact
  of expenses, history of, 1-19;
  income, 26, 96; income shortfalls,
  45, 46, 48, 50, 52, 75, 115; financial security, 44; size of accounts,
  25, 55; impact of fees on , 26, 141
Retirement Heist, 125
Revenue Act of 1978, 39, 45, 68

Revenue sharing, 105, 111; advisor-
  paid-fee, 46; conflicts of interest,
  108, 109, 112, 152, 154, 189, 209,
  212; defined, 111, 218; history of,
  abuses related to, 113, 115, 117; in
  401(k) plans, 106, 118; and ETFs,
  102, 172, 174; scope of, 113, 114,
  116, 214
Regulation, 93-99, 101, 112, 116, 124,
  129, 166, 181, 185-186, 203, 217-
  218, 221, 224, 225, 229, 230-239,
  241, 242
Rhoades, Ron A., 113
Risk, 12, 22, 114, 120, 149, 169, 174,
  182; career risk, 88; defined, 103;
  management of, 41, 90, 91; shareholder assumption of, 45, 60, 94,
  97, 122, 123; transfer of, 45, 125,
  126, 152, 184; risk-free, 179
Riversource, 214
Robinson, Reginald, 21
Rockefeller, John D., 4
Roland Criss, 101, 109
Roosevelt, Franklin D., 20, 22
Roth IRA, 150; defined, 217
Roth 401(k), 150
Royal Navy, 2
Russell Investments, (Frank Russell
  Company), 3, 29, 51, 97

S&P 500 Index, 40, 54, 76, 108, 150,
  152, 178, 187, 191, 199; futures, 195
Sauter, Gus, 188
SBC Communications, 15
Schapiro, Mary, 118, 196
Schedule C, 69, 73, 80, 82
Schultz, Ellen, 120, 125, 128, 207

U.S. Federal Reserve, 13, 135, 170, 186, 191, 193, 197
U.S. Supreme Court, 3
U.S. Treasury Bonds, 13
U.S. Treasury Department, 14

Vanguard funds, 57, 90, 91, 108, 150, 151, 178, 188, 208
Volatility, 18, 26, 38, 60, 88, 110, 120, 149, 150, 167, 170, 185, 187, 192, 195
Von Bismark, Otto, 2

WAMU (Washington Mutual), 197
WBTB-TV, 157
Wal-Mart, 128, 132, 160, 202
Wall Street, anti-sentiment, 160, 202
Wall $treetWeek, 158
Wealth accumulation, 90, 185, 233
Wealth destruction, 47, 119, 133, 135, 138, 145
Wealth managers, xi; xii
Wealth transfers, 123, 126, 144
Windsor I Fund, 86
Wellington Fund, 83
Wells Fargo, 139
Whitney, Richard, 6, 212, 213
Wholesalers (see mutual fund wholesalers)
Williams, Senator Harrison, 11
Wilshire Associates, 15
Winks, Steven, 93, 102, 103
Wizard of Oz, xv
Worker productivity, 2, 3, 11, 141, 214

Y2K, tech bubble, 167, 168

For more information, visit:
www.mutualfundreform.com

or contact the author at:
epstein.chuck@gmail.com